Inside Clubbing

Inside Clubbing

Sensual Experiments in the Art of Being Human

Phil Jackson

Oxford • New York

First published in 2004 by
Berg
Editorial offices:
1st Floor, Angel Court, 81 St Clements Street, Oxford OX4 1AW UK
838 Broadway, Third Floor, New York, NY 10003-4812, USA

Berg is an imprint of Oxford International Publishers Ltd.

Library of Congress Cataloging-in-Publication Data
A catalogue record for this book is available from the Library of Congress.

British Library Cataloguing-in-Publication Data
A catalogue record for this book is available from the British Library.

ISBN 1 85973 708 0 (Cloth)
1 85973 713 7 (Paper)

Typeset by JS Typesetting Ltd, Wellingborough, Northants.
Printed in the United Kingdom by Biddles Ltd, King's Lynn.

www.bergpublishers.com

For
Mum and Pam,
still loved, still missed;
and Dad
for being the best

Special thanks to
Doktorinna Karin Charlesworth and
Doctor Edward 'Buck' Schieffelin –
two complete stars

Contents

Acknowledgements ix

Introduction 1

Section I: Inside Clubbing

1 Snapshot: Saturday Night Out on the Town 9

2 Dancing 15

3 Music 25

4 Sex 35

5 Dressed to Thrill 47

6 Drugs 55

7 The Vibe 87

Section II: Sensual Experiments in the Art of Being Human

8 Knowledge in the Flesh 115

9 Sensual Experiments in the Art of Being Human 135

10 Back into the World 155

11 Conclusion 171

Glossary 177

Bibliography 183

Index 187

Acknowledgements

I want to say a huge thanks to everyone whose support and determination to party hearty allowed me to complete both my PhD and this book – especially my informants for sharing their experiences and their wisdom. I'd like to thank all the clubs who put me on their guest list, particularly everyone at The Blue Note and The Bedsit (Burnell Penhaul – we're all missing you buddy; the world's just less dazzling without you), Tuppy Owen and the rest of the Sex Maniac's crew, The Thankyou team, Matthew Glamorre, the good folk of Swaraj and everyone else who gave me their time and their illuminating insights into the crazed, chaotic heaven they've all helped to build. I also want to send a big shout-out to my friends (you know who you are, you lovely, lovely people) for their patience, their kindness and their va-va-voom, and to all the other denizens of clubland for their capacity to make the night shine and zing with good humour, passion and a uniquely human beauty. Finally, I want to thank everybody at University College London's anthropology department for turning me on to the delights of learning about people and helping me out with my fees, and the Graduate Fund for assisting me in the purchase of equipment. Thank you, Thank You, Thank You and once again I Thank You.

Introduction

Whores, freaks, saints and angels, we're all beautiful, we're all dangerous, we're all users, we're all takers. This is how our God made us.

(Dirty Beatniks, *Feedback*)

This book is about dancing, smiling, drugging, flirting, fucking, friendship and having a ball. There are two reasons why I've written it. The first is that I love to party. The second is that I think clubbing is an important and complex social experience that merits further investigation. More specifically I believe that by examining clubs you are granted access to a particular kind of knowledge that has either been reviled or ignored in the Western world. This knowledge throws new light upon the way in which our lives are constructed, experienced and lived as we head further into the twenty-first century.

The book is split into two sections. The first section, 'Inside Clubbing', is an ethnographic account of clubbing based on my informants' party exploits and my own fieldwork in the clubs. I focus on the various elements that go into creating the club experience. I examine dancing, music, sex, dressing-up and drugs and then show how each of these aspects of clubbing feeds into and creates the unique social vibe found in clubs, which makes them radically different from other public spaces. The second section, 'Sensual Experiments in The Art of Being Human', explores the social and sensual knowledge that arises out of clubbing and its relationship to the wider social world in which clubbing is immersed. I show how this knowledge is constructed and how it gains autonomy from the club experience itself and the influential role it plays in structuring people's lives even after the party is over.

The knowledge found in clubs is an embodied knowledge that you can feel deep in your guts and it must be lived if it is to be truly comprehended. It is both social and sensual and I will show how these twin realms of experience are more intimately intertwined than is usually credited within our understanding of them. The role of the body in constructing and maintaining our experience of the world, our culture and ourselves provides one of the main lines of inquiry throughout this book. Clubbing is a profoundly visceral and corporeal phenomenon, it is a leisure activity that allows us to shake off the body of the everyday world and subsequently recreate our experience of the world. This sensual shift grants us access to the succulent and carnal modes of social encounter, which arise in the hours of darkness. Here, wrapped within an immaculate bass and flying on a chemical carpet, clubbers begin to experiment with the social and sensual knowledge of the night.

Night-time has a quality all of its own that can alter your whole experience of the world. It can make it more intense and more immediate because darkness is the time of invisibility and transformation where people can become fluid in terms of the activities they seek out and the personas they present to the world. Alvarez (1996: 295) described the city's night in these terms:

> Night in the city is time out – time for leisure and intimacy, family and lovers, hobbies and pastimes, reading and music and television. It is also the time for excitement and celebration: theatres, movies, concerts and party-going, wining, dining, dancing and gambling. For people who hold down boring or unsatisfactory jobs, night is the time when they feel they lead their real lives.

Night is a time of sensual alterity during which the body is unleashed from the rules of propriety that operate in the daylight hours. We are shrouded in night's cimmerian embrace and use this feeling to expand our carnal lives and savour disparate, social experiences.

This sense of expansion provides the foundation upon which my exploration of clubbing is built. I have taken, as my starting point, the idea that our bodies are always immersed in the world and that this point of immersion is structured culturally, ideologically and emotionally so that it orders and even controls our capacity to perceive and experience that world. Throughout this book, I will investigate the way in which clubbing challenges this cultural codification of the flesh by taking us into a writhing, rhythmic and chemical realm of social encounters, virulent beats and seductive desires, which create a sensual landscape that generates its own modes of knowledge. The wisdom of clubbing is chaotic and passionate; it is grounded in the sensual tension that exists between our daylight bodies and our night-time revelries. In order to capture it and understand its form and the potential impact that it has on people's lives we've got to comprehend the body's role in structuring those lives. This is why I use the term socio-sensual, throughout this work, because it captures the way in which sensual states possess social power. Our social encounters arise out of the body through which we live them. If you wake up feeling angry or depressed you will occupy the world through these emotional states, which will impose a posture upon your body and order your perception of that world. That posture will also play a role in determining how the world sees and approaches you. Through clubbing, people create and socialise through novel bodies that underpin new social practices, which eventually become embodied and taken beyond the club space.

Clubbing has predominantly been examined from within the field of youth studies but the pathways I followed challenged this assumption. My informants were not youths – they ranged in age from their mid-twenties to their late-fifties. The oldest person I came across in a nightclub was eighty-two. The informants with whom I carried out the longest and most in-depth interviews were aged between twenty-five and fifty-five and had been clubbing for years. This opened up the process of clubbing to examination because the way in which my informants clubbed, what they set out to experience and how those experiences were assessed had changed over time.

This has added a more historical dimension to this book that, when combined with the fact that I've been clubbing it up for a fair few years, allowed me to chart the changing dynamics of clubs. My long-term party shenanigans gave me enough knowledge of clubs to provide a wider perspective on clubbing than other studies have used. I can still remember when clubs were predominantly late-night drinking dens, when the sociality they housed was simply a pissed-up version of the every-day world rather than anything radically different. I witnessed the changes that came along with the arrival of Ecstasy. I saw the Ecstasy comedown after people's initial enthusiasm for and faith in the drug waned. I saw the return of cocaine and booze. I witnessed the splintering of clubland from large-scale raves to smaller social settings and the gradual commercialisation of the scene, which made it a mainstream, leisure option. I had observed these changes and I brought that knowledge to the contemporary club space.

I have also explored a wider variety of clubbing styles than any other invest-igation of clubbing. From trance clubs to hip-hop venues, dress-up gigs and fetish clubs, queer clubs and straight clubs, Asian clubs, techno nights, house clubs, drum 'n' bass gigs, soul nights, funk nights, tranny clubs, free parties and saucy sexual soirees. I did them all because I believed that the surface differences they displayed were less important than the hot and funky parties that they housed. This book takes these parties seriously; it interrogates them and makes them give up their secrets by examining the shifting social, sensual and emotional states upon which they are built.

'What the fuck are you on about mate?'

Throughout this book you must never forget that clubbing is essentially about having fun with other people. Everything I say about clubbing arises out of that simple, social fact. However, the sort of fun you have when you club is very different from other types of fun you have in the contemporary world. Although clubbing is very much immersed in British culture it still stands out as a radically different style of public space within that culture. The intensity of pleasure you can experience when you're out and about in clubland marks it out as a sensual extreme, which challenged the traditional British morality. The Christian and especially Protestant attitude towards pleasure was one of intense mistrust; pleasure was of the devil, it drew people away from God and work and so had to be vigorously controlled. Clubbing is almost the polar opposite to such a perspective and, as such, it is a field of practice that has played a role in re-orientating both social and individual perspectives upon and experiences of pleasure. Pleasure is becoming more important as a reference point in people's lives. The social constraints that used to keep pleasure in check by setting sensual limits policed by moral rules have weakened, partly due to the influence of clubbing because it democratised access to Nietzsche's realm of Dionysus as opposed to the Apollonian realm of order that constructs our everyday experience of the world.

There are a number of forces that I explore throughout this book that influence the sober, sanitised and rational body that structures our daylight hours. The habitus is one of the most important. This is a term taken from the work of the great French sociologist Pierre Bourdieu (1977, 1990) who examined the way in which cultures structured the bodies of their occupants through the imposition of practices. These practices encode the ideological and social values of a culture into the flesh and by doing so they predisposed those occupants to recreate that culture. The habitus is why we feel guilt when we break one of our society's rules. It is why men behave like men and women like women. It is why certain classes share particular social traits such as diet or a love of football rather than rugby. Bourdieu shows how these seemingly disparate phenomena can all be linked together through the idea of the habitus. To use Bourdieu's (1998: 8) own terms:

> Habitus are generative principles of distinct and distinctive practices – what the worker eats, and especially the way he eats it, the sport he practices and the way he practices it, his political opinions and the way he expresses them are systematically different from the industrial owner's corresponding activities. But habitus are also classificatory schemes, principles of classification, principles of visions and division, different tastes. They make distinctions between what is good and what is bad, between what is right and what is wrong, between what is distinguished and what is vulgar, and so forth . . .

The habitus makes some things seem right and some wrong, some things seem natural and others weird. It exists as a realm of taken-for-granted knowledge created by a mixture of practices and emotional templates that we embody as we grow up within our culture. It is why something like homosexuality used to be perceived with a deeply embodied sense of moral repugnance, which now seems ridiculous. Although you still find people who will tell you that they don't have a problem with homosexuality as an idea, yet they feel uneasy if they see a couple of boys snogging. This is the true power of the habitus because it isn't an idea in itself – it is a bodily posture that has been linked to an idea and grants that idea its sensual power and imbues it with a taken-for-granted status. Real social change is only effected when the habitus is altered at a bodily level. An idea can be the first step in initiating change but until it becomes embodied and gains its own corporeal posture that idea will always have a tenuous, cultural existence, which predominantly operates within the sphere of language.

I will show that the sensual intensity of clubbing generates an alternative body in which the structuring framework of the habitus is temporarily erased and that this erasure underpins the modified social world you encounter through clubbing. Obviously this is not the reason why people club, they're not sitting at home thinking: 'Right, I'm off out to erase my habitus.' It is an unintended consequence of the drugs, the dancing and the crowds. It is an experience that impacts incrementally on people as the body of clubbing begins to challenge the body bequeathed to them by their own culture, thereby changing the way in which they negotiate their passage through their social realm and relate to the symbolic and ideological frameworks, which govern that realm. This is can be a problematic process – with its dangers, confusions and blind alleys – yet my informants all agreed that the risks they sometimes took while clubbing were worth it because clubbing had added something to their lives that they valued.

In order to understand the workings of the habitus I began to explore the social, biological and cognitive structures that granted the habitus its power. I have drawn upon the work of neuro-cognitive scientists Antonio Damasio (1994, 1999) and Joseph LeDoux (1999) who both examine the role of the body and the emotions in structuring consciousness. Their insights into the relationship between body and mind allowed me to build upon Bourdieu's (1977, 1990) ideas by breaking the habitus down into its constituent parts and viewing each of these elements as a different form of embodied knowledge. I explore the connection between the body and consciousness, the organisation of the emotional memory system and the links between the realm of the flesh and the world of signs. This approach gave me a framework that allowed me to move beyond the club-space, in Section II of this book, and explore clubbing's wider influence on our social and cultural lives.

Section I of the book is based upon the in-depth interviews that I undertook with my informants and my own participant observation in clubs. I employ the work of social theorists including Michel Foucault (1977), particularly his notion of the 'gaze', and Erving Goffman (1990), to examine the social constraints placed upon the body and the modes of sensual expression contemporary culture both tolerates and denies. It is these constraints that are largely abandoned when clubbing, and their disappearance generates the emergence of multiple bodies and even multiple selves over the course of a night out. Mainly, though, I clubbed it up night after night with other clubbers who are, of course, the true experts in this field. I danced and laughed, watched and mingled, got blasted and ground my teeth. I went to pre-parties and after-parties, talked all night with damn fine people and saw many a dawn rise over the city. It was the social rush of clubbing that had the most impact upon me; the fluid sensuous friendships that are forged in the night when you find people determined to live at their best. I journeyed from the centre of clubbing outwards to its edges where it was at its wildest and the rules that govern our everyday experience of the world had most obviously been cast aside. This was a realm of self-expression and creativity, a conspiracy of pleasure, based in a hedonism that had escaped the confines of individual gratification and become a series of social and individual experiments grounded in searing sensual extremes.

Section I
Inside Clubbing

–1–

Snapshot: Saturday Night Out on the Town

I'm out on the razzle, dressed to the nines, and ready to rock. Thank God for Saturday night and clubs like Hush (not its real name). Standing in the guest line I started talking to a group of out-of-towners who always came in for Hush; one of the women looked great in a pink, fake fur outfit, which she had spent all day making. I've always loved it when people create their own image on the cheap and still look amazing and it proved that Hush wasn't a fashion venue, just a make an effort event. We queued for about twenty minutes. It's always a bit nerve wracking waiting to find out if your plans have come to fruition and you are actually on the guest list. My turn: 'I'm on D's list, anthropologist, study of pleasure, spoke on the phone blah, blah, blah.' D not there yet and then: 'OK you're in.' Ha, so glad I dressed up.

Next step, getting past security with my stash intact. The search looks thorough: pockets emptied, brisk frisk, not really worried about the acid, so small that it's virtually impossible to find, but the spliffs are a different matter. I get lucky and I'm waved through.

You enter the club down a dark corridor; the music getting louder as you approach the end; walk into a brightly lit space, which is dominated by a large, pink, music box about seven foot high and ten foot long in which a live ballerina is performing. I immediately warm to the space. This is going to be fun. Grab a beer and catch my bearings. This space is a bar area and overlooking it is a balcony, which is presently empty. Two corridors lead off from the left-hand side, but they're both closed off and everyone is forced to pile into this one area. On either side of the music box lie two small podiums upon which the Hush dancers are already in full flow. Hush hires people to dance and look fabulous for the night in order to get the club moving and impose a glamorous aesthetic upon the space. It is important to get the right look because the Hush team understand the importance of watching and being watched in clubs and their aesthetic encouraged big looks, which gives the event a larger than life appeal. The podiums are full of drag queens, delectable boys and lingerie-clad women and they are givin' it some. This immediately brings a grin to my face; they look great, sexy, fun and their efforts pay off because the gagging-for-it crowd who have been waiting and waiting to get in start to go off almost immediately.

The intensity is already building and I decide it's time to get an edge so I find myself an out-of-the way spot, which isn't easy in such a brightly lit room, and surreptitiously drop a tab of acid. It should come up in about forty minutes to an hour. So I do a little boogying, smoke a few fags, enjoy watching the crowds swirl by and check out the mighty, fine, looking women, dressed to kill and slaying me with every immaculately manicured set of lips. Grrrr – down boy.

The space is stage-managed beautifully using the logic of critical mass. When the bar is packed and people are shaking a booty the main dance floor is opened up. Later on, when folk need a breather, the balcony will flourish. However, people are having so much fun that there isn't a huge rush to get into the main floor, which prevents a lull in the proceedings. The main floor is a much bigger space and dark. The speaker stacks double as podiums and there is a raised platform on the far side; in the middle is yet another podium, this one larger than the others though not higher. (Drug-fucked people have a tendency to fall off things.) The music is loud, banging house, relentless beats that physically invade your flesh. Sweet. The acid is coming up nicely, weaving its way through my system. Colours are crystallising and taking on that dazzling psychotropic intensity. The room looks alive with potential – potential for what I'm not sure. The tallest drag-queen I've ever seen passes by with her entourage. I notice what looks like a group of bodyguards – for whom I'm not sure – they are massive men and I have to get through them to get to the loo. The biggest seems to be four times my width and twice as tall; I feel like a midget; can't work out whether he is truly that huge or if my sense of perception is changing. I smile and say: 'Excuse me.' He smiles back and ushers me through the group.

From the toilet cubicles the occasional sharp intake of breath is the only indication of the night's chemical content. The more trippy I get the more trolleyed everyone else looks. I try to convince myself that I appear sober. Who am I trying to kid? I make another trip to the bar and to my astonishment it's stopped serving alcohol. It's 2.00 a.m. There's another seven hours to go before the club shuts and it's going to be water all the way. Never mind. I decide to head off to the main floor for a spliff in the shadows.

Boom-Boom-Boom, merrily sucking on a spliff, the room's filling up and the speaker podiums are all bagged. On one is a woman in a gold, sequinned bra and mini-skirt, seriously sexy, she's already givin' it some vent. The lights are reflected upon her tinselled muscular body. She looks fabulous changing from red to orange to green, smile plastered over her face, magnificent and strong. The dervishes start to inhabit my feet; this time fuelled by the growing, buzzing energy unleashed by the LSD. My body's loosening up – it feels sinuous, sensuous and strong. You can savour the energy pumping through it, lithe like snakes, erectile and passionate, alive, my whole being feels like a cock hovering at the point of ejaculation. The gap between the music and me has gone; I am possessed by a friendly daemon, but there is no sense of losing myself, if anything I'm me to the power of three: Uber-Phil.

Time has lost all meaning; I have no concept of where I am in the chronology of this event, just music, dancing and people – that's all that matters. I stop for a breather and move out to the other bar to cool down. The balcony has finally been opened; people are grooving up there and watching the party. Some guy is beating out Tito Puente style riffs on the bongos; the crowd has caught the fever. A group of women in multi-coloured wigs pass me by, sucking on lollipops. I have never wanted to be on a stick so badly. Divine madness reigns, but it is so good humoured, so impeccably social, that it seems not only normal, but oh, so right. I slurp down water, mouth parched from dancing, drenched in sweat, but I've moved beyond giving a toss about how I look. The party's got me by the tail.

Work my way over to the corner of the music box; the ballerina has gone to be replaced by the Hush dancers who tower over the floor; living monuments to the joys of self-expression and home-made creativity. Start talking to the guy standing next to me, he's nineteen, lives in a small town in Wales, came down to visit some mates who live in London. His smile is swallowing his head and his pupils are the size of a couple of coal scuttles: 'I've never seen anything like this, it's fucking wild, I want to live in here.' Home from home.

Decide to go for a wander. The place is coming to the boil; wonderful sights dance at the periphery of my vision, then I'm confronted by a luscious crowd of love librarians, perfectly sculptured glamour, all wearing the same type of glasses. They look like pornographic secretaries like the ones found in under-the-counter movies. Delicious. They ice past in a Tippi Hedren stylie. A guy who's dressed in a fetching pink baby-grow wanders past grinning and talking animatedly to a lingerie-clad black woman.

Back into the dark for more bass, sonic stimulation in a technological age, dancing hard, fast and frantic. Such a succulent frenzy. My body feels so good, loose and passionate, feasting upon the glances that dart across my flesh and spur me onto more exertion. A woman in a pink, leather bra and skin-tight, pink, leather trousers walks directly up to me smiles and starts grinding out a lascivious mambo, a pole-dancer without a pole; we dance for a couple of tunes and then, with a grin, she's gone into the crowd. A heavily muscled gay guy stands, top off, flesh bulging, his teeth clenched so tightly together that I half expect them to shatter into dust. His feet are completely still, eyes tranced out, his only movement is the flexing and unflexing of his steroid-pumped torso. I need another breather. So I sit and watch, just getting off on the voyeurism of it all. Then a sparkly eyed pixie suddenly makes a beeline for me from across the room. She looks naughty and smiley at the same time. She looks me straight in the eye and speaks in a voice with a melodic, Irish lilt: 'There's always one more dance left in yer, always.' Then she's off, but oh, she spoke the truth and I hurl myself back into the action.

So it continues – the infectious chaotic thrill of crowds bound by chemicals and rhythms and the urge to party. A governmental nightmare, the order of the anti-system, extreme, well mannered, out of it – or should I say into it. I get talking to a great looking couple; she's tall, elegant and smiley; he's shorter and built like a bouncer; they're both in their late thirties. He's dressed in a dinner jacket, but without a shirt and round his neck he wears a fetching pink dog collar. We chat, enjoying the sights, talking about nothing, just blarney, but that's all that is required.

I'm in the well-lit bar; people are dancing everywhere, including upon the bar itself; hips gyrate, bodies are flushed with carnal energy, music pounds out engulfing the crowd. I'm captivated by the sight of sweat pouring from the semi-naked flesh of the women; all I want to do is lick them. Clubs are so luscious.

Everywhere I look people are smiling big smiles. How often do you get to see that? Faces shimmering with excitement, passion, sheer joy writ large upon the crowd. It's emotionally ripe for the plucking and the human race doesn't seem that fucked up after all. It's all hanging together through a combined act of willpower grounded in the simple intention to have a good time, which grants people a willing-ness to accept others as they are and the expectation that they will do the same. You would have to work really hard to find something to have angst about.

'Do a little dance, make a little love, Get down tonight, get down tonight' (K. C. and The Sunshine Band, *Get Down Tonight*). My ears prick up and it's time to shake my booty again. The room's going fractal, charged with the energy of people in motion, the act of living being done. I wander back into the darkness to find the central podium's packed. I want to play too. So I wriggle my way in. The temperature immediately rockets and I curl around the beat, skanking along with the mass. Wondrous. Arms and legs and torsos weaving and writhing round each other, all held together by that virus known as bass. An inevitable act of aural seduction, guttural sounds, viscous and sticky and inexplicably wise. My body feels liquid. It has gone through so many changes, the tensions of the week melting away, the rushes of energy, the intimate, fleshy cartography of dance, moving how I only ever get to move in a club – expressive, fervent motion, a kinaesthetic freedom that resides in muscles and sinews and bones.

I head off to the loo again; a guy staggers out playing with his nose, eyes twitching, the slight green hue of his skin suggesting that he had imbibed a little too much crystal stimulation. He joins a group hanging around outside and mutters that he might have to leave. I think he was looking for a little sympathy, instead he's greeted with a chorus of 'lightweight, lightweight' from his friends who proceed to drag him off to the dance floor again.

It's happened four times now; every time I try to take a break the same Irish woman pounces out of nowhere to spur me on and every time it works; it's the only communication we've had all night. What a laugh. I don't know the woman, but I've got a soft spot for her; a tiny, trippy pixie making sure I stay with the programme.

I've been dancing for the best part of five hours and I am increasingly in the mood for an ice-cold lager.

Then kaboom the lights go on. Ooooch, harsh. Most people scamper to the main floor, which is still dark, but the clearing out process has begun. This can be a strange time in a club; a sudden jolt to the system as you realise it's over. I decide to grab my coat before the final rush gets going; people are standing round chatting; a few couples are fumbling and necking; it's very mellow though, which is great. It's 8.45 a.m. When I leave the sun's up and I can grab a tube home. The train is weird; sober looking folk going about their business while my brain merrily buzzes away. It always feels deliciously mischievous when you come out of a club with the sun up. You feel part of a vast conspiracy of pleasure, which somehow these other grey-looking folk haven't caught onto yet.

–2–

Dancing

Never trust spiritual leader who cannot dance.

(Mr Miyagi, *The Next Karate Kid* 1994)

Sometimes I think. Sometimes I am.

(Paul Valery 1871–1945)

Dancing is one of the most crucial elements of clubbing because it unleashes the Dionysian body from the Apollonian constraints imposed upon it in the everyday world. Nietzsche suggested a central opposition in human nature and human relations to their own society, which he examined by using the concepts of Dionysus and Apollo. As Bryan Turner (1996: 18) explains: 'Apollo stands for the principles of formalism, rationalism and consistency while Dionysus stands for the realities of ecstasy, fantasy, excess and sensuality . . .'

If he'd got out more Nietzsche would have loved nightclubs because clubbing is a deeply Dionysian practice that has generated its own alternative forms of social order. Dancing is the best example of how clubbing has introduced a Dionysian body into the mainstream of British's culture, so inverting the notions of bodily discipline and control that underpinned the Protestant-Christian perspective on the flesh that dominated our culture for centuries.

The speed with which this ecstatic experience was seized upon and spread via clubbing was remarkable. Dance re-emerged as a mass form of social experience, particularly amongst men, and the majority of them had spent the preceding years standing round in clubs, clutching pints, watching women groove around their handbags and fearing that dancing would emasculate them and leave them open to ridicule by their peers. In 1984, when I first started clubbing, before the Ecstasy-rave movement had begun, I would be one of the few men going for it on the dance floor in clubs, usually receiving scowls from the other men around me. It did not leave me enamoured of the club environment as it seemed like little more than a noisy, angst-ridden, overcrowded pub.

When I went back into clubs in 1989 the floor was heaving with tight-jawed men on Ecstasy, waving their hands in the air and grinning so hard you thought their faces were going to rip. Many of these men were the same ones who had resolutely refused to dance only a few years earlier. The difference was extraordinary; the sheer physical energy produced in the club environment immediately went ballistic and the levels of angst and machismo, which was so noticeable in the past, diminished. Both these alterations were seen largely in terms of the effects of Ecstasy by clubbers themselves, but in reality they were as much to do with the simple act of dancing than any property inherent in the drug. The drug reduced people's self-consciousness and fear of censure to the point where they could enjoy dancing. Men moved from being drunken wallflowers to being very much part of the club environment as they started to discover dancing for themselves.

Some men had, of course, always danced, but the breakdown of partner-based dancing left men without a major role to play on the dance floor. The dance styles that men partook in during the two decades before rave appeared tended to stress aggression (pogoing and slam-dancing of punk) or competition (northern soul, disco and break-dancing). They placed heavy emphasis on the machismo of dance, either through stressing a drunken, violent physicality or by creating styles that had to be mastered before they could be displayed. This left men split into dancers and non-dancers and the visibility of the dance floor kept the majority of them on the periphery, too self-conscious to step forward and risk making fools of themselves.

The arrival of Ecstasy and the rave scene altered the face of dance by rejecting the adoption of any particular dance style and by placing it in an environment that viewed macho posturing as a complete waste of time and energy. It was as if the music itself underpinned a physicality that men felt comfortable with. The thumping bass and accelerated beats of the drum machine were exhilarating enough to drive drugged-up men onto the floor and, once there, they generated a muscular, vigorous and sweat-drenched style of dance that replaced outward aggression with a form of internal frenzy. It felt masculine and men could get on the floor and do their own thing without fear of censure from either men or women.

The inclusion of men on the dance floor also had a positive effect on women's dancing; suddenly they were no longer dancing under the watchful eyes of sexually tense men who were only in the club to get pissed and pull. Instead everyone was in it together and the general air of delirium granted both genders an increased sense of freedom on the dance floor as the sheer sexual and sensual aspects of dance resurfaced via this on-going liberation of the body from the judgmental gaze of the gendered other.

The Dionysian rush of the rave environment allowed both women and men to savour the sheer physical seductiveness of their own and others' bodies in a safe space. All my female informants stressed this level of safety as being a hugely important part of their clubbing experience. For them finding a space in which to sense their own bodies as both sensual experiences and erotic objects without having to worry about some 'idiot boy' getting the wrong idea and hassling them was one of the main draws of clubbing. As one informant suggested:

I get to be sexy. It seems silly, but I really enjoy it. When I'm in a club dancing my whole body feels hot and horny and alive. I can dress-up in a way that I could never do on the street or in pubs because I think in clubs people will accept that you're doing it for yourself. They can watch you and enjoy you, but that's as far as it goes. It's playful, rather than serious and it feels safe, much safer than other places where it might cause hassle. I feel more in charge of the situation, less threatened by people watching me. You know that some guy might be getting turned-on by the way you dance, but in a club that feels less dangerous because you expect the men to not behave like arseholes. If they're just smiling at you and watching you and enjoying you or dancing along with you, then they understand that it doesn't necessarily mean you want to fuck them. It's just part of the night, part of the fun of clubbing. (Female 41, 19 years' experience)

The other side of the coin came from an informant who said: 'I love to watch women dance in clubs, all glammed-up and looking beautiful. It's a big part of clubbing for me, enjoying women enjoying themselves. They're so fucking horny' (male 26, 8 years' experience).

The Social Dynamics of Dance

Only the most confident or intoxicated clubbers walk straight into a club and directly onto the dance floor. The majority of punters must first accustom them-selves to the space itself and start to relax into it. This social anxiety means that dance floors must build with the social buzz of the club and they pass through various stages over the course of a night, which reflect this buzz. The model laid out below is drawn from observing hundreds of dance floors. I must stress that this is a general account of the process and that the whole thing can change if a particularly up-for-it group suddenly arrives and throw themselves into the thick of the dancing, which will accelerate the whole process. In general, though, this five-stage plan held true in the majority of club spaces, regardless of the specific identity of the club itself.

Stage 1 is the pre-dance stage where punters begin to settle into the club. They congregate at the peripheries of the space, around bars, at the edge of the dance floor. Standing with their mates, scanning the crowd to see who's there, they drink, giggle and watch. Some are waiting for their drugs to come on and, at this stage, the crowd is still anxious about the night. Will it be a success? Will they have a laugh? Do they like the look of the crowd? Are they going to feel comfortable in that crowd? Yet, because clubbing is a sensual practice, these doubts are answered sensually: bodies start to alter and shift their postures as the drugs take effect; the crowd builds as does the noise and the heat; people begin smiling and laughing; the music starts to infect their bodies and movement. They are beginning to occupy the space, to feel emotionally at ease, physically energised, but relaxed. They start to enjoy the crowd and feel less threatened by it. Once this first stage is well underway then people begin to head for the dance floor.

Stage 2 is the point where a dance floor tentatively begins. Dance floors can take time to form because in their initial empty stages they are the most visible space in the club. Very occasionally they erupt out of nowhere because the DJ drops a club favourite or a confident party posse arrives in force. More often than not, though, they begin to build incrementally going through a stop-start process as people surreptitiously start to dance at the periphery, move into the visible space and then retire back to the edge. Usually the floor is surrounded by would-be dancers who are gagging to get boogying, but can't quite take that first step because they are still feeling too self-conscious about moving from the safety and anonymity of the crowd to the visibility of the floor. However, the infectious nature of the music gradually permeates their bodies: heads nod, feet tap, hips wriggle, torsos bounce. No one's dancing out in the open yet. They're chatting, watching, teetering on the edge, but they are beginning to move into the dance by experiencing the music as an irrepressible embodied force. People would rather be in a group at this stage so even when they do begin to move out onto the floor they will stay close together concentrating on one another and attempting to remain as invisible as possible. A logic of critical mass applies on a dance floor once it reaches a certain level of participation, usually two or three separate groups of people dancing, then it will suddenly explode into life and the balance between the dancers and the watchers is rapidly equalised as the punters realise that the night's taking off.

Stage 3 is the warm up period where dancers start to physically work themselves deeper into the dance. The temperature rises, muscles warm up and bodies relax as the music becomes a tangible presence deep within their flesh. This sensation of feeling yourself moving is almost like a sixth sense, the kinaesthetic sense, a sense of self and others in motion. The crowd nourishes you, each person linked by rhythm and movement, the pounding of the bass-bins and the rapid-fire riffs of the drums, enclosing the group, pulling you deeper into the succulence of the beat. Each dancer is different, unique, adopting different tempos in the music, some dancing with their arms, others from their feet or their hips, some standing almost completely still, except for the shiver they exhibit each times the bass hits. The joy of dancing in a club is that there is no wrong way to dance as long as you're getting off on it. The only bad dancer is a miserable one.

The perfect dance floor is one that coalesces and begins to dance together, where people dance with strangers, friends and lovers alike. People look beautiful when they are dancing and relishing it. Once their anxieties have fled you seem to catch sight of the life pumping ecstatically through their veins, empowering them, changing them, allowing them to pack every ounce of themselves into this space, this time, this electrostatic moment of carnal living.

Stage 4 is the point where the dance floor reaches a critical mass of bodies. It is the hottest and most intense stage in terms of being amongst others. Full dance floors can become static; they reduce the range of potential movement. This is the hands-in-the-air stage when you have to focus your movement vertically, rather than horizontally to avoid collisions. As one male informant explained: 'Dancing on a really packed floor that's really going-for-it can feel like leaping into a bucket full of eels; it's great. Hot bodies everywhere, all just squirming and getting sweaty; it's great.'

On a crowded dance floor dancing can become more akin to wriggling. This has its own charm – you sense the sheer closeness of the bodies next to you and the sensation of moving *en masse*. Your kinaesthetic sense is externalised by being transferred from your own body into the body of the crowd. Although you are physically moving less it can seem as if you are moving more because the whole club arena is in motion. The room ceases to be occupied by strangers, instead it is filled with party folk all satisfying their need to *be*. The heat can be overwhelming as the energy level rises with each tune the DJ drops. The sweat, which pours from your skin, cleanses you, draining out the toxic residue of frustrated plans, niggling worries, stupid arguments and petty insecurities. Nothing matters, but the beat, the crowd, the dance. Glorious.

The crowd has worked together to create this moment. It has put time, energy and hard cash into the night, but most importantly it has generated a sense of social camaraderie within the club that underpins the clubbers' ability to cut loose amongst the people who surround them. The dance is one way in which that sensation manifests itself in both individuals and groups by allowing them to possess a different physicality in the world; one that is strong and fervent, relaxed yet powerful; one that has shed the body of the drudge.

Stage 5 is the time when crowds have thinned out. The dance floor still rocks as the end of the night looms, instilling an extra urgency to the proceedings. The lightweights are leaving; the party hardcore remains. This is where the dance die-hards are most evident; pushing themselves through exhaustion, refuelling on drugs or simply dragging up reserves of energy and feeding upon the kinetic charge unleashed by the music and crowds; they continue to cut a serious rug. For these people the dancing won't end until the lights flick on. Some will have danced all night, barring the occasional fag break and trip to the bar or loo. I have seen people hit the floor for five or six hours at a time. In many ways these people are the energetic heart of a club because without a dance floor to provide a central point of reference the energy in the space swiftly dissipates. Hence the importance placed upon DJs in clubs; they must tease this energy out and sustain its presence because if the dance floor dies the club will soon follow. There is usually a look of shock upon these dancers' faces when the lights come on. They have been occupying time via their bodies and emotions and this warps the chronology of the event. It seems like a continual present in which time passes in rushes or minutes expand out into hours. This temporal disorientation is an important part of the experience because it is grounded in a sense of emotional immersion into the club space and the crowds. I overheard one group at the end of the night summing it up like this: 'It can't be six o'clock. It feels like two o'clock. Fuck we've been dancing for ages, has the bar shut? Shit, where are we going next? Will Trade be open?' Off they went still visibly boogying looking for another dance floor on which to finish their night.

Sensual Landscapes

Dancing in a club especially under the influence of Class A drugs is a special species of dance. As one informant explained:

> I was trained as a dancer, I worked as a dancer, I have always danced, I've always enjoyed dancing, but I never really felt like a dancer until I started taking drugs and dancing in clubs. That taught me more about dancing than any other experience of dancing ever has. (Female 41, 19 years' experience)

This informant is speaking of the sheer social, sensual and emotional intensity that marks club dancing out as a Dionysian practice. To fully comprehend these Dionysian extremes we've got to see clubbing as a particular co-ordinate in people's sensual landscape by which I mean the whole range of bodily practices that they encounter as they pass through their daily lives. As one male informant revealed:

> I work in front of a computer all week, sitting on my bum staring at this headache-inducing screen with one eye on my boss. I quite like my job, it's not that so much, it's just that it's so still, but you can never really relax because it looks like you've fallen asleep or something. Then I get to go out at the weekend and dance and it's stunning, just moving and the music and the heat and my body feels like mine again.

The body of capital is a rigid body, the mechanised body of work: upright and ordered. For some it is a sedentary body, which has its buttocks firmly rooted to a chair. For others it is a repetitive body carrying out the same tasks over and over again or it can be the strong but tired body of physical labour. Each body is ordered by the requirements of its work, by the expectations of bosses, by the rules of the corporation, by the habiti of each job. People's bodies are controlled in time and in space, too still or slouched and they're lazy, too manic and they're disruptive. They must sit or stand for hours at a time looking the part of the worker, even when they're dreaming of Caribbean seas and oral sex. Our minds can flee our jobs; our bodies must pass their allotted time in the space of work, even when we can't be bothered to actually do anything.

The clubbing body stands in opposition to this Apollonian body; it is seduced beyond its boundaries. One female informant described dance in these terms: 'Well the best way to describe dancing is it's the next best thing to sex; the feeling of your whole body being completely connected together and fluid and moving and you can just feel energy flowing right through your body.'

When I asked one informant about her enjoyment of dancing she was fairly frank in her reply. 'I haven't had sex for almost two years and dancing allows me to enter a wonderful sensual place. It's almost as good as sex in terms of making your body feel fabulous' (female 42, 5 years' experience).

I heard such sexual analogies used again and again by clubbers and they reveal just how erotic this body feels. As the night progresses punters become less self-conscious about this body, they climb onto podiums and become flirtatious and these actions are applauded in clubs, which is one of the very few spaces in British society where you are allowed to savour such visibility. These activities add to the club night and help draw other people in, as one informant explained:

> I don't do the display thing for me; well I don't feel like I do it for me. I do it for the fun of it and I try and get people to interact with me. If I'm strutting round the dance floor like a cockerel it's because I want other people to come out of themselves. It's not showing off; it's trying to provoke and tempt people to go further. It's not about performance; I don't want people to look at me; I want them to interact with me, to be with me, not stare at me. The display thing is all very silly really; it's a game. (Male 32, 14 years' experience)

This game is about giving something to the club; it is about using it to its full potential. The space itself can grant you the freedom to become bigger, more expressive, more outrageous and the more people participate and reveal this freedom through their participation the easier it becomes for others to follow suit.

The music unleashes a sensuous fever that infects the crowd, leaping across the floor with incredible rapidity, luring more and more people into its virulent grasp. The embodied residue of the week, your weaknesses, anxieties and strengths are channelled into the dance and so transmuted into movement, energy and heat. They are not simply forgotten their form is altered and their shadows are expunged from the flesh. The dance floor is on-one and I don't mean drugs, I mean living, not in the physically and emotionally confined spaces of everyday life. Grey flees the building to be replaced by vivid reds, burning oranges, iridescent blues and a slither of topaz. You ain't in Kansas no more. You're on a dance floor and it is fearsome fine.

At times this can literally feel transcendent; it is a physicality that takes you so far beyond the everyday experience of your own social body that it feels like a sublime manifestation of self-in-world. As one male informant said: 'If you haven't fucked God on a dance floor, then you've never truly danced.'

In terms of its physical intensity club dancing does seem comparable to the possessionary rites of Candomble or Vodun. I have taken myself elsewhere on a dance floor, I have inhabited a carnal and exhilarated body that has felt transcendent. However we must be careful when making using such an analogy, as Bataille (1985: 236) explains:

> While it is appropriate to use the word *mysticism* when speaking of a 'joy before death' and its practices, this implies no more than an affective resemblance between this practice and those of the religions of Asia or Europe. There is no reason to link any presuppositions concerning an alleged deeper reality with a joy that has no object other than immediate life. 'Joy before death' belongs only to the person for whom there is no *beyond*; it is the only intellectually honest route in the search for ecstasy.

There was no God on my dance floor, there was no cosmology of possession, no expectation of spiritual ascension, just people, booze, drugs, grins, music, all packed in on top of one another combining to produce an experience that becomes more than the sum total of its parts. 'It's the bollocks' just about sums it up. If you only focus on these moments of intensity, as Malbon (1999) does in his discussion of the 'oceanic experience', you can miss out so much of the dance experience. In fact for older clubbers the 'oceanic' is little more than a sensual trick that is seen as being less important than the Dionysian sociality of the dance floor. As one informant put it:

> I have a huge respect for people who do tango and really sexy partner dancing, but club dancing's different. It's an expression of exuberance and once you've got the basics down, if you can follow the beat, you express your exuberance about the beat in any way that you feel fit. You don't dance with one other person; you dance with everyone else on the floor. You rotate a bit and dance with someone else or dance with several other people. It's a big mass of people dancing and enjoying each others' dancing. (Male 32, 14 years' experience)

Another male said:

> One of my favourite things about dancing is that point when you catch someone's eye on the floor and you're both obviously getting off on the music. So you start to dance together and you dance for the track, but when it ends you've just got to hug them or thank them because it felt so good to share that thing with them and no I'm not talking about being pilled-up. It's just giving that moment you've shared some recognition and thanking them for it before you dance off. It's about openly enjoying other people.

These points of social interaction are a massively important part of clubbing and the dance floor is one of the best spaces for them to occur, but even simply watching other people dance has its own rush. As one informant explained:

> I do love watching dancers going off on-one on the floor. When you're just sitting down having a break and watching someone completely go-for-it and you see them have a really good time that's fab to watch. It's much better than anything you can watch on TV. (Female 41, 19 years' experience)

The ability to express yourself physically without fear of censure in a club was demonstrated by a number of incidents that I observed on the dance floor. On one occasion I watched a lone male simply stand on the spot and leap up and down grinning as hard as he could at everyone around him. He looked like he had popped a few Es and for a moment his physicality became that of an excited child. His sense of exhilaration was instantly communicated to the strangers who surrounded him, he ceased to be separate from the group, he became a physical emblem of the club's growing euphoria. On another occasion I witnessed a young, heavily-set guy suddenly burst into a reasonable and extremely energetic interpretation of Irish dancing. He looked like he weighed around eighteen stone, but in an instant his body began to defy gravity and his feet flew, sweat poured off him, his eyes were clenched tight shut and his face radiated sheer joy; it looked both majestic and deliciously silly. These incidents give some indication of the level of physical freedom tolerated in clubs. You don't have to look good when you dance; it is enough to simply dance and express your passion for dancing and this freedom is one of the most important qualities of clubs.

Summary

Club dancing is an expansive and Dionysian practice in that it moves people beyond their everyday social, sensual and emotional boundaries. It is therefore a form of knowledge: a way of occupying the world that challenges the sensual limitations imposed through the habitus and the imposition of the gaze, which is why my informants found it so liberating. This knowledge does not simply evaporate when people leave the club space, but rather it becomes a particular co-ordinate within clubbers' sensual landscape, a point of reference, which throws the bodily practices of the everyday world into relief. The constrictive nature of these everyday Apollonian practices ceases to be taken for granted, to use Bourdieu's (1977, 1990) terminology in relation to the habitus, and the knowledge gained through engaging in these practices can be transferred to alternative sensual activities. As one informant pointed out:

I wouldn't have sex with a man who couldn't dance. You watch a guy who can dance and who is an imaginative dancer, a sexy dancer, and you can see that he knows how to move; he knows about rhythm. He understands his own body and from my experience men that can dance are a lot better in bed than men who can't. They seemed to have learnt about sex by dancing. (Female 29, 13 years' experience)

A number of informants suggested the same thing, which suggests that people accumulate the socio-sensual knowledge they discover through clubbing and use it to intensify other points of sensual engagement with their world.

Music

There are only two types of music: good and bad.

(Duke Ellington)

Without music life would be a mistake.

(Nietzsche)

Every culture has its music; it is a human universal and music has a profound effect on those cultural worlds. In this chapter I will primarily examine the sensual aspects of club music, its kinaesthetic and emotional dynamism, which makes it capable of uniting crowds and underpinning passionate and intense social experiences. The soundtrack of clubbing is eclectic and inventive; each musical style offers a subtle alteration in the experience of clubbing, from the soaring anthems of house, through the two-step beat of garage, to the luscious complexity of Asian beats and the sheer rhythmic force of Drum 'n' Bass. Music's sensual potential is embodied through the writhing dynamism of the crowd. The sheer power of music to bring people together and radically shift the social and emotional timbre of clubs is truly awesome. Its ability to act as a form of sonic adrenaline that consistently re-energises the night is equally impressive, as this example from my diary reveals:

> Five o'clock in the morning, party's dying down, handful of dancers on the floor, everybody else crashed or chilling-out. Then the DJ changes and shift into techno, those around the floor perk up, the dancers pick up the pace and then whoosh bodies start tumbling into the room and we're off again. Another lull, half-past seven in the morning, everybody's looking wasted, DJ changes again, I don't hold out much hope for resuscitation, but I am wrong, deep funk this time, another stampede and away we go. Eventually crawled out at ten o'clock. Brain a bit blistered from the whizz and the E, but without the music the drugs wouldn't have been enough on their own to keep me going.

In *Club Cultures,* Sarah Thornton (1995) examines music as a form of subcultural capital, an approach that reduces music to a set of signs and symbols that are used as an alternative form of cultural knowledge. This is music as fashion and music as 'distinction', a way of showing off your 'hipness' (to use Thornton's terminology).

In its most extreme form this approach ends up as the 'trainspotter' view of music and amongst my informants this 'trainspotter' reflex was predominantly viewed in a negative light. As one informant explained:

> I don't like those hardcore techno nights that are full of nodding blokes going: 'Yeah tune, really obscure Derrick May remix, blah, blah, blah.' And all that trainspotting shit. I hate it when people get all tight arsed about their music. When they can't just kick back and let themselves loose because they're too busy trying to spot a sample or guess the label so they can show off how much bloody useless and obscure musical knowledge they know. (Male 32, 14 years' experience)

So, although music does generate its own forms of subcultural capital, this is not its only or indeed its most significant role in clubbing. To truly understand the relationship between music and clubs we must return to the notion of a sensual landscape, which we began discussing in the last chapter, and examine the way that music impacts upon this landscape in order to generate the euphoria and intensity of clubbing, which brings the crowd together and alters the way they experience both one another and the night as a whole. This aspect of music arises directly from its ability to become embodied by that crowd and to bring about profound changes in their emotional states.

Embodying the Beat

> If you think about the tunes too much you loose the ability to feel them and you've got to feel them. You've got to let them in, if you're really going to know them. (Female 34, 16 years' experience)

The intensity with which music can move people emotionally has been recognised by numerous commentators over the years. Both Schopenhauer and Nietzsche at various stages in their philosophical careers suggested that music could grant people profound and almost transcendent experiences, which provided one of the few ways in which life could be given meaning. One of my informants said:

> Music is one of the most important things in my life. It connects me to people because I know I share this passion with them. It makes me feel incredible; it inspires me to dream; it helps me to make sense of my life. I couldn't live without it. (Female 34, 16 years' experience)

The trainspotters can talk about music until their tongue's ache and their hips coagulate, but music only really begins to exist when the listener embodies it. Your heart soars, your spine tingles, you are infected by a beat that unleashes a profoundly emotional and utterly physical response. When a stunning new tune is dropped onto the deck it is like climbing into bed with somebody for the first time; you're hungry for the experience; you want that tune to become part of your body. You often don't notice this process occurring until you're right there in the centre of the beat givin' it some for all you're worth, only then do you fully appreciate just how physically potent music can truly be. One informant described her relationship to music in these terms: 'Sometimes the music makes me insane; I can't stop dancing; it feels like my heart will pop; I'm covered in sweat, but the beat keeps driving me on. I HAVE to dance, there's no other option the music's in control' (female 32, 9 years' experience).

In their book *Music Grooves,* Charles Keil and Stephen Feld (1994: 56) make an interesting observation:

> Common sense and day to day observation of children learning by doing as much as by thinking . . . have demonstrated quite convincingly that our muscles are perceptive. Somehow muscles remember . . . could it be that in many cultures children learn to listen when they learn to dance?

This statement suggests that dance expands your affinity to music by allowing you to build deeper and deeper physical relationships to it. Music ceases to be something that washes over your ears by becoming a corporeal force that is expressed in your whole physical response to the tune.

The social elements of clubbing are hugely important in terms of how you experience the music itself. Sharing music intensifies the way in which it affects you and the presence of music alters the way in which crowds relate to each other. The crowd and the beat nourish one another and the music exists as much through the body of the crowd as through its audible presence. As the crowd comes alive, so do the tunes; you begin to see the looks of amazement and excitement spread over people's faces. The sudden rush of recognition that sends someone hurtling onto the dance floor; people singing along; givin' it everything they've got, all wallowing in the passionate embrace of the music.

The sheer volume is one of the important differences between club sounds and other music as it literally amplifies the music's presence in your bones. As you pass through the door of a club the boom of the bass slaps you in the face. It is a wake-up call to the fact that you have entered an intense sensory environment where music, rather than existing as a background hum, has leapt to the foreground of perception. Within clubs music is largely inescapable; it ceases to be heard, instead it becomes a visceral, seductive form that has the power to 're-arrange your internal organs', as one female informant so succinctly put it. The glorious combination of amplification, sub-bass and accelerated beats charges the club environment with a palpable surge of sonic adrenaline, which has the power to unleash the Dionysian reflex in all, but the most jaded of souls.

The seductive power of music is the force that allows it to become a form of subcultural capital. Music is not imbued with its sense of meaningfulness for people via the endless labels and categories through which it is classified, but rather because it has the ability to generate and manipulate the realm of the sensual. It moves you physically, emotionally and mentally and, as the next informant reveals, clubs can deepen these properties:

> Clubbing's changed my attitude to music. I don't often listen to club music at home, but I'm more emotionally involved in all the music I listen to and I use music in a different way. I listen to all sorts of odd things. We played Robert Palmer yesterday. He's a bit of a joke now, but in the 1970s he wrote some of the most beautiful soul music the world's ever known and I'm prepared to give everything a go. I find myself buying all sorts of different music from different decades and getting emotionally involved and attached to it in ways that I wouldn't have done had I not gone clubbing. It's not about only listening to clubbing music; it's about allowing music to get that close to you. You get very emotionally involved in music in a club and it seeps into your life. Once you've felt the real power of music in a night-club where you're allowed to express the way it moves you, then forever more you just experience music more intensely. I bet you find that most clubbers have really interesting top tens. I bet Burt Bacharach is in a lot of clubbers' top ten because he creates beautiful songs. Even though club music breaks down the verse/chorus pattern and strips music down to a beat you still get into the musicality of it. So when you're at home and you fancy a bit of verse/chorus you can appreciate it more. It made me less tolerant of the pop stuff. Me and my friends who go clubbing when we're at home we tend to listen to real classic great songwriters while people who don't go clubbing they're prepared to put up with Blur or Steps. (Male 32, 14 years' experience)

Clubs made him experience music differently because of the way in which it affected him at an emotional level while in the club space. This is music as a viscous, material force that penetrates deep into people's sensual core and either radically alters or powerfully reflects the way they feel in the world. Club tunes uses certain techniques and technical resources to intensify the already potent effects that music can have on both individuals and groups. In the next sections, I want to examine the way in which these technical advances have played an important role in shifting music's experiential parameters and so altered the sensual landscape of those who encounter it in clubs.

Bass

If I believed in a God, then that God would take the form of a bass beat. Raw, guttural and sublime the bass enfolds and possesses, it is the heartbeat of clubbing, both archaic and wise, infusing both time and space with the organicism of a living thing. The arrival of sub-bass heralded an intensification of the cult of bass, once only explored in its most extreme manifestation via Dub it began to creep into the realm of dance music as more and more musicians recognised its awesome power to envelop people. The advances in sound recording and reproduction, which have occurred in the current electronic age of music, allowed bass to reach a visceral zenith that sank deep into the flesh of those who experienced its intoxicatory allure.

Such a bass has the ability to sculpt air and charge it with an electrostatic frisson, which makes it akin to being touched . The driving power of this subcutaneous force is a source of energy in itself, it hits your gut, genitals and chest with a kinetic surge of desire that can at times become so intense that it is physically overwhelming and you are forced to turn away for fear of puking. A pumping bass beat launches you onto the floor before you've even thought about it. Its immediacy is lascivious and virulent and the rhythm it carries infects entire rooms. A Rastafarian woman I met at a Dub night explained that: 'Bass is a communal thing for Rastas; it immediately links you to people and to Jah. There is obviously no scriptural reference to bass, just a shared feeling that brings you together and makes you all one.'

The emotional power of bass is derived from its material quality, which enfolds the listener within the tune. Sometimes it is heavy and dark like someone's creeping up behind you possibly with an axe clutched in their sweaty, psycho paws; at others it is exhilarating like the kick bass of techno that imbues you with instant energy and makes dancing feel like a form of sonic surfing. One informant explained how she:

> was knackered before I came out and I wasn't in the mood for drugs, but I knew I'd have a good time when I got here, so I made the effort, even though I didn't feel up to it. The minute the bass hit all that tiredness just went and I was off. I can't resist it. I just love hearing that bass.

The act of living is rhythmic from the beat of our hearts to the ordering of our time. We adopt rhythms in the form of habits: the way we walk down the street, how we pass our working day, when we eat and sleep, they all become rhythms that suffuse our sense of being-in-the-world. These everyday rhythms are embodied in our physicality and our movements, yet they can be disrupted by a counter rhythm and the force of the bass beat has the power to create such as disruption. The deeply sensual quality of bass, its material succulence, penetrates the flesh like an alternative heartbeat that initiates a new physicality. Dub uses slow, stoned rhythms, but drum 'n' bass or techno combines the power of bass with an acceleration, which lifts the body. This force is infectious; it drives you on and energises the entire club space. As an informant commented:

> You can completely feel bass and nine times out of ten when you're drug fucked they could turn the treble off and you'd hardly notice it had gone. You don't follow the treble when you're dancing; you follow the mid-range and the bass. With bass you can get so

immersed in the sound that you can't even see; it just fills you up. (Male 26, 8 years' experience)

Clubs encourage such physical change, the intoxication, the crowds and the music all work together to create new physical and emotional rhythms that underpin an alternative experience of self-in-world. Bodies shift, they throw off the rhythmic constraints of everyday life, they mutate physically as they gradually embody the beat to the point where they feel energised, potent and powerful. One of the hallowed mandates of clubbing is that clubs are places in which you can be yourself, but that self must cast off the fears and insecurities that are carried within the physicality of the body and that restrain our ability to openly express ourselves. As a male informant explained: 'It feels so different in a club than anywhere else. Your body relaxes, but it's not a sinking form of relaxation; it's full of energy and a lot of that comes from the beats and they just power you on. You feel strong, if you know what I mean.'

Acceleration

Western music has become faster; the combination of clubs, the drugs and the technology behind the music itself has radically increased the BPM (beats per minute) of clubs' tunes. One informant explained that BPM rates manifested themselves as alternative styles of club music:

Different styles of music attract different people for different reasons. The regular house, garage scene is sort of 130 BPM, which is roughly one and a half times the resting heart rate of the average person. It's easy to get into; you're not getting too hot and sweaty; you can have a little dance. It's slow enough that the women get to shake their booty without losing it.

Then you move onto the underground garage of today, which is again about 130 BPM, but as it's a two-step beat it feels slower. It's not slower, if you hook up a BPM counter to it some of it's coming in at 140, 145, which is Trance, but because it's a two-step beat you only hit every other beat, so you can still give-it-some without getting too sweaty. That's the thing with this sort of crowd, if you go to a house or garage club they're very much into the way they look. They have to look very neat, precise; they've got their D and G, dodgy banana; they've got their Ralph Lauren's and Moshino and that's fair enough, go-for-it, but they don't want to drench it in sweat, so they end up looking a bit bedraggled, do they?

Then you get House music. For the purists like Progressive House it's a little bit faster, but it's mainly for people who are into the technical thing; they're listening for the mix, this bit, that bit; they're not really there to enjoy themselves. Ninety-nine times out of a hundred they're with the media, coked out-of-their-brains; you know the ones that get media flu on a Monday morning.

Then you get Trance and Progressive Trance, which is what the latest Trance DJ thing is called, that's the euphoria-level-three stuff. It's fun; it's faster; 140 BPM; you're dancing around bang, boing, boing, boing. Once you get passed that stuff then you start getting into Hard House, Hard Trance. For me, when you get somebody who knows what they're doing on the decks with Hard House and Hard Trance that's my level. It's also NRG, which means they play it slightly faster, 140 record banged up to 155. That's when you can't care how you look; you're listening to the music; you're going-for-it. People are supposedly into Hard House this year. Mixmag defined Hard House as a bassier version of House, but anyone in London who knows Trade knows that Hard House is faster and less jangly, less piano more bonk, bonk, bonk. It's kind of grit your teeth music, but you can still smile as you grit them. (Male 26, 8 years' experience)

The process of acceleration increased the intensity of the music – not at an emotional level (all forms of music are capable of unleashing profound, emotional responses and that quality isn't related to its speed) – rather, it intensified music at a kinaesthetic level. The musicologist Gabrielsson (1987) suggested that all rhythms possessed inherently kinetic properties; a classification he has extended to cover both real and implied motion. This implied or imaginative motion is increased in the accelerated realm of club tunes. When you're watching a trance crowd go off they don't necessarily seem to be moving any faster than a house crowd, particularly on a crowded dance floor, but from my own experience, and from watching countless crowds, accelerated beats seem to intensify the sense of self-in-motion in the mind. The implied kinaesthetic quality of the beat makes people feel they're moving more than they actually are. In a crowd situation this is intensified even further because your own movements occur within a sea of movement. As one informant said after seeing herself dancing on video in a crowd:

I was really surprised at how little I was moving. It felt like I was really going-for-it, but my body's actually moving quite slowly and I'm moving my head much more than I thought I was, but I remember that particular point in the night and at the time it felt like I was really pushing my dancing. (Female 30, 11 years' experience)

The kinetic qualities of the beat intensify your perception of your own body and add to your sense of bodily acceleration. The beat infects both body and mind; it exists as a combination of mental schema and bodily practice that together creates the experience of dance. The faster the beat the more frenzied your dancing feels; it magnifies the sensation of the body. It is important to remember that the BPM is not the only connection that people make to a tune. Music has different characteristics, speed is only one dimension of dancing, and dancing won't necessarily feel better or more fulfilling because you're dancing to fast music. We are simply talking about a sense of frenzy here and not everybody wants to experience that sense of frenzy. One male informant described his experience of accelerated beats on the dancefloor in these terms: 'When the beats really get cranked up it feels like a sonic strobe light going off in your head; it just pushes you on; it feels chaotic, but it's great.'

As the beats become faster the experience of dancing to them changes; in general the faster the beat the more internalised the sense of dancing becomes, which alters the social dynamic of the dance floor. People enter their own world of dance, there's less direct social contact, but you can still feel the weight and presence of the crowd, so it is still a social and shared experience. As you push the kinaesthetic limits of your own body and feel the passion of the music suffusing your flesh your consciousness contracts. As one informant explained:

I love losing it on the dance floor when I'm just going-for-it and it's hot and I'm just feeling the music and my dancing and that's all that seems to exist really. (Female 41, 19 years experience)

I watched one woman dancing on top of the speakers for at least four hours, stopping only occasionally to drink some water, physically matching the beats, staring out over the crowds, but seemingly without really noticing them. However, you can feel the crowd moving around you and that crowd is linked through the experience of the beat; it is a tangible kinetic rush that drives them on and on and on. As one informant commented:

To a certain extent you make yourself as an individual smaller, less, and you become part of this mass. It's a collective experience in the same way as the hypnotic-type, voodoo, drumming ceremonies. It is the nearest contemporary Western people can get to those quasi-trance experiences and time does funny things to you and you get this feeling of pure energy. Energy in yourself and feeding off everyone else's energy and feeding off the music, the rhythm of the night. (Male 32, 14 years' experience)

This is a point of deep sensual connection to yourself, the crowd and the music. The sense of energy flowing through your veins makes you feel exquisitely alive and supercharged. Acceleration offers another point of sensual expansion, another intense physical encounter that has become a mainstream experience in the contemporary world.

Chemical Beats

There is a symbiotic relationship between music and drugs. They make sense of one another in many ways as they alter the way the music occupies your body, particularly when dancing. The accelerant quality of drugs has played a role in making dance music sensually comprehensible by generating a physicality that could match its intensity. As one informant explained:

I just didn't get dance music when I first heard it, especially the real hardcore stuff. It was only after I listened to it in a club on drugs and danced to it that it began to make sense to me and now I love it and I can listen to it without being drugged-up. (Female 31, 13 years' experience)

Another male said: 'I don't know what it is about drugs and music, but they work together; it's like the drugs help you let the music in.'

Music's capacity to challenge the parameters of our sensual landscape can be seen by the impact it has on cultural worlds. The arrival of rock and roll or even the Charleston both created moral panics because of their impact upon the body. Both Elvis's wriggley hips and the spectre of coked-up debutantes gyrating wildly were perceived as a threat to the moral order of the day because they radically challenged the constraints placed upon the body in Western society, which demanded discipline, rather than ecstasy and frigidity, rather than sexuality. Lord knows what the powers-that-be would have thought about club tracks if they could be sent back in time. They'd certainly be seen as the work of the devil, but then Old Nick's renowned for having all the best tunes.

The drugs, music and dancing triptych allows people to build different relationships between these three seductive forms. The music affects the dancing, the drugs effect the music and the dancing alters the way people feel the drugs and the music. All these new relationships arise as practices, rather than ideas and people encounter these practices as moments of heightened sensual intensity within a radically altered social framework. They become deep participants, but this level of participation is a bodily technique that can move beyond clubs. It can permanently alter the way music is received by the listener; they learn how to listen to and feel music in different way.

Part of this shift in relationship has a Pavlovian quality; the beats exist not only as a type of music, but also become inextricably linked to the emotional experience of clubbing. As one informant pointed out:

I love dancing to good music that just makes my body tingle and it makes you stand up and wriggle; you just can't sit down to this tune. Yes, there are points when you're just too tired to get up and dance to it, but you can still wriggle in your chair and wobble and feel it pulsate through your body. It has the effect that if you dance to a good tune for the first time and it's fabulous and you peak out, then when you hear it on the radio or something a week later those feelings rush back into your body. Not at the same level, but you definitely feel that euphoria again, just by listening to the music. Your body seems to clock it before your mind does. (Female 41, 19 years' experience)

Music is at its strongest when that music becomes part of a person's biography. Hearing a dance tune in another environment could still bring back at least some of the euphoria of clubbing. It becomes an emotional marker, a trigger like Pavlov's bell, but this is an act of self-conditioning arising out of a subcultural body. It becomes a point of connection back to the good times; you find yourself smiling, bouncing along and generally feeling groovy as you reconnect to the sensual states that clubbing underpins. It reminds you that life can feel good, even when the situation you're in may not be so hot.

Summary

Music has always been imbued with passionately sensual and emotional qualities for the listener. The club environment and advances in musical technology have intensified some of these qualities. The viscous and energising properties of bass, the shift into accelerated rhythms and the influence of drugs has altered the sensual landscape through which music is experienced by clubbers. It has become ecstatic in that it has gained the capacity to underpin a radical shift in the way people experience a social body, which is empowered by subcultural rhythms that challenge the Western focus on bodily discipline and control by seducing people into a state of frenzy. This state of frenzy can take two forms in the sense that it can be both an individual experience of deep immersion into the beat or a more social encounter created through the emotional power of music, which binds people empathetically to one another.

The club experience and the music combine in memory. Club tunes can unleash an almost Pavlovian response because they are intimately linked to the sensual biography of clubbers. They reignite part of the rush of clubbing, its kinaesthetic and emotional properties, and this experience brings the sense of having lived and of having had a good time back to clubbers. The music exists as a soundtrack of pleasure, of being amongst people, sharing good times with them and feeling good. It helps keep the sensual knowledge of clubbing alive by acting as an emotional referent, which can be experienced at other times and other spaces away from the club environment. This is important because the realm of the sensual is not remembered in the same way as ideas. The memory of the emotional content of clubbing can dissipate over time. It can leak from the flesh. Music can reverse this process and bring it all flooding back, even if it does so in a somewhat gentler form.

−4−

Sex

Humans are erotic beings and they need somewhere they can go to celebrate and share that side of their nature.

(Tuppy Owen)

Love is the answer, but while you are waiting for the answer, sex raises some pretty good questions.

(Woody Allen)

I want to examine sex as part of the sensual fun of clubbing by paying special attention to the highly social, expressive and voyeuristic forms of sexual play that people engage in within club spaces. The search for sex, companionship and intimacy suffuses the sensuality of clubland. Yet, we should be careful when we define the sexuality of clubland because the club arena provides a space for at least four forms of sexual experience. The first is the search for sex that plays a large but curiously unsung part of the desire to club. The second is the sensuality of expressing your own sexuality, of feeling sexual, of displaying your own body for your own satisfaction and enjoyment; again this is not limited to sex clubs. As we saw in the chapter on dance, it is part of the whole field of clubbing. The third is the creation of communities based around a shared sexual orientation like the gay or lesbian scene. The fourth is sharing sex, being amongst sexual people, engaging in sexual play, exploring and discovering new aspects of your sexual-self in a specifically sexual environment. This aspect of sex is most highly visible in the sex club scene.

The sex club scene is far smaller than the mainstream club scene but it is growing rapidly. The aesthetics of fetishism have become part of the mainstream media's visual arsenal. The latex and leather look has become the symbolic expression of sexual power games and sexual difference, the height of sensual chic with Gucci, jewelled wrist restraints selling out within days of their arrival in the store. The sex club inverted the history of sexual morality by creating a sublime social tolerance that filled this clubbing arena with the added erotic frisson of sexual expression. Taboos were smashed by becoming visible and shared but retained just enough of their transgressional allure to keep them saucy and passionate. All of the other elements of clubland remain intact and not everybody has sex. People dance, talk and chill out as in every other club space, but there is enough visible sex to move the space one step further away from the everyday world and so challenge the habitus, which provides the socio-sensual framework through which we encounter sex in that world.

The Sexuality of Clubbing

Sexual desire is a clubbing constant, regardless of race, age, gender or sexual orientation; the only difference is how much it is expressed in the visual make up of the club. I had been asking an informant questions in the queue and he told me he was mainly at the club for the music, but when I met him again inside the club after he'd had a few beers he said: 'I'm here to try and get laid; I think most people are; you just don't admit it because somehow it's not cool.'

One of the promoters I talked to reiterated this idea while also revealing the important role of finding a sexual partner plays in people's desire to club:

> People club for different reasons, but the hope of finding a partner is always there. It's quite funny, when you're on the scene you see people turn up every week for a few months, going out every night, having a wicked time, going to all the different places on a certain scene, say a Drum 'n' Bass scene, telling you that they're mad for the music and the scene and then they meet a girl or a boy and they don't come very often. It's part of that finding a partner process and a club is a good place to find a partner because people are showing off, people are looking good.
>
> Is there less of a drive to pull in clubs than there used to be? It has changed, but it's still one of the elements. It is just not as blatant in a lot of clubs, but it's one of the driving forces in all clubs that will never go away. (Male)

The men and women of clubland enjoy the sexual frisson that hangs in the air of a club. They want to be checked out sexually; they want to flirt; be admired for their looks, their dancing, their seductive allure; it is all part of the fun of clubbing. The sexual gaze plays a huge role in intensifying the experience of the party in all club spaces. The phatic communication of eyes devouring flesh; the smiles that keeps such looks from becoming oppressive; the sensual exuberance of the night all combine to raise the temperature of the event. Like drugs, sex is becoming a leisure pursuit that is gradually being deproblematised in terms of the Protestant-Christian perspectives, which viewed it as a morally degenerate social force. People fuck for fun; it is part of the sensuality of clubbing, the cherry on top of an already delicious cake. As one informant explained:

> I love watching women and men dance; I love watching sexy people doing sexy things. I mean actual sex shows are damn boring. I've seen girls dancing and they're turning me on like a bastard. I'm sitting there thinking: 'Oh fuck, the things I want to do to your body.' Then I've seen live sex shows, full penetration, double barrels, the works and I'm

sitting there going: 'Big deal this is boring.' If I've gone clubbing and I've had way too much speed or E to have sex, but I've had a fantastic night, then it doesn't bother me if I don't get laid because I'm feeling really fucking good anyway. It changes the rules of the game in some ways. I've been talking to girls before in a club and I like them and we're getting on and it's come to the point where you know you're getting somewhere, but when it's come to the crunch I've had to turn round to them and say: 'Look I'm really sorry, but there's no way on earth I'm gonna be able to have sex with you tonight. I am completely drug fucked, even a miracle from the lord wouldn't give me an erection, but I still think you're absolutely fantastic and lovely. So if you stay over tonight, we can crash out, chill, talk, watch vids, whatever and in the morning we can fuck for as long as you want.' And it's worked and when I've had good drugs, the night before, the next morning, shit, I'm gagging for a fuck, so we get to spend the day in bed. (Male 26, 8 years' experience)

This statement is interesting for a number of reasons. Firstly, it gives a good picture of just how sexually charged clubs can be and how punters enjoy being part of this sexually seductive environment. Secondly, it reveals how the sensual intensity of clubbing can make finding a sexual partner less of a priority at times because clubbers are already experiencing a high level of bodily immersion into the space, the crowds and the experience as a whole. Hence my suggestion that sex becomes the cherry on top of the cake; a metaphor I suggested to the same informant who replied:

Yeah, I think that's very valid. You'd rather have the whole cake than just the cherry and you can fuck-up a night if all you're trying to do is eat the cherry and ignore the cake, but then sometimes you really do just want to go out and get laid. So I guess a lot of it depends upon your mood and how horny you're feeling, but I can see what you mean.

The visceral nature of clubbing can be as intense as sex in the level of physical immersion and participation people experience when clubbing particularly through dancing. It is obviously not the same thing as sex, it can just be as physically and emotionally intense as sex, but in a different way. When this sensual intensity becomes the bodily platform out of which the process of seduction and sexual consummation arises, then sex itself is intensified beyond its own more sober sensual parameters. However, I am specifically speaking here of regular dance clubs. Sex clubs provide a far more overtly sexualised environment, which immediately eroticises the experience of clubbing to a higher degree by making its sexual nature more visible.

Arc: Snapshot of a Sex Party

This was a fundraiser for a charitable organisation, an illicit night that involved making multiple phone calls to find the venue. We'd got our tickets in advance but it still took a while to find the party. This particular night was spent with my girlfriend K and a friend M.

The house it is based in is great by managing to be both exceptionally ugly, but wonderfully sleazy in a 1970s porn film sort of way. It's started raining outside and the kitchen roof is leaking badly. We drop a tiddle of Ecstasy and M heads off to the loo to honk down a line of cocaine. He returns with that distinctive spring in his step.

This particular group has an etiquette code, which is applied at all their events:

1. Stewards are available to advise and help our guests to feel relaxed enough to be themselves, so have a chat.
2. Never touch or intrude upon someone uninvited and move on if asked.
3. Discreetly indicate to stewards any guests who behave disrespectfully to others before any serious security problems arise.
4. Safe sex – our stewards will happily supply you with a free condom if you're caught on the hop.
5. No swastikas or racist symbols – even as a kinky fetish; they cause serious misunderstanding and justifiable offence.
6. No cameras and no press: This event is private.
7. No litter-please, use the receptacles provided.
8. Be discreet in the neighbourhood when arriving and departing.

The crowd is mixed: white, black, Asian, straight, gay, lesbian, bisexual, transsexual, transvestite, young, old and wheelchair users are all having a fine, old time. We find ourselves some space in one of the dance rooms, which is fairly empty at this point in the proceeding. The carpet is an ageing shag pile that makes dancing feel a little odd because your feet keep sticking to it. We neck some beers and then the three of us start to boogie, goofing off, celebrating the fact that we'd actually found the party. A few people join us, some familiar faces arrive, we start to relax.

It's time to head off for a nose around. The room next door is larger and has a sunken pit in the centre. This is the tantric sex/theatre room. The pit is a space where anyone who chooses to obey the rules can enter. The rules are displayed on the wall: no wanking, no spunking, no shoes. People are in various states of undress, they roll around stroking, caressing, kissing. It is all touchingly innocent and relaxed and the crowd round the edge chats, watches and smiles.

There are four main room upstairs: one is for dancing, another for chilling-out, the third is the dungeon and the fourth is the couples' room, which single people are not allowed to enter. Just off the chill-out room is the gay men's cupboard, a tiny, little space that is packed fit to bust. We opt for some dancing; it's a Latino rhythm and the room is packed. Two women in sequinned stars and stripes bikinis are grooving-on-down in a particularly saucy stylie. The E has connected and K, M and I flog our bodies with the beat. A rather irritating man who's dressed as a school teacher in cap and gown keeps trying to cane my butt, obviously over-excited by my rather splendid sequinned frock and I politely, but firmly, send him on his way. K's started chatting to a couple of women; they're heavily tattooed and wearing tight, tight corsets and ultra, high-heeled fuck-me pumps. They've got the giggles because their heels mean that they can hardly stand, never mind walk, and their corsets won't let them sit down, but they're still having a good time, feeling sexy and happy. They're both in full-time employment and this is the way they choose to spend their wages, hanging out with people who are 'fun-loving and laid-back'. I start talking to the guy sitting next to me who is completely naked, which seems totally normal in this space, even though most people are dressed. He's been coming to these parties for years and loves them because they're so friendly and sexy. The event certainly has the social feel of a party in someone's home; a lot of people know each other already and it just doesn't feel like you're surrounded by strangers.

We head off again; there is a lot of milling around, people shuffling past each other down corridors, a constant flow of human traffic, all seeking something – sex, companionship, fun, laughter, love. The atmosphere is starting to chill out, just like every other party this takes time. We come across 'Diamond Lil's Incredible Cunt Show'. It costs a pound and the money goes to the charity's war chest. I decide to give it a whirl. The show consists of a box, which has a magnified panel in the front; upon payment the curtains open and Lil's cunt is proudly displayed and magnified to TV screen proportions. She has a very pretty pussy and I do the only thing a gentleman should do when presented with such a sight: I cheer and whoop resoundingly as Lil holds herself open for inspection. Cunts are so very beautiful. Lil pops her head over the box to see who is responding so well and then I get an *encore* for my efforts. By the time the show has finished there is a queue lined up behind me. K's dissolved into giggles. I should have gone into PR.

M returns from checking out the dungeon; he's been such a naughty boy he had to be punished. We're dancing away again with a group. One woman wears a kitty-suit, which is open across the breasts and crotch; the man accompanying her is in vivid Lycra; an older guy, about seventy, wanders past in a fetching rubber g-string. M is dancing with a woman who's wearing a tiny, white, see-through, baby-doll dress; he looks ever so happy. We sit down for a spliff; next to us a couple is kissing, then the woman's boyfriend appears and taps her on the shoulder so he can grab a ciggy. The guys talk while the woman searches her bag, they compliment the woman on her kissing skills and then she hands over the ciggy and with a smile her boyfriend wanders off leaving his girlfriend to continue snogging her new friend.

Over the other side of the room another couple is getting passionate. He's looking sharp in Armani; she's looks like a gloriously pornographic, Barbie doll with bottle-blonde hair, steel-tipped heels and crotchless, rubber shorts. She sits astride his rather large cock, fucking him like a freight train on heat while his eyes flicker into the back of his head and his hands encircle her breasts. Around them people are talking and chatting away; a few people watch and enjoy; everyone else just lets them get on with it without batting an eyelid. They continue for maybe fifteen minutes and then she rolls off him; he hasn't ejaculated and he just pops his willy away and they head off to get a drink, looking relaxed and reinvigorated.

There is a moment's commotion around the theatre pit as one participant tries to get in without taking his shoes off. The hippie in the fishnet body-suit who seems to be in charge of this particular slice of space stops his drumming and demands the person leave the pit; there's some muttering, but the interloper is eventually ejected. The rules laid down in the party charter provide a set of boundaries within which people can interact. The sexual content of the space can leave people feeling a bit freaked so it's important to create a model of social interaction that they can hold onto and through which they can engage with others. The most important rule is obviously consent and the right to refuse or stopping what's happening at any point is continuously stressed within the organisers' literature. This is particularly important in a sexual arena where people can get confused and over excited if they're not use to such behaviour.

We end up in the chill-out room, skinning up, gabbing away. The DJ's naked. This is a gentle room as chill-out spaces tend to be; the music is soothing, rather than frenetic, everybody looks stoned out-of-their-gourds. We decide it's a little too laid-back and head out to the action. At the top of the stairs we pass the white, baby-doll woman who beams at us and waves. She has two boys licking a breast each while another guy kneels in front of her nuzzling her panty-clad pussy and running his fingers over her thighs. She says one word: 'lovely' as we walk by; her smile is a colossal beaming testament to the pleasures of the flesh.

The dungeon's busy; two women clad in expensive lingerie are using one of the whipping posts. One stands legs astride while the other deftly crops her cunt and thighs producing moans of pleasure. They look beautiful. In the corner a more intense scene is going down: a women is caged with a piece of leather restraint wrapped around her throat, she's sitting on a guy's lap and a crowd surrounds them. Her 'Top' is controlling the proceedings with skill. The mixed crowd have their hands pushed through the bars, covering her body, stretching her nipples, running over her pussy and legs, exploring her ass while she groans and cries out for more. Her eyes have rolled into the back of her head; sweat is pouring from her and the recognisable rush of an orgasm flickers across her musculature. She's revelling in the attention; fantasy has become reality and her passion is radioactive, charging the space with a sizzling sexual buzz.

Most of the actual sex at this event took place in either the gay men's cupboard or the couples' room. The couples' space looks a little daunting, it's a darkened room that is policed by one of the party's stewards to ensure that single people can't enter. Inside, though, it's relaxed; people are stretched out on cushions; it's languorous and lush as the dressed-up punters snake their bodies around one another. Most of the action is one on one with the occasional threesome and foursome. We just sit there for a while, a bit shy, but the infectious, seductive charge of the space is drawing us in and kindling our passion while simultaneously relaxing us and making us feel less self-conscious. The guy next to us licks his wife's asshole while she roots in her handbag for lube and condoms. A woman in a wild, red hat and stockings gently dildo fucks herself, putting on a show for her wheelchair-using partner. Hands wander up skirts and into waistbands. A lascivious mambo of desiring bodies getting off on themselves and the presence of others. I'm getting my cock sucked; it's hot, giggly fun and I relax into it, savouring the visibility, letting my eyes wander to catch glimpses of faces burning with passion, invigorated by the charge of sexual tension and the amiable glow of fulfilment. It's honey sweet and whisky warm.

Downstairs the theatre has stopped and people are just hanging out talking, laughing, joking. In the corner of the room a transvestite is sucking the foot of a leather-clad dominatrix who's drinking champagne. The toe-sucker is writhing like a playful kitten, obviously turned on; the Dom is being cool until with a flick of her foot she sends the transvestite on his way. He thanks her and leaves the room presumably searching for more perfectly manicured feet. Everyone looks so laid back and charming; this is a truly tolerant space. I get one of those rushes, which have occurred throughout the fieldwork period whether on drugs or not; this is human beings at their very best creating a social space that is gentle, supportive and happy.

We eventually crawl out at about 8.00 a.m. The three of us are feeling groovy and we end up lounging around in the living room, smoking weed, swapping tales and laughing until 11 a.m. when we eventually tumble into our beds, exhausted, but happy. Just like after a day's hard physical labour a night of intense partying makes you feel like you've worked to achieve something. Its presence suffuses your flesh, a visceral reminder that at least for a few hours you have stepped beyond the mundane.

Sex Clubs

The sex club has its own genealogy, which lies outside of the rave culture discussed in most of the texts about clubbing. Sexual spaces have always existed in our society, but their growth as a social arena has accelerated since London's first commercial sex club opened in 1986. The sex club adds an extra dimension to the club experience. The crowds are there to revel in this overt, social sexuality and they will tolerate more extreme forms of sexual display than you'll come across in a regular club. The imposition of a code of etiquette formalises the basic, social practices of clubland into a more rigid social framework that is designed to both protect and liberate the sexual nature of the event and the operation of strict dress codes attempts to ensure that the gawpers are kept out. This exclusivity is necessary because the environment of the sex club is another step further removed from the everyday world and some people can just find it too much: they get scared, feel insecure and threatened, morally outraged or just plain freaked out and over excited to the point where they get legless, abusive and intrusive.

Sex clubs are not orgies where simply walking through the door will guarantee that you'll get laid. The same social rules that operate across the rest of clubland also operate in this space. Not everybody who attends wants to fuck or flagellate. Many are simply enjoying the expression of a particularly sexual persona that allows them to wear what they like, behave in especially sexual ways, explore their fantasies and exhibit their desires. They can do these things for themselves without necessarily wanting to share them with anyone else.

I met a lot of couples in clubland who relished the chance to glam-up and savour one another's seductive allure. They got to witness a different version of each other's personas that can so often be forgotten during endless nights of watching television in the living room while scagging around in shapeless casuals. The joys of watching your lover dressed to thrill and getting slinky on a dance floor as eyes feast upon their flesh is a potent act of re-sensualisation that can reawaken desires numbed by the sensual mundanity of the everyday world. As one informant explained:

> I love it when we [he and his wife] get all dressed-up and come out. Look at her she's amazing, but these are the only places we'd have the confidence to dress like this and fuck she turns me on when she does. It gives you an excuse to be really sexy, to make that extra effort; you get tarted up and flirt and dance and just enjoy being with all these funky, sexy people. We always shag like bunnies when we get home; we're so turned on. (Male)

It doesn't have to go any further than this; simply being in a space where people celebrate and savour sex where they dress to arouse both themselves and others has its own sensual rewards. However, other people do take it further; they enjoy sharing their lovers with others and experimenting with sexual desire. Take this example from the Sex Maniacs' Ball, as recounted by its organiser Tuppy Owen:

> We had a lot of space that year so we'd set up a drive-in movie area with some cars and a screen with porn films playing. One couple got into a car and things started getting fairly hot so that a crowd gathered. The couple were fucking away, obviously really turned-on and they kept it up for hours. The crowd would change, but they didn't stop. Anyway I saw them at the end of the night and they were really excited. They came over and said: 'Thanks.' And how great the night had been, then they said that they'd never really imagined that they could have got off on doing such a thing. The Sex Maniacs was the first sexually orientated party they had been to. They thought it would be an adventure, but they got the surprise of their lives at how turned-on they'd got. Anyway,

a few months later I heard from them again; they had set up a club in their hometown and it was doing really well and they were really enthusiastic about it. So just from that one discovery they had changed their lives fairly dramatically and it was permanent change; they'd discovered something about themselves that they hadn't known existed.

This is sex as a shared adventure; a process of discovery that turns vague, often unarticulated desires into socially sanctioned realities. You can find desires in sex clubs. You can witness sexual scenarios that you may not have considered and find yourself becoming aroused by them. You get to see sex as a game played by consenting adults, rather than a practice bounded by the rules of monogamy and sexual propriety.

One of the first things I noticed about the whole sex club scene was how quickly you became used to it. It ceased to look strange after twenty minutes in the space because the social vibe was so obviously benign. The level of participation varies amongst the crowds; everyone is dressed-up because that is an entry requirement, but not everyone will engage in some form of visible sexual practice. So some punters will use the dungeon and put on shows for others. Some will enjoy being sexual creatures and revealing themselves as such to the world. Some will end up having sex. At one night I ended up sitting next to a couple who looked in their late forties; the guy was naked except for a cock-strap and a snakeskin jacket; the woman was wearing lingerie and sat beside me while giving the guy a blowjob. It felt a bit odd for a while, but they were just enjoying themselves. They were luxuriating in the attention as people glanced at them or stopped to watch and they carried on for about ten minutes before stopping and moving off to the bar. This wasn't hardcore sex; they giggled as they headed to the bar; it was sexual play in a safe space.

The majority of punters tend not to engage in public sex; they are there to enjoy the sexual vibe of the space, to dress-up and delight in an alternate sexual reality, to savour its erotic edge. It is a world of seductive glances and lascivious smiles, of overtly sexual bodies getting down on the dance floor, people smiling and laughing and getting turned-on. It is also incredibly courteous, some of the most polite spaces in clubland. This sensuous sociality is as important as the sex itself, it creates a conspiratorial edge grounded in a movement away from the moral sensibilities of the everyday world and as such it socially sanctions this alternate moral perspective in which consent is the foundational rule upon which the environment is built. Sex ceases to be a furtive, private act; it does not have to 'speak' (Foucault 1981) in order to justify itself, but can simply be a Saturday-night, leisure option wherein its passion and playfulness become visible and celebrated by those present.

The sex clubs also had the greatest age range of any of the club scenes; it was not rare to see people in their seventies enjoying the delights of the space and the crowd tended to be older in general. There were a number of reasons for this shift. Firstly, these older crowds were more socially confident so they could dare to be overtly sexual in public. Secondly, they had more money; they could afford to spend a couple of hundred pounds on a latex cat-suit and up to £25 just to get through the door. Thirdly, as Tuppy Owen explained: 'A lot of people begin to explore the fetish clubs or swingers' scene when their children have all grown up and left home. It's something they can share together once they've stopped living their lives through their kids; it's an erotic adventure.'

This age range from between twenty to seventy gave these clubs an eclectic feel. They revealed that the search for socio-sensual pleasure didn't end at twenty-six, but continued for as long as people were willing to make the effort to get out to these spaces.

Sex and Drugs

The last dimension of club sex I want to look at is the relationship between sex and drugs. This is a relationship that occurs in all areas of clubbing; in fact sex clubs often seemed less druggy than other clubs did because their primary focus was on sex. Drugs can radically alter the way people experience sex because they shift the sensual and social parameters of those sexual encounters.

Certainly, sex on Class A drugs is very different from sex on alcohol, which can often boil down to twenty minutes of rather uncoordinated rumpy-pumpy followed by immediate collapse. Sex on drugs tends to go on far longer; you can afford to relax more, you have more energy. Ecstasy does not diminish sexual desire; that desire simply travels down an altered socio-sensual path. It is articulated and experienced differently; just being touched feels wild as does kissing, licking and watching. There's also the communicative quality of the club drugs that when part of a sexual encounter changes the way people talk about sex, they are franker and more open about it. Sex becomes less antsy and more relaxed.

Some male informants say they have problems sustaining an erection on drugs, others don't. It depends upon the drugs and how long they're actually engaged in sex. As one explained:

> Your hard-on can come and go when you're having sex on Ecstasy or any other drug really, partly because of the drugs, partly because you spend so long fucking that it gets tired and disappears. It doesn't matter though as you just change what you're doing or have a break, maybe a spliff and a laugh. Penetration stops being the be all and end all of fucking; you get more imaginative and inventive. I've probably learnt more about fucking by losing my hard-on than I would have if it had stayed because even when it's gone it doesn't mean the fun has to stop. When you're drugged-up your whole body can feel like a dick so the fact that your six inches of prime love has gone wonky isn't so relevant. (Male 34, 16 years' experience)

Another said:

I enjoy having sex on cocaine, but sometimes I really can't cum. It's like your dick turns into a dildo. It can stay up, but it goes numb so orgasming is really difficult. It used to drive me mad, but I've got my head round it now and I just get off on what's happening. I can always finish off next morning when the feeling's back in it. (Male)

You can certainly take too many drugs to be able to have or enjoy sex particularly as you get older. The sensation of numbness, my informant speaks of is not an uncommon one but if you don't overindulge in them drugs can alter the socio-sensual experience of sex quite dramatically. Cocaine and speed can give you the energy of a sexual dynamo and the numbness, which can accompany them doesn't mean you necessarily loose your erection; it can stay, but it just does not feel as intense. The upside is that sex goes on for longer because premature ejaculation isn't a problem. An informant said:

I like sex on E because it's more relaxed. It's more like a long and intense session of foreplay than a quick fifteen-minute shag and I prefer that. You touch and stroke and fuck and touch and laugh and fuck; it's not so mechanical; it's far more fluid; it lasts longer and feels different more intense. (Female 34, 16 years' experience)

Sex and drugs can complement one another and radically alter the sensual intensity of people's sexual encounters at a physical level in terms of how their body feels during sex and at a social level in the way people interact with one another during sex. A number of informants said that they enjoyed smoking marijuana before having sex because like a couple of drinks it relaxed them and one of my female informants stressed how much she enjoyed sex on LSD. A point of view reiterated by Timothy Leary (1990: 127):

I'm saying simply that sex under LSD becomes miraculously enhanced and intensified. I don't mean that it simply generates genital energy. It doesn't automatically produce a longer erection. Rather, it increases your sensitivity a thousand per cent. Let me put it this way: Compared with sex under LSD, the way you've been making love – no matter how ecstatic the pleasure you think you get from it – is like making love to a department-store-window dummy.

From my own experience I would add that a high degree of trust between partners and knowledge of the effects of LSD were as important as the drug itself during sexual encounters. Otherwise they can become confusing because of LSD's ability to warp the way you feel and see the world. As one informant explained:

Sex on acid can get a bit freaky; you can't work out where you end and the other person begins. You look at them and they can mutate in front of you; they can seem skeletal or wolflike. It can take you a moment to recognise them, but if you're with someone you trust, then these feelings just add to the sex because they don't get scary, they're just exciting. (Female 41, 19 years' experience)

For the vast majority of clubbers the relationship between sex and drugs is explored away from the club space, but it is an important part of the club/drug experience that radically alters the socio-sensual parameters of sex. When combined sex and drugs alter and intensify the experience of each other, but as one informant pointed out:

Fucking and drugging's great, but you have to be careful; you can get careless. I've been so out-of-it that I've forgotten to put a condom on and that's risky. So now I like to get prepared, have plenty of condoms, unwrap a couple so I've got them at hand, take my time. It just means I don't have to wake up in a panic the next day. (Male 32, 14 years' experience)

Summary

Sex is an important part of all clubbing it suffuses and eroticises the sociality of clubs. In sex clubs this sexual element is made overt and visible; it becomes the sensual practice around which the club coalesces and the social rules of sex clubs are designed to both liberate and protect the sexually expressive nature of the event. Sex becomes public and playful; an adult game based upon open and honest consent between punters. The sexual vibe is as important as the amount of actual sex housed within Sex clubs; it acts as a seductive force, which binds the crowds together and marks out the sensuality of the space in opposition to the sexual codes that operate in the everyday world. When sex and drugs are combined usually after the club event itself, then they intensify the way each is experienced and radically shift the socio-sensual parameters of those sexual encounters. My informants valued these shifts and enjoyed sex on drugs as a heightened experience of sex that allowed them to expand their sexual world.

–5–

Dressed to Thrill

Beauty beyond the call of duty.

(Transformer's epitaph)

The truly fashionable are beyond fashion.

(Cecil Beaton)

Dressing-up plays a significant role in all areas of clubbing. For many clubbers, putting on their glad-rags is one way of marking clubs out as different from their everyday world. There were various degrees of dressing-up operating across clubland ranging from putting on a new dress or shirt to people wearing big-looks and completely altering their public persona for the night. There was a crossover between the fetish club scene and the most extreme dress-up clubs: they both stressed expressivity and imagination, had door codes to ensure a high level of participation and were grounded in creating spaces of safety and tolerance wherein punters could risk experimentation.

There was a curious paradox at the heart of clubland's attitude towards dressing-up because clubs that had no dress codes tended to produce crowds that looked predominantly the same whereas clubs that had dress codes created big variations in the way people looked. When left to their own devices people tended towards conformity but when they were pushed into participating they created difference. The dress-up clubs examined in this chapter were not fashion venues as their exclusivity didn't arise from enforcing an economic distinction based upon the labels of the fashion world; this was a particular style of dress-up club that I never gained access to. Instead, the dress-up clubs I visited were spaces that demanded an effort from their punters; they celebrated personal creativity and expressivity over the dull conformity of label culture.

Putting on the Glitz

When I go out I dress-up and wear something skimpy and dance outrageously; it makes me feel better. You go out and feel special for the evening, rather than just being stuck in your drab, work clothes. There's a whole ritual about getting ready, making yourself feel good, getting dressed, getting your makeup on, putting your glitz on if you like. I have a whole clubbing wardrobe, which isn't just comfort clothing and that's important to me. I don't like going out straight from work in the same clothes; it's never as much fun. I went through a stage of wearing little cut-off tops under my work stuff so I could transform when I went out and anything that goes mad under UV light is always good because it glows when you get into a club. I like that; it stops me feeling grey. (Female 32, 9 years' experience)

The above quotation is interesting for a number of reasons. Firstly, it gives us an insight into the process of personal transformation that plays an important role in marking the club night out as a special event. Secondly, it reveals that this transformation is about making my informant feel different by shifting her from her 'drab' everyday-self into her 'glitzy' party-self. Thirdly, it shows that this shift into wearing something 'skimpy' is an experience my informant enjoys and values; it makes her feel 'better' about clubbing. Fourthly, she mentions that she has clubbing clothes that aren't necessarily designed for comfort but, rather, for their aesthetic impact. Together these statements reveal that my informant's clubbing self is constructed through a process of sensual objectification; she creates this version of herself in opposition to her 'grey', 'comfortable' work-self.

In *The Presentation of Self in Everyday Life* Goffman reveals how the world of work shapes the way we present ourselves. To use Goffman's (1990: 83) terms:

Firstly, it often happens that the performance serves mainly to express the characteristics of the task that is performed and not the characteristics of the performer. Thus one finds that service personnel, whether in profession, bureaucracy, business, or craft, enliven their manner with movements which express proficiency and integrity, but, whatever this manner conveys about them, often its major purpose is to establish a favourable definition of their service or product.

Clubbing offers the above informant the chance to change the way she expresses herself in public and her bodily presentation is intimately linked to the clothing she wears. Freed from the representational requirements of her work she can stress different aspects of her own personality by revealing herself as an altered social object. This process is more sensual than symbolic; she feels the transformation wrought by her choice of clothes, which in turn alters the way she encounters and relates to other people in clubs. She mentions the 'ritual' of putting on her 'glitz', the process of making herself more desirable, seductive and visible; she wears skimpy revealing clothes; she can be more glamorous and outrageous; she has dressed to party.

Yet, this is not an act of symbolic resistance to her other work-self. Such an idea is too simplistic. Rather, it is a process of sensual expansion, which moves her into and allows her to occupy the alternative socio-sensual landscape of clubbing.

These visible-selves are created through altering the way in which people experience and express their own bodies, particularly in the way they construct that body as an object and so change the way it encounters the gaze of others. At work, at home, on the street or in a club people objectify themselves in different ways. They reduce or increase their physical presence; they move from public anonymity to public display, depending, as Goffman (1990) points out, upon the social situation they're in at any given time.

Fetish clubs often have changing rooms for their punters so that they can negotiate the street in relative anonymity before transforming into their visible clubbing-selves because for many punters the street is simply too exposed to risk standing out. The safety of the club arena allows them to take risks and creatively play with the expressive medium of clothes. The way a crowd dresses adds to the aesthetic of clubs; it marks it out as different from the everyday world. There are degrees of difference operating in club spaces. As one informant pointed out:

> Well some crowds could be anywhere, they look like they're dressed to go shopping or something and then other crowds look like they've come from another planet. I prefer that; it makes sense to me because clubs are one of the few places that you can get away with really dressing-up. It's one of the freedoms clubs offer, but it's only pushed to its limits in certain clubs, which is a shame because dressing-up is fun; it adds a lot to the night. (Male 33, 17 years' experience)

This statement reveals another important aspect of the dressing-up process as it is fun in itself and people enjoy playing with the way they look. As one informant pointed out:

> The dressing-up thing, the changing the self, I don't always go out as myself exactly, I quite enjoy not going as myself. I went through a stage of dressing slightly like a ballroom dancer, co-ordinates wise and stuff. It didn't last too long, thank God. That was a character I didn't even particularly like, but I was just enjoying the bizarreness of it for a while. I don't just try and look the best I can or something in fact I sometimes enjoy doing the opposite. (Female 30, 10 years' experience)

So, looking 'good' isn't always the goal. People experiment with different looks, different characters, different visible selves that range from looking great in a more conventional sense to looking downright bizarre. At one club night known as The Bedsit the extraordinary host, Transformer, provided a dress-up box for punters. He was the absolute king of dressing-up; nobody in London (maybe even on the planet) could come close to him; his costumes were all handmade and all spectacular works of art in themselves. Yet, these works of art had a personality – they lived and breathed, entertained and cajoled and seemed to unleash the creative potential in everyone around him. After all nobody could upstage Transformer so they were freed from the fear of going too far. The rest of the punters mutated over the weeks; they experimented with their looks and styles and pushed themselves beyond their own limits and insecurities. The dress-up box was always packed with people trying on clothes they would never usually dream of wearing and then partying in them for the night. It was a night of absolutely delirious fun and the freedom to wear what you like and then change your persona in relation to what you were wearing underpinned this delirium.

However, not all clubs could cope with these experiments. Take this example from my fieldwork notes:

> Saturday night at Club V, which prided itself on not having a dress code and being a 'real' clubber venue. A woman walked in, she had immaculately bleached hair, cut short and was wearing a vivid-red, very-tight, glamorous-looking dress and a pair of red heels. She looked great. It was her birthday and she was wearing her presents and had just had her hair done. They were all looking forward to a good night. A couple of hours later, well before the end of the night I saw the woman and her friends about to leave the club. I asked them why they were leaving early. She replied: 'I don't feel comfortable, everybody keeps staring at me, I don't feel like I fit in. There's just load of attitude going on.' I went back into the main section of the club and looked around, on this Saturday night in the middle of the most diverse metropolis in the country in a club that claimed that you could wear what you wanted everyone looked the same.

This woman was made to feel uncomfortable because she didn't fit into the idea of clubbing that the space was grounded in. She was too glamorous for this crowd to handle. Her visibility itself was the problem as it caught the eye and drew them to her, but she didn't experience the looks it brought as friendly and supportive. The presumption of crowd mutuality is challenged by this visibility because the crowd is only the crowd if no one stands out from it. If they do then the perspectival nature of the gaze comes into play as it is focused upon this difference and its unwavering stare whether it intends to or not annihilates this difference by making the person experience the sensual weight of being visible and standing out. This incident needs to be put in perspective as this was not an unfriendly crowd and I don't believe they had intentionally ostracised her. They just couldn't stop looking at her and this made her uncomfortable. However, because of the current range of different clubs people can usually find an arena in which the ways they want to express themselves will be tolerated and celebrated.

Uber Drag and Rubber Nurses

The dress-up clubs I visited allowed clothes to become fun again and celebrated individual expression as an important part of the crowd-making process. People create characters and alter egos and they perform these alternative selves within clubs, which becomes their stage for the night. Drag-queens are one example of this phenomenon: they perform constantly, they adopt names and personas, they add theatricality to the club event, which again marks the space out as different from the everyday world.

When dressing-up becomes a major part of a club's identity, then it moves beyond the simple act of putting on your 'glitz'. Everything we said about dressing-up in the previous section is intensified. There is a fancy dress feel about these spaces as clothes become costumes in dress-up clubs. They are an integral part of the aesthetic of clubbing and people get to alter their public persona to a far greater degree than in other clubs. Big-looks need big spaces in which they can be contextualised otherwise they can bring too much attention from the rest of the crowd. However, the door codes operating in these spaces guarantee a mutual level of participation in terms of getting everybody to make the effort to dress-up. As one door picker explained:

Some people arrive in a pair of jeans and a T-shirt and then get all arsey about the fact we have a door code and you try to explain to them that it's what the night's all about, dressing-up, having a laugh, we're throwing a party here. There're loads of clubs that don't have a door code, but they want to come here because they've heard it's a great night, but it's only a great night because the crowd makes a fucking effort and some people just can't get their head round that fact. They want to be part of it, but they don't want to make the fucking effort to become part of it. (Male)

The club creates the context both socially and aesthetically and by demanding a certain level of participation they ensure that people won't feel uncomfortable or become too visible in the crowd, unless they want to be in which case they have to push their look even further. Dress-up clubs expanded the parameters of what people will dare to wear.

Once a crowd has gained the confidence to start dressing-up it swiftly becomes an integral part of their clubbing experience. I have seen people dressed as: rubber nurses, leather bishops, go-go girls, cowboys, dandy highwayman, wonder woman, a hammerhead shark (accompanied by a Furby), carnival queens, freakish clowns, ringmasters, Victorian schoolteachers, voodoo priests, devils, bunny girls and boys, drag-queens, transvestites of all shapes and sizes, big babies, angels, pantomime horses and 1940s film stars – and they were just the looks I could vaguely categorise. One of my favourite costumes was simply a guy who'd stuck multi-coloured scouring pads to his head and wore them with a black suit; every time the light caught him the scourers would glitter like jewels: simple, cheap, very effective.

This was a highly creative club environment; many of the looks were home made and people had put a great deal of effort into their construction. They were big, imaginative costumes that challenged the basic conformity of the world of fashion. This was not the space to feel glamorous in a little black Gucci dress because you would have simply looked dull in comparison to the rest of the crowd who'd eschewed the classificatory labels of fashion in favour of personal expression. As one informant explained:

> I have a PVC cheerleader's outfit I made myself a while back. It's beginning to fall apart so now I wear it looking all fucked-up. The arm got split because I've buffed up since I made it and I thought: 'Well either I don't wear it or I use it.' I put this cross belt thing on it, strapped toy guns on my legs, then gaffer taped a couple of light pens onto the shoulders. It was my 'Columbine High Cheerleader' look. There's a lot of creativity in clubs and personally I find it a more valid form of creativity than most of the stuff I've seen in the Tate Modern because people aren't being up their own arse. They're being true because the only place this creativity is coming from is themselves. They do it for themselves and for the party. You know call me cynical, but I have a nasty feeling that the art world's just about money and bullshit nowadays while this is just about people making stuff for the joy of it. (Male 26, 8 years' experience)

This statement further stresses the creative aspects of these nights and their role as an alternative arena for expressing this creativity, which exists well away from the confines of the art world. These nights reveal the importance of this creativity in people's lives because they stress that clubbing is an arena of production as much as consumption because in the last instance only the crowd can make the night.

Transformational Skins

Clothes change the way your body feels. Whether this is the comfort of cosy casuals or the fetishistic allure of leather, latex and fur, clothes impact upon the body and alters its presence in the world. In Hebdige's (1979) analysis of the clothing styles of punk, his emphasis on the symbolic obscures what, for me, was the most important aspect of the punk look. When I went through my punky stage around twenty years ago my mohawk, fishnets, doctor martens and leather mini-skirts changed my body at a visceral level and gave me the body of a punk. They acted as armour so that they both got me looked at, but also steeled me against the ensuing gaze by giving me confidence. It was a total and profoundly sensual aesthetic, rather than a cluster of symbols to be read. Looking different confuses people because they're not sure how to deal with you. The clothes changed the way I carried myself in public, I felt bigger, more in the world. The clothes I wear now are very different, but they have the same effect on me. Getting dressed-up to go out is an act of bodily transformation through which people can playfully engage with their public persona and the symbolic frameworks that surround this persona. I don't believe that my own experiments with the punk look was anything to do with resistance; it certainly never felt like that anyway, but rather my experimentation with the way I looked was more closely related to a notion of expansion. I presented myself to the world in alternative ways, part drag-queen, part tough-looking son-of-a-bitch, when in fact I was neither. However, through the practice of dressing-up I learnt to experience the gaze in different ways and this became part of my sensual landscape; an emotive bodily memory that allowed me to become less fearful about the prospect of standing out in a crowd. As I matured, my adolescent need to be noticed diminished but my enjoyment of dressing-up remained to the point where I was dressing-up for myself, not to make an impact on others, but rather to make an impact on me by shifting the way I experienced my own body via the clothes I wore.

So the feel of those clothes became more important, comfort for the daytime, outrageous at night. Fabrics changed, silk, leather, rubber, PVC, yet I never considered myself a member of the fetish scene. I wore dresses, but I never looked feminine. I took to wearing bright, acidic colours, not because I wanted to be noticed in them, but rather because I like them and I wasn't scared of being noticed, which allowed me to put them on. If I was resisting anything it was the notion that clothes are serious and that they define me, rather than being fun.

At the Arc party, I mentioned two women who had dressed-up to the point where they couldn't stand or sit down comfortably. Yet, they felt good in black, rubber corsets, five-inch heeled fuck-me pumps, micro minis; they weren't on-the-pull – in fact I got the impression they were lovers. They had dressed for themselves and each other and, despite their discomfort, they had become seductive creatures. I use the term 'creatures' because the notion of objectification demeans humans. It only allows them to become a constellation of signs to be consumed by others, whereas I am speaking of the sensual rush of becoming a sexual creature, the internality of the experience, rather than its external symbolism. I could have 'read' their clothes symbolically: as signs of power, as symbols of conformity to the media's portrayal of sexual women, as a subcultural statement, but I didn't because I was too busy desiring the women who wore them and who were obviously enjoying wearing them. I wanted to ravish them more than I wanted to analyse them.

Summary

Clothes are often analysed as cultural symbols, yet within clubs these language-based structures become fluid and are often replaced with a more immediate and emotive lexicon. Clothes make people fuckable, approachable, desirable, lickable, glamorous, aloof, funky, playful, fun, slinky, seductive, passionate, invisible, bizarre and beautiful. These classifications reflect an immediate emotional and sensual response to the total look that somebody has created, which in the lived reality of the practice-based present subsumes the observational distance required for symbolic analyses. This reaction to clothes is potent because of its immediacy; it rushes through you, capturing your gaze, igniting emotional responses that draw you to or distance you from the wearer. I have witnessed people being both excited and extremely disturbed by big-looks,

Wearing such clothes takes a degree of confidence but clubs offer spaces where people can set about gaining that confidence in a relatively safe environment. How you wear clothes is as important as what you wear as they become an extension of the flesh; your posture must suit the clothes you've got on; they must feel like you, but they can also change you by stressing different aspects of yourself. They can be sexual, playful, imaginative, glamorous, colourful or comfortable; they can be tongue-in-cheek or serious. Whatever they are they must make people feel good and in clubs they must make them feel like partying and this is a deeply embodied sensation.

–6–

Drugs

No drug, not even alcohol, causes the fundamental ills of society. If we're looking for the source of our troubles, we shouldn't test people for drugs, we should test them for stupidity, ignorance, greed and love of power.

(P. J. O'Rourke)

Drugs may be the road to nowhere, but at least they're the scenic route.

(Anonymous)

Drugs, by which I mean all intoxicants including alcohol, play a huge role in generating the socio-sensual shifts that mark the club arena out from other forms of public space. The arrival of Ecstasy on these shores radically altered Britain's attitude to leisure and pleasure. This process can be problematic; drugs are basically tools that are worthless when they become habituated in practice or used to shore up insecure egos and keep the realities of the lived world permanently at bay. My informants understood this, but they also valued their drug experiences – they felt that those experiences had added something important to their lives, they felt that they had gained access to alternative forms of knowledge through using them.

It is these forms of knowledge that I want to explore in this chapter, because they represent the other side of our current simplistic rhetoric about drugs, which basically classes drug users as the deluded victims of drugs, instead of being active participants in their own lives who are exploring their relationship to the world through drugs. This process does not generate ideas but, rather, lived practices. I am talking about the way people engage with each other socially, particularly with their friends; people's knowledge of how their world can feel and the limits of their own pleasure in that world; their capacity to know and perceive of their own lives from alternative emotional perspectives. They are testing the socio-sensual limits ingrained in the habitus to experience what may lie beyond those embodied boundaries if only the knowledge encountered by using drugs can be translated back into their everyday sober world.

This act of translation is not an easy task to accomplish and, for my informants, it was predominantly manifested within the social networks that had been built while using drugs. If we begin to look at drugs as social tools, rather than experiences in their own right, we gain a far deeper understanding of both their positive and negative impact upon the contemporary world. The drugs I am concentrating on in this chapter are alcohol, Ecstasy, cocaine, amphetamine, marijuana and to a lesser extent the psychedelics like LSD, because these are the drugs most commonly used in social situations. My informants did not use heroin or crack because they are not social drugs. Heroin is too insular and a club full of crackheads would swiftly become a Dantesque nightmare of paranoid scowls and hair-trigger emotions rather than a laid-back, fun place to be. Smack and crack have a tendency to destroy social networks instead of opening up those networks to new shared experiences because their addictive qualities make the need for the drugs more important to users than people are.

Drug use is nothing new in human terms as many cultures use the capacity of drugs to warp reality in order to create social rituals and spiritual experiences. However, in the West drugs have never been granted any social or religious worth and so their usage has occurred within illicit, social and secular frameworks. This refusal compounds many of the problems we associate with drug use because users are either left to create their own frameworks or gradually find themselves alienated from the social world in which they are embedded.

My informants' relationship with drugs had altered with age and experience. This allowed me to view a long-term pattern of drug use that transformed with the changing lives of my informants. What drugs they took, how they took them, what they wanted from them and the impact they had on other aspects of their lives all shifted over time. They tailored their use of drugs to create a range of different experiences, rather than only seeking to get out-of-their-boxes and push that drug experience to its limits. They had been there and done that, but repetition had dulled its impact and they began to place a growing importance on being able to fully socialise and relate to people while under the influence of drugs. They believed that this was where the real significance of drugs in their lives lay.

'Every fucker and their dog take drugs'

> One of the problems we have is that drug taking has now become so commonplace it is widely regarded as socially acceptable. (Plant 2001)

All but one of my informants used drugs to varying degrees; for some of them clubbing was inextricably linked to taking drugs, which provided a foundational part of the experience. They recognised the potential pitfalls of drugs while still valuing what they offered and the types of experience they underpinned. The majority of my informants said that their drug experiences were largely positive; they were glad that they had discovered and taken drugs, even when they had ceased to do so. This perspective is obviously at odds with the accepted view of drug use that is articulated by legal and medical authorities. Drugs are a 'scourge', a 'plague' and the irrepressible enemy in an ongoing 'war on drugs' and the very possibility that they offer anything of value is consistently and vociferously denied. User's become increasingly cynical about the authorities' pronouncements on and attitude towards drugs, as Lee and Shlain (1992: 129) point out in relation to smoking cannabis, but which holds true for many other recreational drugs:

> When you smoked marijuana, you immediately became aware of the glaring contradiction between the way you experienced reality in your own body and the official descriptions by the government and the media. That pot was not the big bugaboo that it had been cracked up was irrefutable evidence that the authorities either did not tell the truth or did not know what they were talking about. Its continued illegality was proof that lying and/ or stupidity was a cornerstone of government policy.

The statistical data available is contradictory. Surveys from the Institute of Alcohol and Health Research show that drugs are just as prone to going in and out of fashion as anything else. In 1995 British teenagers exhibited the highest use of drugs in Europe. In 1999 drug use seemed to be dropping off again as Ecstasy went out of style and the government's propaganda machine scared people away. However, the result of people becoming bored with or scared of Ecstasy was a steady rise in heavy drinking amongst the young and particularly women, as the Institute reported in (2000). Britain remains a nation in search of a hit and the wheel of drug fashion will continue to turn.

The main reason I would contend that drugs are becoming a mainstream part of our culture arises from the way in which people talk about them. They are no longer associated with a small group of rebels and outlaws who exist at the edge of society. They are not the preserves of bohemians and artists or sad, broken people trapped in appalling lives and desperately seeking escape. They are not even particularly rebellious although their position outside of the law means that they have maintained some kudos as a criminal activity amongst younger users. This gradually disappears as users age and their illegal status is perceived as a 'bit of naughtiness' or a 'pain in the arse', rather than a counter-cultural statement.

Drugs have woven themselves into the social and aesthetic fabric of our culture. Late-night television, in particular, uses styles of humour that my informants classed as 'utterly stoned' and visual techniques that were 'tripped out'. As one informant explained:

> Why do you think the 'Clangers' are on at four in the morning; it's got sod all to do with nostalgia; it's because it appeals to drug fucked people who've just got in and their heads are still fizzing. You can see the change especially at the weekends; the programmes start when the pubs kick out; they tend to be viewing for drunks and as the night goes on they get less drunk and far druggier. It's comedown TV for a drugged-up nation and the TV

companies know their market and cater to it. They'd never admit it of course, but it isn't very surprising considering the amount of drugs that the media world consumes; they're like Dysons stuck on maximum suck so of course they know what's going to appeal to their fellow druggies. (Male 31, 13 years' experience)

This statement suggests a hypocrisy within the media's relationship with drugs. As one branch condemns them another caters for this mainstream, drug-using populace. Evidence of drug use has been uncovered everywhere from the Royal Opera House to the Houses of Parliament. Drug use occurs in all social, economic and ethnic groupings (I met one dealer who supplied cannabis to grateful pensioners in an old people's home) although there are differences in the types of drugs used and the patterns which surround their usage.

Club Drugs

In this section I want briefly to examine each of the club drugs in turn in order to tease out the differences and similarities between them as well as the types of experience that they play a role in creating.

Alcohol

After a very brief and partial displacement in the late 1980s and early 1990s as the drug that fuels people's leisure activities, alcohol has come back into vogue in clubland. It has to be said that rumours of its demise were certainly premature and outside of the Ecstasy-fuelled rave scene it was still the drug of choice for the majority of Britain's population. For most of us alcohol is our first introduction to intoxication and it is through alcohol use that we discover our ability to alter the way we feel in a particular environment. It is the most socially acceptable of all the drugs to the point where people who espouse a virulent anti-drug philosophy will become quite upset if you decline a drink from them and will view it as an anti-social act. Drug use is classified in terms of an intoxicant's illegality; most drinkers don't perceive of themselves as drug users. Research aimed at drugs often ignores the presence of alcohol. When positing a relationship between soft and hard drugs alcohol is conveniently left out of the reckoning and cannabis is used as a baseline for the soft-drug side of the equation. The idea that alcohol teaches people about intoxication and so makes other states of intoxication comprehensible at a bodily level would challenge the assertion that only illegal drugs play a role in creating people's knowledge of drug use.

As we have seen, the social feel of Britain's nightlife radically altered with the arrival of raves and Ecstasy as it shifted away from the social models surrounding alcohol, which underpinned drinking clubs. Alcohol was very much part of the system, easily accessible and socially acceptable, except when linked to violence or alcoholism. The licensing laws that surrounded its use meant that clubs shut down at 2 a.m. and pubs at 11 p.m. and this created a situation in which a large part of the club experience was based around finding a place to keep drinking, rather than searching out anything novel or even fancying a dance. So the vast majority of clubs were far more an extension of the pub environment than a completely separate space offering a radically different experience. As one informant explained:

> I don't think you can connect those old, lager-fuelled clubs with club culture as it stands now; it was completely different. The arrival of Ecstasy took it to whole different worlds; it got rid of much of the violence. The Friday and Saturday night 'get lagered-up and have a fight thing' blighted clubs. Younger clubbers don't realise how far clubs have come, how different they are. I used to find myself in pissed-up clubs thinking: 'Shit I just don't want to be here, this place feels vicious.' (Male 25, 8 years' experience)

Although drinking has returned to clubs it has changed because now it is often a chemically assisted practice as people drink and take drugs – something that went out of fashion when Ecstasy was at its height because Ecstasy and large amounts of booze don't mix very well. However, cocaine and speed can easily be mixed with alcohol. As one informant told me:

> Drink and speed mix really well. You become an indestructible drinker and you don't get that downer, maudlin bit that drink on its own can give you. (Male)

Cocaine actually binds with alcohol to produce a chemical blend of ethanol and cocaine called ethocaine, which means that booze and cocaine complement one another. As one informant said:

> I like a few beers when I'm on coke; it's a nice combination; it mellows the buzz and anyway I like the way you can wash the coke that trickles down your throat away with the beer; I like the taste as they mix. (Male)

The energy both these drugs supply changes the experience of drinking quite radically. It reduces the depressive qualities of alcohol and keeps drinkers energised long into morning. The first people to leave a club are often the ones who are only drinking and there seems to be a point at around two to three in the morning when they collapse leaving other chemically assisted clubbers still rocking the dance floor. One of the most common drinks in clubs was vodka and Red Bull, which tastes like the worst cough medicine you can imagine but has the advantage of supplying caffeine and taurine, both of which are uppers and this holds off alcohol's depressant quality – although nowhere near as effectively as the Class A drugs.

The return of alcohol into clubs has made clubbing a more accessible experience to many people, particularly the ones who had been kept away by the relationship between clubs and drugs. Whereas a drinker would have felt out of place in the old, Ecstasy-orientated clubs, which sometimes didn't even have a bar where you could buy booze, they can feel completely at home in contemporary clubs. There is a definite split between the vibe you get in a club that's predominantly dependent upon alcohol as its intoxicant and ones where other drugs are being used. This split is created in two ways: firstly because of the actual effects of the different drugs and secondly because of the alternate social models that surrounds their usage. As Maryon McDonald (1994: 13) asserts:

A state of drunkenness will be defined differently cross-culturally, the meaning of drunkenness varies, and the behaviour which alcohol induces is a cultural matter, rather than a question of the inevitable or natural consequences of ethanol entering the bloodstream . . . drunkenness is *learned* behaviour.

This gives us the strong version of the cultural constructivist view of alcohol. However, after reading the text, I can't say I came across any real indication that people got drunk in vastly different ways depending upon where they lived. I would have to temper this perspective to say that cultures construct different models of intoxication but they do so within the parameters of the physiological effects of the chosen drug. Models of drinking are distinct from models of drunkenness as once people reach that point, then their behaviour seems startlingly similar across cultures, but the way that behaviour is perceived and interpreted is radically different. The social models that surrounded alcohol use in this country have been around so long that they were largely stagnant. They were heavily gendered and predominantly masculine models of behaviour, which reflected ideas about class, taste and social decorum. In *Alcohol, Gender and Culture,* Dimitra Gefou-Madianou (1992) shows that women's drinking was viewed more harshly than that of men's. Heavy drinking was still perceived as a predominantly male activity and men were granted a certain licence for their behaviour when drunk whereas women were not extended the same luxury. In Britain the social model of drunkenness recognised the disinhibiting potential of alcohol, but our Protestant-Christian heritage made legislators constantly fearful and suspicious of these changes in people's behaviour. As McDonald (1994: 17) points out: 'When we talk disapprovingly about 'drugs' we are talking in priority about perceived threats to the social and moral order, threats which have been medicalised and on which a whole scientistic edifice has been built.'

Drunkenness was associated with promiscuity, violence and self-destructive behaviour as much as it was linked to people having a good time. The model of the social drinker was always linked to sobriety more than it was connected to the state of drunkenness. It was a model of control and propriety with no space for such notions as abandonment and the radical intensification of pleasure. People ignored these models frequently as they found a sense of liberation and the experience of an altered social-self by drinking, but the nature of the alcohol hit is eventually depressive and it can't offer the same rushes of energy associated with other drugs that in themselves can radically alter people's experience of their world. You can find abandonment, excess and a damned good time through booze, until you reach the point where your co-ordination has gone and the room is spinning or you've become completely unaware of what you're doing. One informant made this comparison:

> You get a loss of inhibition on other drugs, but not in the same way as alcohol because you're still much more aware of what's going on. Alcohol blunts all the edges whereas E, speed or cocaine doesn't do that. They intensify and magnify your experience and your awareness and alertness is far greater for far longer. (Female 32, 9 years' experience)

The difference between drinking now and drinking prior to the growth in illegal drug use is the added edge of the uppers. We've moved from being a nation that uses a depressant as its party drug of choice to one that wants a decidedly more upbeat experience when they're in the club environment. Clubbers don't want to collapse at two in the morning because they want to party all night and alcohol alone tends to restrict that possibility rather than facilitate it.

From Alcohol to Ecstasy and Beyond

The arrival of Ecstasy changed the social and sensual feel of a night out. It intensified the whole experience and introduced more and more people to this intensity while setting it within a radically altered social framework. Clubs ceased to be late-night drinking dens with dancing and developed their own identity distinct from the pub model of social interaction, which had dominated the social realm of clubbing up until the late 1980s. As one informant explained:

> Pubs are quite territorial. I've never really met anyone in a pub. That's not why I go there. I go with my friends and I stay with my friends and people don't mingle like they do in a club. So you never get that feel that everyone's there to just go-for-it. I find pubs quite boring to be honest. Drinking crowds don't seem to gel like druggy crowds in that people can behave very differently from one another when drunk, some get talkative and excited, some get depressed, some lose their co-ordination completely or become aggressive and leery. Even clubs get that cattle-market feel back when people are just drinking. They lose a lot of their energy if there are too many people who are just drunk. I think a lot of that is to do with the fact that alcohol is a bit of a shit drug really in that

it can't keep up with the club buzz. It gets too messy and people lose control. After all club spaces weren't really designed with drunks in mind were they? They were designed to house drugs and they didn't really appeal to drinkers, but now they're getting swamped by drunks. (Female 32, 9 years' experience)

Alcohol is an old drug and the social models that surrounded its use have been around for an equally long time. However, Ecstasy was a new drug, which spread with amazing rapidity and its physiological effects such as raised empathy and a loss of inhibition and fear played a massive role in altering the dominant, social model of what made a good night out. Its swift incorporation into the rave/party scene altered the social experience of these spaces so profoundly that those ravers derided alcohol use and abandoned it on mass. The loved-up vibe of Ecstasy gave clubs an inclusive feel and attracted a crowd who'd had been put off them because of their snobbery, economic exclusivity and drunken violence. They had found an alternative experience of socialising with other people, particularly strangers, but also their own friends. In the early years of rave/club culture that social experience and the sheer Dionysian excess of the parties themselves was revelatory and it generated highly idealistic and Utopian dreams of the future. By the mid-1990s these dreams became far more pragmatic until clubbing became viewed as an intense leisure option – one amongst many – but certainly not a revolutionary practice. However, as my next informant points out, the nightlife experience had changed:

I think the atmosphere's changed in dance clubs in particular, even when they're not all on Ecstasy. If you go to, say, an Indy club you realise how much better the general atmosphere of dance clubs really is. You really do. Even the dance clubs that you think are a bit moody and underground still have a much better atmosphere than other clubs. I think Ecstasy showed people that a night out didn't have to end in a fight. (Male 27, 10 years' experience)

When the hardcore, clubby, druggy crowd started pulling away from the Ecstasy gig and moved back into drinking and taking cocaine they brought an altered social model to that drug combination. They still wanted to be in a social space that maintained some of the qualities of the Ecstasy experience in terms of how they interacted with one another by smiling, being tolerant, an absence of violence etc. However, they set about achieving this social experience through drinking and snorting a few lines. Cocaine and speed are incredibly chatty drugs although they don't imbue that chattiness with the same emotional openness and sense of trust that is associated with Ecstasy, but then neither do they leave the user as fragile and vulnerable as Ecstasy can. When mixed with alcohol the accelerants provide a socially intense yet less psychedelic experience of clubland that doesn't initiate such a radical shift in their sense of self. Compared to the mutational rush of

Ecstasy or the psychedelics the booze and upper mix can feel like a relatively sober experience after night after night of being E'd up or tripping 'out yer gourd'.

Ecstasy

3,4 methylenedioxynmethylamphetamine, MDMA, Ecstasy – the drug that underpinned many people's experiences in raves and then clubs – was invented in 1912 by the German pharmaceutical company Merck but was never marketed by it. Although the use of Ecstasy has increased over the years it would be wrong to try to continue to use the Ecstasy experience to sum up people's club experiences. I visited plenty of clubs where Ecstasy wasn't the predominant hit or where it was not even used and others where people were under the effect of a variety of drugs in a single space. Nevertheless when you do come across a room full of people whooping it up on Ecstasy then you find yourself looking at a space that bears the most obvious relation to the original rave experience. The average price ranges from £3 to £7 a pill, depending on how many you buy.

In this section, I will use my informants' descriptions of their Ecstasy experiences to illustrate the social and individual changes that Ecstasy facilitates. I have broken these down into three sub-headings that reveal different aspects of those experiences.

Unravelling Fear, Experiencing Trust

I've always maintained that what Ecstasy really does to me if I'm honest is that it turns me back into a six year old. It's a childlike state; you don't have the worries, just like children. You put a group of children in a room and they just get on with it really because they don't have the same inhibitions and everything is new and wonderful. It assails the senses. The inhibitions you can have about who you're talking to or what you're doing just go. It's like free association. You feel really happy and empathetic. You connect to people, even though you might not be able to hold a conversation for more than two minutes. You can hug and kiss people without them thinking you're coming onto them. When I'm in a club on E I'm looking for a pure, pleasure experience, it's just pleasure, nothing else. When I'm happiest is when I'm really chatty and I have loads of energy and I can exploit the whole club thing as much as possible. That whole state arises from the feeling that there is nothing wrong, everything's OK. It doesn't have to be everything's completely blissful, just that it's hunky dory. I'm loving the people I'm with and I have the ability to express that, to say: 'I love you, give me a hug'. On one level I've always recognised that there can be a superficiality on E, but saying that I always managed not to do that in terms of not doing it to people who I wouldn't normally do it to. So it's not falseness, just a sense of release. You feel happy about saying these things and connecting with your friends and you let them know how much they mean to you and you know they'll be receptive to it. Then there are the people you've seen, but you don't know well, but you feel you'd like to know them better and you have an opportunity to and it's safe to do that because you have an excuse. It's almost expected. (Female 32, 9 years' experience)

This description captures the social experience Ecstasy helps generate within clubs and has much in common with descriptions offered by my other informants. The most important consequence of taking Ecstasy for these informants was the way it altered their experience of and interaction with people and I began to look for an explanation, which could account for these effects. I discovered two explanatory frameworks from two different disciplines that, when combined, accounted for a large part of the Ecstasy experience. The first was derived from the work of Damasio (1999) whose investigations into the human brain have stressed the importance of emotion in structuring human consciousness. One particular example stood out in relation to this study the patient S who had a disease known as Urbach-Wiethe, which causes calcium to be deposited in the amygdala and this is how Damasio (1999: 64–5) describes the effect that this calcification had on his patient:

> S approached people and situations with a predominantly positive attitude. Others would actually say that her approach was excessively and inappropriately forthcoming. S was not only pleasant and cheerful, she seemed eager to interact with most anyone . . . shortly after an introduction, S would not shy away from hugging and touching . . . it was as if negative emotions such as fear and anger had been removed from her affective vocabulary, allowing the positive emotions to dominate her life, at least by greater frequency of occurrence if not by greater intensity . . . (*this behaviour was*) mostly caused by the impairment of one emotion: fear.

The similarities between this description and the behaviour of somebody on Ecstasy especially a novice are astounding and this suggests that Ecstasy affects the amygdala or some other part of the brain's fear system in some way. S lived a life without fear and that occasionally made her vulnerable to manipulation by others; her judgement of other people's motives was impaired, as Damasio (1999: 67) explains: 'Immersed in a secure Pollyanna world, these individuals cannot protect themselves against simple and not-so-simple social risks and are thus more vulnerable and less independent than we are.'

Unlike S, Ecstasy users do not experience this state of reduced fear constantly; they know people can be untrustworthy and manipulative; they have experienced it and so the Ecstasy rush is mediated by this autobiographical knowledge. However, experiencing even a temporary and partial dip in the feelings of fear and anxiety, which suffuse much of our social experiences, can bring its own rewards. It allows users to experience the sense of 'happiness', 'empathy' and 'connection', which this and other informants reported. Ecstasy allows them to experience a socio-sensual state in which fear is minimised. Fear is a curious emotion because often what we fear is the unknown, which in turn keeps the unknown unknowable. Take away the fear and you reduce the emotional distance between yourself and that which is unknown. It becomes approachable. If you approach an object, an experience or a person without fear you approach them from within an entirely altered sensual state: your body looks relaxed; you do not exude threat; you smile and by making your approach in such a way you instantly reduce the chance of experiencing negative feedback because you're not perceived as intimidating or threatening. It is a technique of the body, which has profound social effects. However, part of this reduction in fear arises from the assumptions people make about the 'set and setting' in which Ecstasy is taken. Ecstasy does not remove fear completely it just reduces it and this reduction has been woven into the social model of Ecstasy use, which in itself helps to further reduce people's sense of fear. So the drug and the social model support one another and intensify one another. They turn this reduction in fear into a shared social event. I must stress that no clubber talked about the term 'fear', but like Damasio's assessment of patient S they stressed the positive emotions they both felt and shared during their Ecstasy experiences, which Damasio was able to relate back to S's lack of fear.

The knowledge that she was in an Ecstasy environment allowed my informant, from the beginning of this section, to make certain presumptions about the crowd's behaviour. She could assume that they would be approachable and friendly. She also mentions the 'superficial' nature of the drug. There are two forms of social interaction taking place on Ecstasy in clubs. The first was the way people interacted with the friends that they arrived with and this was not seen as 'superficial' because it was part of an ongoing social network that existed outside of the club space. The second was the way people interacted with strangers and this was seen as an important part of the 'pure, pleasure experience' my informant was seeking. My informant makes it clear that there are limits to these stranger interactions and that she wouldn't want to treat a stranger in a club in the same way as she treated her close friends. She wanted to be chatty and friendly to strangers; she wanted to enjoy strangers, but she didn't want to be 'false' by saying inappropriate things to them that meant she was treating them like long-term friends. I would again relate this split between friends and strangers and the potential sense of superficiality, my informant identifies, to my hypothesis that a diminution in fear is the key to understanding the Ecstasy experience. Over time people begin to recognise that the social encounters they have on Ecstasy are marked out by the level of immediate closeness they feel towards someone. They have learned that this is part of the drug's effects upon them, but unlike Damasio's patient S they have autobiographical memories that alert them to the fact that this is a special state of relations between people. They retain a critical function in relation to their own behaviour and they realise that the way people behave on Ecstasy may be very different from the way they behave when they are not on it. So they channel the most intense effects of the drugs into their own social groups and simply enjoy chatting and laughing with strangers for the sheer fun of it without expecting anything to necessarily come of these social encounters. They are enjoying the moments for what they are. As another informant explained:

> Meeting people in clubs is a very immediate thing; it's fun. I've told strangers they were beautiful because at that time I thought they were and it's just like paying them a compliment and I don't really expect anything in return. I'm not making any big statement; I'm not trying to make them into my friends; I'm just being complimentary because that's how I feel and often that's how people look. I've never told a stranger that I love them and they were my best friend in a club; I wouldn't like to do that; it would be bullshit because it takes time to get to know a friend. So I think club crowds are less utterly loved-up, more just gentle and excited and complimentary towards one another whereas with close friends the experience is a lot deeper and I've enjoyed both sides of that. (Female 29, 12 years' experience)

The urban environment is extreme in itself. It acts as a pressure cooker that intensifies experience; you negotiate it with your guard up. In many ways Ecstasy is the direct antidote to the sense of underlying anxiety that infects urban life. It allows you to experience the crowds, which make up a huge part of the urban experience in a very different way. Certainly part of this encounter arises from the social rules that surround much of clubbing, but Ecstasy allows you to experience those rules fully as an embodied force because those rules were created from within the Ecstasy rush. Once you have experienced this embodied state, once you've learned what those social rules feel like you can go onto recreate those experiences to some extent without the drug because you know how far you can go in a club and how to interact with people while in the space. Which is why I was constantly being mistaken for an E'd-up party animal when I'd only had a couple of beers. Once you've become confident in clubs, once you can just let your hair down and go for it, then you look like you're on E. You have created an embodied emotive model that underpins the reality of the rules of clubbing.

I must reiterate that I'm not talking about people feeling scared and then taking E to relieve that fear. That is not what happens. Rather, by taking Ecstasy people release themselves from the body by which they hold the anxieties of city living at bay. They resist this anxiety by creating a resistant body that allows them to negotiate the social reality of the metropolis without it becoming experienced in mind as the idea of fear. It is held in the body, it is a particular musculature, a set of emotional parameters, a subconscious physicality that arises from the anonymity of our social encounters, which take place in the stranger led world of the city. It is most evident on the tube: silence, no eye contact, a studied invisibility within the mass of commuters, very few people smiling, all the things that are altered in a club crowd. This is not fear as an overwhelming force; it is fear as a general level of anxiety about other people's possible intentions and actions. As LeDoux (1999: 177) explains in

The Emotional Brain: 'Bigger brains allow better plans, but for these you pay in the currency of anxiety.'

Energy

> For me a lot of the drug thing is about energy. When I've done a full week at work and I'm going out, then I need the extra energy if I'm going to have an awesome night, rather than an OK night, I'll honk a gram of whiz or pop a pill and suddenly the night's alive and I can concentrate on the whole party thing without having to feel tired and half thinking I want to go to bed. (Male 26, 8 years' experience)

This informant stresses the energising quality of his drugs of choice the way in which they can banish tiredness for hours at a time. This is important for two reasons. Firstly, because the sensation of that energy rushing through your body immediately intensifies your experience of the event and it imbues you with a radical physicality that can in itself feel liberating. Secondly, it allows you to seize your leisure time with both hands. Leisure is time for the self and clubbers want it to be far more intense than the time that they give to their working lives. They want to be on form, not exhausted and drained by their jobs. They want their own time to feel different from the time that they give to other more controlled aspects of their lives. This informant did not hate his job – he thoroughly enjoyed it, going so far as to describe himself as a 'workaholic' but he still needed to experience this sense of changing gear that made his time more sensually intense than the time he gave to earning the money he needed to support himself. This desire has expanded leisure time and the chronology of the night has been altered and the boundaries surrounding the world of leisure have shifted. The licensing laws have been changed as a direct result of the rave movement. Many clubs are open all night and drugs allow people to savour this change by keeping them awake and empowering their nocturnal reveries. However, as the same informant suggested this can also have negative effects: 'I think a lot of the downside to taking drugs arises from sleep deprivation after all it's a recognized form of torture isn't it?' (Male 26, 8 years' experience).

The downside is sleep deprivation and exhaustion, but people are prepared to put up with these at least for a while because they get to experience their own lives accelerated to a point of passionate intensity, which feels very different from the ordered mundanity of the daylight hours. You can't live it large if you feel like the dormouse in Lewis Carroll's *Alice in Wonderland,* constantly wanting to snuggle down for a snooze. The effects of exhaustion are accumulative and if you don't get the balance right you can reach the point where the world of work can become almost dreamlike; you feel disconnected from it; its niggles and pressures are intensified by tiredness; it can become harder to deal with. This is one of the main reasons clubbers leave clubbing or begin to slow down and alter their nocturnal patterns. They re-address the balance; their clubbing becomes more occasional; they give themselves more time to recharge their batteries without having to abandon clubbing completely.

Touch

> One of the best E hits I had was at a party when my friends X and Y were in a particular friendly mood. I was dressed-up, feeling great and being very tactile, dancing around, being gentle and a bit lascivious in the club, but then we went back to mine with a gang and X, Y and I went to bed together and we were being deliciously feely with each other and I love that. Ecstasy's a sensual drug, rather than a lust drug. You get to touch people for the pleasure of touching them, of feeling their skin and making them feel good, but you're not striving for a fuck. It's more playful and less desperate than that. (Male 32, 14 years' experience)

My informant's statement captures the tactile quality of the Ecstasy rush. Touch becomes electric and deeply satisfying and the Ecstasy rush itself is an incredibly sensual experience. As you come up on Ecstasy you feel your body changing and once this rush has levelled out your sensual-self is altered and my informant points out how this sensual shift changes the way in which you interact with people on a sensual level. This is an important difference between socialising on Ecstasy and socialising in the everyday world. In the preface to *Touching: The Human Significance of the Skin*, Ashley Montagu (1986: xiv) suggests that:

> The impersonality of life in the Western world has become such that we have produced a race of untouchables. We have become strangers to each other, not only avoiding but even warding off all forms of "unnecessary" physical contact, faceless figures in a crowded landscape, lonely and afraid of intimacy . . . The world of Western man has come to rely heavily for communication on the "distance senses," sight and hearing, and of the "proximity senses," taste, smell, and touch, has largely tabooed the latter.

This tactile rush arises from two sources. Firstly, the actuality of touching other people, putting your arm around them, giving them a hug and dancing with them. Secondly, from the sensual intensity of the club space itself, the crush of bodies, the heat, the sexual buzz. This all impacts upon the body of the clubber with such force that it feels like being touched, even when you're not actually being touched. This is a somewhat synaesthetic experience. It is as if the sensual weight of the club crowd rests upon the skin. People on Ecstasy do touch each other more than people using other drugs; touch becomes informal and gentle; it is used as a way of communicating between people on Ecstasy; it becomes playful and, as Montagu (1986) suggests, this is a rare experience in the contemporary world.

Accelerants

The major club drugs all share a social edge, a feeling of being hurled head first into the world. In the case of the accelerants particularly amphetamine and cocaine this feeling arises from the sensation of energy they unleash in the body that is in itself empowering. In fact one of the main reasons people move from Ecstasy to cocaine is that they begin to see the Ecstasy rush as naïve, whereas cocaine is perceived as a more active, in-your-face drug. However, cocaine was first legally marketed as a wonder drug and adverts proudly proclaimed that it was the perfect cure for 'young persons afflicted with timidity in society' (quoted in Grinspoon and Bakalar 1976: 93).

So it can be seen that both Ecstasy and cocaine can help us overcome self-consciousness and fear, but they just work in different ways. Cocaine immunises you against self-consciousness and doubt and lets you come out from behind your mummy's apron by imbuing you with a sense of strength and certainty. As Sigmund Freud once proclaimed in a letter to his fiancée Martha Bernays: 'You shall see who is stronger, a gentle little girl who doesn't eat enough or a great wild man who has cocaine in his body' (Grinspoon and Bakalar 1976: 33). This quotation captures the visceral bodily rush of cocaine that underpins the states of mind which users report. Amphetamine achieves a very similar goal at a fraction of the cost. Yet, there are some subtle differences not least the social models that surround their usage. Cocaine has become the drug of success as its price alone, which ranges from £40 to £60 a gram, ensured its association with wealth and prestige and made it so popular with celebrities. This is important because fame and celebrity themselves are becoming significant aspirational models in our contemporary social world and, rightly or wrongly, cocaine is perceived as being part of that model because its price makes it the drug of success. Cocaine provides an embodied experience of energised visibility and individuality that make living the high life easier by making you feel like you would imagine a superstar would feel in public: confident, visible, secure. An informant suggested that 'Cocaine's always really popular when people have got too much money and too much to prove. It's a lifestyle thing, a confidence thing really, a way of sharpening your ego and facing the world; powdered popularity if you like' (Male 34, 16 years' experience).

It is this aspect of the cocaine rush that leads people to label it 'a bullshitter's crutch', even amongst people who enjoy cocaine. It is the drug of 'front' that allows people to present a particular version of themselves to the world. However, not every cocaine user subscribes to this social model; some take the drug simply because they enjoy its effects even though they have no pretensions of fame and fortune; it is a treat, something to be savoured and shared with friends.

Amphetamine, on the other hand, is seen as a street drug: cheap, effective, utterly unglamorous, the working-class version of cocaine that costs £5 to £10 a gram. The basic currency of the accelerants is raw energy and the feeling of this energy surging through the system alters the accelerant user's relationship to the world. Externally the world remains much the same, but from an internal psycho-physical perspective it becomes charged with a potential for engagement. Speech becomes strident, ideas explode into the mind and you feel like you can communicate at warp speed. This is an emotionally intense language, somewhat evangelistic in its passion by being grounded in a sense of certainty that can on occasion seem almost aggressive. Bodies become empowered and revitalised as their rhythmic structure quickens and they develop that restless coke and speed physicality: constantly playing with their noses, eyes darting around the space scanning the room to see where the action is, a positive tension between self and world. It is exhilarating; you feel turbo charged and fuel-injected, the human equivalent of a formula-one car.

If you overdo the accelerants the sense of tension between self and world can become overwhelming. You can become so visible in the world that you begin to believe that everyone must be looking at you and talking about you. The hyper-vanity of acceleration and expansion makes you feel like the centre of the universe around which the space is revolving, which is groovy when you're having a great time feeling witty and wonderful, but not so hot when you've gone that step too far and are beginning to feel tense or out of control. This sense of self-importance means that everything relates intensely to the self; it all matters because you are the central referent, but this feeling comes in short lived bursts. As one female informant explained:

> Cocaine makes you feel really energetic and big, but I think you constantly have to fight a comedown because the rush only lasts forty-five minutes. You don't really notice it if you've got enough to keep going, but if you only have a line or two and that's all you've got, then I find that it can leave you tireder than you would be if you hadn't taken it. I mean Ecstasy lasts five to six hours; you can do a lot in that time, but to get the same effect on coke you've got to snort a fair few lines to keep going.

One possible explanation for this sense of mastery and confidence is offered in the book *Cocaine* (Grinspoon and Bakalar 1976), which suggests that:

> The heightening of the sense of self – 'The greatest ego-inflating drug there is' – may be a correlate in the mind of the sympathomimetic action of stimulants. For in moments of stress and danger the organism . . . must *realize* its own distinctness from the world and discourage any tendency toward a relaxed merging with it. In the mind this may produce a strong sense of individuality and of power and control. (Grinspoon and Bakalar 1976: 95)

Cocaine actually mimics how people feel in response to a fear-generating stimulus, but because there is no actual stimulus people just get the sense of being empowered and ready for action, which helps reduce their sense of self-consciousness and so, like Ecstasy, alters the body they use to keep their sense of fear in check. However, overindulgence can produce intense paranoia and agitation and this arises from putting yourself in that 'fight or flight' mode. It is possible that some part of your brain is primed for the stimulus that would have normally initiated this physical and emotional state. If you're having fun with your mates and everything's OK, then this aspect of the drug will remain dormant. However, if the situation changes or you take too much of the drug to be able to keep its effects under control, then you can begin to interpret people's actions negatively because of your own altered emotional state. An informant gave me an interesting description of this process:

> I've only really got the heebie-jeebies on drugs a couple of times and you learn how to deal with them after a while because you know it's just the drugs, but when it first happens it's fucking weird. I was at this club having a really good time, having a few lines and then, shit, I can't even really remember what set me off, some misunderstanding or other, and I start feeling paranoid and I'm looking at people and I think that they're talking about me or looking at me funny. I saw people sort of talking into each other's ears like they were whispering, which is ridiculous because they must have been shouting over the music to be heard, but I thought they were whispering about me and then when they laughed I thought they were laughing at me and I started to feel really tense and I wanted to leave and suddenly the whole club looked completely different, everyone looked intimidating. Then one of my mates came back and I told her how I felt and she just smiled at me and told me to chill-out because it was just the coke and that made me feel a bit better and I had another beer and just sat and talked to my mate and after half an hour or something I felt fine and the club looked all right again, everyone looked normal and I relaxed, but I laid off the coke for the rest of the night. (Male 27, 8 years' experience)

This is an interesting quote because it reveals the way my informant's emotional state affected his perception of the social environment he was in. He began explaining people's actions through that emotional state by creating explanatory narratives that related to his own sense of threat and tension. As coke users are already so hyped-up this negative reaction can get real nasty, real quick if there is nothing to calm things down. The presence of cocaine ups the ante and overindulgence can put people on a hair-trigger that can have some fairly ugly ramifications. This isn't an inevitable outcome of using cocaine as it arises from people abandoning their control over its use or taking it in the wrong 'set and setting'.

Psychedelics

The full-blown psychedelics like LSD, psilocybin and ketamine have the ability to warp the world radically. The LSD dosages used now are generally far smaller than the average hit taken back in the 1960s, which means people can communicate more successfully on LSD even in intense social situations. However, there are a number of differences between the psychedelics and the other club drugs. Whereas Ecstasy seems to imbue most users with a predilection for seeing things positively, you have to create that positive element with LSD, mushrooms and ketamine, which is why Leary (1970) stressed 'set and setting' so strongly. This explains why Ecstasy took off amongst more people than LSD in many ways it is an easier drug to handle and to understand.

There is no convincing framework for the psychedelic experience in the West. When people have tried to make sense of psychedelics they have turned to Eastern mysticism and new-age philosophies in an attempt to create such a framework. So if you're a hard-headed rationalist with no spiritual beliefs, then these frameworks can look fairly lame. Ecstasy's effects, on the other hand, were quickly socialised by becoming part of raves so there was no need to create any other explanatory framework for the experience beyond having a good time with people. This changed people's perspective upon LSD and they ceased to view it as a quasi-spiritual experience and just started to take it for fun.

Clubbing changes the way you experience psychedelics because getting amongst the crowd externalises their effects and stops them from becoming a predominantly internal journey. As one male informant said:

> I have no time for pixies, Gods, earth mothers and spiritual enlightenment, but I do have time for people and I find that tripping with them is just a really good way to experience them. It's funny and freaky. It's like sharing a holiday with someone; it brings you together in the same way.

The holiday analogy is interesting as psychedelics have the ability to make you feel like you've been elsewhere, which is why taking LSD is often referred to as tripping. Just like a holiday abroad you share a radically different world from the one you normally occupy. It is 'wilder', 'freakier' and more intense than your everyday experience of the world. LSD doesn't always induce hallucinations, particularly at current dosages, but it can still radically alter your emotional and sensual experience of the world and completely change the way you interpret that world. Colour, in particular, becomes incredibly intense. In fact the world just seems more sumptuous, vibrant and lucid all round. The faces in the crowd change, sometimes to the point where everybody looks utterly bizarre, which can be disconcerting, but also exciting. Dancing on LSD is incredible; it provides an even more radically altered experience of your sensual-self than Ecstasy. Your body bristles with energy; it becomes lithe and empowered and each of your senses is intensified. The following informant said:

> Acid's my favourite drug. It's incredible; indescribable really; I love it. Dancing on it is wonderful. It's like being possessed though it can make being in clubs quite difficult sometimes. It can all get a bit too odd and it can make talking to people hard. Having sex on it now that's utterly outrageous; it's completely changed the way I think of sex; I never realised that it could be so intense, so ahhhhh. You can't really put it into words, but having sex with someone you love whilst on LSD is a slice of heaven on earth and it's become an important part of my relationship with my boyfriend. Just setting a week-end aside where we shut ourselves in our bedroom and have sex for hours on a fairly hefty dose of acid is an incredible way to experience each other. (Female 41, 19 years' experience)

This informant was focusing on the sensual aspects of the LSD experience rather than its hallucinogenic and predominantly visual side. This sensual element can be used for dancing or, as this informant points out, sexually, but in either case it radically intensifies the sensual dynamic of the experience.

Psilocybin is not a common club drug, unless you're raving-it-up with the ciderdelic crews in Devon. It is similar to LSD but, from personal experience, I would suggest that it is more consistently hallucinogenic and provides less energy than LSD; psilocybin has always left me feeling like a pixie.

Ketamine use is growing particularly within the free/squat party end of club culture. I've never used it myself, but from my informants' descriptions I gained the impression that a great deal of its psychedelic effect arose from the sense of disembodiment, which ketamine's anaesthetic qualities generated. It seemed comparable to descriptions of entering a sensory deprivation tank when the body's presence is diminished in mind. Ketamine seemed to produce the most internal and unsocial experience of all the club drugs. Informants described it as 'a mind drug', which made them feel 'disconnected', and some suggested that they had under-gone 'out of body experiences' where they felt like they were 'floating over the dance floor'. It certainly takes you completely 'out of it' and the clubbers I have spoken to who were on it had real problems communicating because they were so spaced out (and often drooling). This put me off trying it because it seemed so insular and unsocial, a little like smack's schizophrenic, younger brother.

Cannabis

Many clubbers smoke dope and it is often used in conjunction with the other drugs to relax the rush that those drugs create, particularly when clubbers are coming down and want something to smooth this transition out. However, it can be hard to smoke dope in clubs because it is so easy to smell. As one informant pointed out:

> It's ridiculous the law on dope. It makes it really hard to smoke in clubs because you can smell it a mile off. Some places are all right about it, but others aren't. You can end up in the situation where you're in a room full of people who are all on drugs, but because you like the smelly one you end up getting hassled, even though it's nowhere near as strong as the other drugs. I'd love to just be able to go out have a couple of joints, a beer and a dance. That would be great, but it's easier to stick to Class A drugs because they're less hassle in terms of getting them in and taking them. (Female 29, 11 years' experience)

The difficulty in smoking dope in public spaces means that drinking or the dance drugs are the only real option if you want to go out. Dope smokers tend to do most of their smoking in their homes or around at their friends. It is not such a publicly social scene although there are some clubs where you can get away with having a spliff as long as you're discreet about it.

Marijuana is predominantly a giggly drug – far more so than alcohol in that I have seen people convulsed with laughter and completely unable to control their laughter while stoned in a way I haven't witnessed while drinking. Dope doesn't provide the energy offered by the other club drugs, which is why people often use it in combination with those drugs while in clubs. With the arrival of 'skunkweed', which is hydroponically grown weed with a heightened tetrahydrocannabinol content, the marijuana rush was intensified. This was not always a positive experience for users; they could become lethargic or paranoid on skunkweed and one male informant suggested that: 'Skunk's like the Tennants Super of the dope world, fine if you want to be a stoner zombie, but it's got not subtlety or style'.

Smoking dope relaxes the body and gives people a certain emotional distance between themselves and the world. Drawing from my own experiences this distance translates into a particular perspective upon the world. The easiest way to describe it is that the inherent absurdity of life is made manifest and its appearance is funny. Life is absurd. Ha, Ha, Ha.

The Rhythms of Drug Use

In this section I want to explore the actualities of drug use from users' perspectives. My informants were not youths and they had been taking drugs for a number of years, which meant they could explain how their relationship to and experience of drugs had changed over time. This long-term perspective allowed me to construct a four-stage model of drug use based on the following categories:

1. discovery;
2. honeymoon;

3. excess;
4. reassessment.

The list above is not a natural progression as one stage does not necessarily lead to the next. Drug experiences, like every other experience, alter as people change; they are intimately linked to what's going on in people's lives when they are not on drugs; they occur within people's worlds and people bring their dreams, aspirations, desires and material circumstances into their drug use. The club drugs are also deeply social and people's experience of that social world has a huge effect on the way they experience drugs. If the club sociality they encounter when using drugs doesn't blossom if it remains disconnected to people's worlds when they're away from the club, then the drug/club combination can become frustrating, shallow and false. If on the other hand these drugs become so much part of that everyday world that people are only ever communicating with one another when out-of-it, then this too can cause serious problems. I want to now examine the categories laid out above.

Discovery

Learning how to take drugs is not a sinister process; none of my informants had been sold drugs in the playground or tempted into drug taking by 'evil' strangers; they'd discovered drugs with their friends. All my informants had taken some form of drug before they ever entered clubs and they had started taking drugs for a number of reasons. The main one was curiosity; they were part of a world in which drugs existed and they wanted to try them out. They had seen people enjoying drugs, some of their friends took drugs and, contrary to the rhetoric that surrounds drugs in the everyday world, these friends were not screwed up, sad or desperate people; they were simply friends. There is an element of peer pressure operating here of wanting to be part of the gang, but this pressure dissipates over time:

> My motive now is to have a good time; it's purely a hedonistic experience. Before I'd just want to do what my friends were doing, peer pressure if you like. When I was at college if you said no to going out you became a party pooper or whatever. I was also looking to meet guys, but when I was younger we were more insecure. A lot of the going out thing was about proving how good a time you were having to other people, rather than just having it for yourself. (Female 32, 9 years' experience)

As we can see, this informant recognised that initial peer pressure, but also felt that it no longer played a role in her own drug experiences. She had gone beyond being pressurised and taken control of those drugs. She decided when, where and how she would use drugs, even though she was part of a group that regularly took drugs together. Drugs are something for the gang to do, a leisure option, and outside of cocaine and heroin they're a relatively cheap leisure option.

The first drug all my informants indulged in was alcohol. It was booze that showed them how much fun they could have when intoxicated. Once they'd discovered that simple fact they could begin to value the sociality of intoxication; the way it could change their relationship to the world and other people. From then on it was a case of coming across alternative drugs and witnessing people having different styles of drug experience, which appeared very different from the times they were having on alcohol. As one informant explained:

> I started clubbing in the sense of taking drugs and clubbing in 1990. Before that I had been in clubs. In fact I remember going to The S Club, everybody else was on drugs and I wasn't and everybody was out-of-their-heads. I was looking at them thinking: 'I don't get this really. Why is everybody jumping up and down really enjoying this? I just don't get it.' Then later, as I said in 1990, I went in and a friend gave me some E and suddenly it was: 'Oh now I get it, now I understand, I know why they're jumping up and down and smiling so much and having such a great time.' (Female 29, 10 years' experience)

This is an example of discovering the socio-sensual limits of alcohol. My informant was going to clubs and drinking but she still didn't 'get' clubbing, which in the early 1990s would have been orientated around Ecstasy. Drink could allow her to engage with the club experience to a certain degree, but she obviously didn't feel that her experience was as intense as the rest of the crowd's, who looked like they were having a better time than she was. It was only after taking Ecstasy that she understood why they looked this way as her own experience convinced her that they were indeed having a better time than she was. This recognition is an important part of discovering drugs as when you come across people who seem to be having a better time than you and who don't seem to be having any problems connected to their drug use, then you begin to reassess drugs before you even take them. As one informant explained:

> I'd smoked weed and hash, but I'd always been nervous about the other drugs. Then I went to Australia and met up with a group of people there. They were a great bunch, successful, professional people who enjoyed taking Ecstasy and acid. They were just so sensible and straightforward about it and they were having such a good time that I just decided to give them a go. So I did and I had a really good time too and I've been taking them on and off since then. (Female 41, 19 years' experience)

Once people realise that alcohol isn't the only way to become intoxicated, then their curiosity is whetted even further, but drugs exist within social networks and these networks have their own rules about what drugs they will or won't take. However, these rules change over time, new drugs are introduced and old ones abandoned as people's relationships with drugs change. The utterly simplistic idea that you have a joint one week and then end up taking heroin because one drug somehow leads to another is ridiculous. Drugs are part of socialising and these social groups dictate the type of drugs that people come across more than any craving to become more 'out of it'. People are introduced to drugs by friends.

People who are thoroughly enjoying their times on drugs swiftly discount the rhetoric of the legal and medical establishment that 'drugs are bad'. By linking all drugs under one banner this rhetoric distorts the very real differences and potential problems of each drug. However, in this discovery stage any potential problems people will experience with drugs are a long way off. People are discovering new ways of enjoying themselves, new ways of being around one another, a new sense of self and new ways of communicating. The impact this has on their social world, the way the intensity of taking drugs binds those worlds together and shifts them beyond a feeling of mundanity is as important as the drugs themselves.

When the discovery of drugs coincides with the discovery of clubs then an extra level of intensity is added. Clubs, house parties and parties have always been associated with intoxication. You won't find people queuing for hours to attend a teetotal party. Yet, clubs are not the only spaces in which people use drugs. I met a number of people who no longer went to clubs, but who still took club drugs – they just did it in different social groupings and settings. Just as people drink at home, in pubs and clubs they also take drugs in a similar manner. Clubs did not cause people to take drugs; all my informants had taken some form of illegal drug before they ever clubbed. Neither did they prolong people's use of drugs because people continued to take drugs once they'd left clubbing. Yet, it is undeniable that clubs are good places to share drugs with people; the intensity of the environment itself matches the intensity of the club drugs and allows people to savour and express that sensual rush to its fullest potential. As one informant explained: 'You don't have to take drugs to enjoy clubs; I've had great times clubbing just drinking a few beers, but when you do take drugs then it adds to the experience because it makes it more intense' (Male 33, 17 years' experience).

Honeymoon

For a while after my first trip I really did think I'd discovered the meaning of life, even though I could only grasp it when I was in the middle of one. (Male)

That first year of pilling was such a fucking scream; I was having a big time; it was exciting. I didn't think I'd ever stop doing them or that my life would ever be the same again. (Female)

Cocaine made me feel like super-girl; I was fearless; I felt like I'd always wanted to feel, confident, strong, in your face; it was great. (Female)

The honeymoon period of intoxication is the period of maximum enthusiasm for the drugs themselves. It is best illustrated on a macro-scale by examining the large-scale arrival of Ecstasy use in Britain, which was greeted with an almost evangelical enthusiasm, mirroring the arrival of LSD in the 1960s. People believed that something special was happening, that the world was changing; the soulless greed of the 1980s was viewed with contempt; the communist block crumbled through largely peaceful revolutions and Ecstasy caught the *zeitgeist* of the times. Take this example of Ecstasy evangelism from Matthew Collins's (1997: 153) *Altered States*:

> The estate where we come from, drinking's the thing, get proper out of it and have a top chuckle with your pals . . . We had a base in Wythenshawe where every activity in the world was going on from. One hundred young lads in there on beer, but all of a sudden five or ten of them had gone wayward, they're coming in with fucking bandannas tied round their heads. From 1988 to the end of 1990 we didn't touch a drop of alcohol, not one fucking drink. After Sweat it Out, for two years we went on a fucking mission from God, we were like Jehovah's Witnesses going out promoting it. Telling our parents it's going to change the world and all that.

This was the Ecstasy honeymoon and, as in the 1960s with LSD, the drug and rave combination offered an experience so radically different from anything people had encountered before that it made them feel that change was imminent. However, the comedown from Ecstasy's honeymoon period made people more aware of the limitations of all drugs so the nature of the honeymoon changed. Nowadays, it is extremely rare to hear people talking about E in such evangelical terms. The E experience has gained a future and a past; it has been contextualised and people talk about it more knowingly with less fervour and more awareness of its downside. On a smaller scale, though, this honeymoon period can be encountered with most drugs at a more personal level and in less radical contexts. No one believes cocaine can change the world, far from it, but discovering cocaine can be exciting if you've never sampled it before. Newcomers to drugs can still find them passionate and radical because those drugs offer such an alternate experience of people's own social worlds. People feel that something has been added to their lives, those lives have become more passionate and exciting. As one informant explained:

> I knew I was really living and life felt so electric. It was the best time and I don't think I'll ever have better times. I was with people I cared about and it was just an adventure, going out, taking the drugs, dancing, laughing, feeling really connected to one another; it felt perfect. (Female 34, 17 years' experience)

All my informants agreed that drugs were best experienced socially and that predominantly taking them alone just like drinking on your own was 'a bit sad really'. Drugs were valued for the social experiences they helped create and these social experiences were as important as the drugs themselves in underpinning this honeymoon period. You and your friends are out and about having a series of adventures that bind these friendship networks together at a deeply sensuous level.

The honeymoon period is also the period where the effects of taking drugs are having a limited impact on people's lives away from the club space. In the last instance the life outside of clubbing exerts a controlling influence on most people's intoxicatory practice. The more connected people are to that everyday life the more negatively they will begin to experience the effects of 'caning' drugs and staying out all night because it gets in the way of their everyday lives. People's priorities can change over time with age. For a while they focus all their energies into partying but eventually they must find a balance between the parties and building a life outside of the party and this is when the honeymoon starts to come to an end.

Excess

The road of excess to the palace of wisdom leads . . . You never know what is enough unless you know what is more than enough. (William Blake, 1978: 96–7)

We had a system: we'd start the night with a couple of lines of speed and then go out drinking after that we'd take a pill and club-it-up. Once the pill was starting to fade we'd drop a tab of acid, which would see us through till the next morning. Then it was more speed and off to the pub on the Sunday for a booze up. By Sunday night we were all completely wasted; no one had slept we must have looked dreadful, but it was hardcore. We were unstoppable party machines for a while there, but after a while we had to slow down; we were all completely mashed and it was getting out of control. (Female 29, 12 years' experience)

I took Ecstasy virtually every weekend for ten years until it got to the point where I wasn't starting to feel OK afterwards until the following Friday. Then we'd go out and pill it for the weekend and the whole cycle would start again. It had to stop. I don't regret it, but it had to stop. (Female 34, 17 years' experience)

The above quote by Blake gives us another perspective upon excess because he stresses the way people learn from their own excesses. People have very different ideas about what constitutes excess; it is more of an experience than an idea or a set of weights and measures; it is the recognition of your own personal limits, which is the element to which Blake was alluding. Those limits arise from the amount of drugs you take in any given night and the amount of nights you spend drugged-up in total and the effect this has on other aspects of your life. When excess arises from a desire to go further and to live faster and longer because it is such a laugh, then it actually seems to be easier to recognise the point when it has got to stop because it starts making the rest of your life less pleasurable and more difficult to cope with. When excess arises from desperation, a need to stay up because the world you re-enter and your experience of yourself in that world is just too unpalatable then to use the drug terminology: 'You're fucked mate, utterly fucked. It's like flying a plane, no point in taking off unless you've got a place to land' (male).

When I talk about excess I'm not talking about addiction. In fact many of my informants were fairly derisory about the whole notion of addiction when applied to certain drugs. As one explained:

> Smack's addictive though you have to work bloody hard to become an addict. It doesn't happen overnight that's just a myth. Fags are addictive. The rest of them well addiction's just an excuse, a way of wriggling out of taking control of them. It's just a bit of prop-aganda that means people don't have to admit that they were weak and stupid and fucked-up royally. They can just blame the drugs. 'It's not my fault mister, honest, I'm a victim of the big bad drugs.' It's pathetic. You've got to keep an eye on how many drugs you're using and be honest about why you're using them or else you're in for a bloody great fall into a hole that you dug yourself. (Male 28, 10 years' experience)

Excess is more about doing too many drugs for too long and it usually arises from people having so much fun that they don't want to stop. Then everything catches up with them – not just the drugs, but the lost sleep, the thrashed bodies, the hangovers and comedowns and their lives outside of the party become more and more difficult to negotiate. Addiction is a luxury of time derived from not having to negotiate the world fully, either because you're on its fringes and denied access or you're wealthy enough to insulate yourself from it. The generation of clubbers I've ended up meeting are in neither position; they have to and want to support themselves; they are part of the social system; they work; they have aspir-ations and so their drug taking occurs within that external everyday framework. Their drug experiences can alter what they want from that world, it can change their perspective upon the world, but they haven't completely disconnected them-selves from the everyday world because that world is still a necessity for their survival.

So a sense of excess arises from a relationship between self and world and it is recognised through the body in how that world feels and is experienced. As one informant explained:

> I'd got to the point where work was just this thing I did to pay for clubbing. I was tired and ratty and everything started getting on top of me. After the partying the rest of my life felt flat and dull, but I was too knackered to do anything about it or to change any-thing. It made me question what I was doing and what I wanted from my life. (Female 29, 11 years' experience)

This is the bodily state of excess, clubbing's sensual doppelganger, the point at which clubbing makes the rest of your life more difficult to cope with. I must stress the almost mundane nature of these experiences of excess. They don't usually involve a sudden rush to the hospital or a month cleaning toilets at the Betty Ford clinic. They are sensual negotiations between self and world; the realisation that by focusing all your energies on clubbing you are leaving yourself too little time to create anything else you can take pleasure in. The next informant places this lack of dramatic content into perspective:

> People fuck-up on drugs because they have an addictive personality. People fuck-up on drugs because they haven't got anything else to do with their time. People fuck-up on drugs because they're stupid and they've got no discipline. Most of the reason people fuck-up on drugs is that they're only ever told that they're dangerous and they shouldn't do them. Then they find out that drugs are fun and they think: 'Oh why can't I just cane them.' They have to find out the problems for themselves. The bugbear image that you're presented of drugs is you will take this pill or snort this line and have a dodgy reaction and die that night or you'll end up selling your ass in alleyways to pay for your crack habit. Whereas, I think it's astounding that no one really says that if you take too many drugs you will turn into a boring person and become insecure, which is the front line. The thing that most people will come up against and recognise first as something that is a warning signal is when you're starting every fucking conversation with the phrase: 'I was so out-of-it.' Because you think it makes you sound like an interesting and exciting person, then that's the first stage in becoming a drug bore. (Male 28, 10 years' experience)

This is an interesting statement because it reveals the disparity between the medical and legal authorities' view on drugs and the problems discovered by drug users themselves. The constant dramatic stress on death and addiction and lives utterly destroyed through drugs within this rhetoric actively obscures these other far more common and more mundane indicators of excess. When people get to the point where they can't perceive of having a good time without drugs; when drugs are all they talk about; when their drug use makes the rest of their lives difficult to negotiate, then they are approaching a state of excess. Yet, they can experience all these things without ever becoming addicts who crave drugs everyday and steal from their granny's purse. There is also a social element to this process, as the next informant explained:

> What happened was we'd go out and do an E or half an E and either club-it-up or party at home, but when it was just E we didn't do it all the time. Then a friend introduced our group to cocaine and then things began to change because cocaine's not as intense as E. It's easier to cope with and that's when things started to change because for about seven to eight months every time we got together we'd take drugs, sometimes Ecstasy, sometimes cocaine, sometimes speed. There were times that I deliberately planned to

stay away from drugs by having a meal round at mine or something, but people would bring some coke or E and it was like, oh shit, I just wanted a nice quiet evening and a nice meal not this madness. In the end we had to make a real effort to stay Class A free, just so we could have a different time together, something more mellow and relaxed. (Female 32, 9 years' experience)

This informant didn't want to spend all her social time completely out of it; she wanted a range of experiences, rather than just staying at a highly intense point of social intoxication. This group worked it out together; they changed their social patterns. They still went out and went wild but they also created other situations where they could meet up. Getting intoxicated to an extreme level had become a habit, rather than a choice. As the same informant explained:

There was a time when I didn't have the slightest qualm about it all. I really enjoyed it and I had no worries about it and then that feeling started to change last year. One of my friends was constantly giving me a hard time about it saying: 'I don't want to go out with you because all you do is this, all you talk about is that.' And being quite critical. I was having big weekends and ending up shagged out and I'd say: 'That's it, I'm going to have a break.' Then the next Friday would come and I'd go out again. Then this friend would 'phone me and remind me that I was going to have a break and I had no answer to that. Now it's planned so it's less spontaneous and I've been doing that since September and I've had really good nights. Each time I've done it I've really enjoyed it and it's been like a holiday. It's made it all special again.

Reassessment

The experience of excess can lead to people abandoning the drugs and clubs completely. For all my informants, though, their excesses made them wonder what they were doing and what they wanted from the world. None of them had given up going out or getting intoxicated but they had begun to build alternative lives for themselves in which partying nevertheless still played an important social role. As one informant said:

I can't see myself ever stopping partying; I just love it too much. Over the years the crowds change, the drugs change, I've changed, but that's all part of the process. I don't get as legless as I used to; I space things out a bit more; the people become more important; they, rather than the drugs make or break the party. I suppose it's always been like that, but you focus on different things at different times. After all you can't simply enjoy the same thing over and over again so it has to develop as you change or it just becomes boring and unimaginative no matter how amazing it initially feels. (Male 59, 43 years' experience)

Partying gives people an alternative socio-sensual environment where their world is intensified. They value this experience and over time they learn to weave it into the other parts of their lives, which also hold things that they value. As one informant explained:

> It's all about balance. It's really fucking important to get that balance; you've got to be able to deal with your world sober and enjoy that world. You can't just club-it-up and drug-it-up to keep the world at bay otherwise you'll end up fucked. So you learn to balance things out the best you can. Meeting my boyfriend was important to me. It stopped me worrying about ending up on my own on a Saturday night if I didn't go clubbing. So some Saturdays we stay in and chill-out and others we go out and live-it-up. It gives you an option and the more options you can create the better because you've got more choices to play with. (Female 29, 11 years' experience)

Balance was stressed by a number of my informants and at the level of the body this balance must be sensed as a sensual equilibrium between these disparate experiences. One informant explained this tension in these terms:

> I liked getting to the point where I felt like I was earning my parties that I deserved to have a blow out. I space them out more and when I do go out I enjoy it more because I'm not battling with tiredness or even that sense of: 'Here I am again doing the same thing over and over again.' I'm more confident and adventurous now. I try and find new experiences, new ways to have a good time, but I'm also more confident in other parts of my life, my work, my relationships and that's given me other things to focus on and enjoy. (Female 30, 12 years' experience)

This process of reassessment is pragmatic; my informants were all dedicated party people, they wanted to enjoy themselves but this was no simple case of fitting your intoxication and party experiences into the growing demands and constraints made upon you by the everyday world. It was also about taking what you'd learnt from clubbing out into that world. The next informant said:

> I don't want a split personality for a life. I don't want to only feel alive on the weekends. I want a passionate life, but if you get over reliant on the drugs to make your life passionate, then they cease to be of any use and they become destructive. I think the whole clubbing thing teaches you a lot. I learnt a different way of being with people; I learnt just how good life can feel. It sounds funny, but once you've experienced the rush of taking drugs and going to clubs it gives you a different perspective on things. It made me realise I want to spend my time enjoying people and not constantly battling with them over stupid trivial things. You can get caught up in all the trivial shit. It becomes a way of life and clubbing and drugging gives you a break from it. You see it for what it is, bullshit, boring tedious bullshit, rather than thinking it's the only way the world can be. You learn to handle it, but you don't respect it because it's not your only experience of people. (Male 34, 17 years' experience)

The process of reassessment is a two-way street; the everyday world encroaches upon clubbing because that world becomes so hard to negotiate that people realise they've got to cut back. However, those that don't abandon clubbing completely retain an alternative perspective upon that everyday world and they set about negotiating it with this perspective in mind. They are attempting to bridge the gap between their clubbing and their everyday experience of the world.

Chemical Literacy

One of the major changes that come out of this period of reassessment is a shift in people's perspective on and usage of drugs. They cease to be an end in themselves. So rather than striving to simply get out of it all the time they alter their patterns of drug use to ensure that they can communicate with and enjoy the other people who are sharing the night with them. As one informant said:

> Getting completely bollocksed out-of-your-box can get a bit boring after a while. You want to be able to talk to people and dance with them and if you get too fucked-up you can't because you're just gurning like a loon or so fucked-up on cocaine that you can't shut up and listen to anyone; you're talking at them not to them. So I've cut back; I take a bit of E, then later on I might have a couple of lines of whizz, just to pick-it-up or I'll a have a bit of acid and then a bit of coke, few spliffs if it's cool to smoke, few drinks. It's enough to keep you in there to keep you dancing and awake, but it allows you to keep it under control as well. I think a lot of it's confidence; you learn that and when you've learnt it you don't need so many drugs to feel part of the club. (Male 34, 16 years' experience)

My informants had become so familiar with the drugs they took that they could tailor their consumption to suit their particular desires for the night; they used combinations of drugs; they paced their consumption so that they could seize all the different aspects of the club event. They had discovered which drugs they enjoyed and which they didn't. Which drugs mixed with other drugs and the altered effects that such combinations produced. It is a similar process to learning to drink; you get very drunk early on and then learn to control your drinking over time. My informants were attempting to maintain a point of maximum engagement with the party. They wanted a sense of clarity from their drugs, which allowed them to socialise. The following informant explained that:

> You become more aware of the drugs you take over time. You begin to understand them more, their different effects and influences both in terms of clubbing, but also how they effect you beyond clubbing. I recognise that something like E influences the way I think when I'm doing it regularly and I've got it together more. I've got a better idea of what I want from them and what they do for me. They help me access particular experiences

that I enjoy, but if I take too many of them they can destroy those experiences as well. There's clarity to the way I take drugs now that I didn't have for a long time. (Female 32, 9 years' experience)

This informant stressed that her knowledge of drugs has grown over the years and that this knowledge isn't simply related to her time clubbing but also to the way drugs affect other aspects of her life. She had become chemically literate in that she understood the role she wanted drugs to play in her life. She didn't take them every weekend because that had become a habit, rather than a decision. She gave herself breaks and had created other leisure activities, which weren't drug related. She had developed the discipline to refuse drugs if she wasn't in the mood or the timing wasn't right.

If drugs become a habit then their usefulness rapidly diminishes. They begin to limit people's experiences because instead of shifting them from one socio-sensual state to another users simply remain caught up in a single sensual landscape, which is the experience they were trying to wriggle free from in the first place. In order to understand drugs users need to know why they're taking them, what they want from them and how to be sober and still cope with the world. If they don't gain this knowledge they will never become chemically literate and drugs will become either destructive or users will get bogged down in them and become dull.

Summary

Drugs in all their forms, legal or illegal, play an important role in creating the socio-sensual intensity of clubbing that makes clubs feel radically different from other times and spaces in people's lives. The club drugs help generate a range of experiences. They each have different properties and propensities that will be heightened or occasionally destroyed by the 'set and setting' of the particular club they're taken in. Ecstasy was important in shifting people's ideas about what constitutes a good night out and its arrival revitalised the nightlife of this country. It facilitated the change into an alternate social and sensual experience of the night in opposition to the booze-fuelled sociality that preceded it. That shift defined the model of what a club should feel like for punters and made them more intense spaces. This model has shifted as fashions and drugs changed. Ecstasy is only one drug amongst many that now plays a role in generating the party.

Intoxication changes over time. It has a pattern and people's knowledge of their chosen drugs deepens with experience. Rather than ending up 'completely screwed' by years of taking drugs my informants have become chemically literate. This is a problematic process and it has its risks and its dangers, but my informants believed that these risks had been worth taking from their own personal perspective because the times they had spent intoxicated had added something important to their lives.

–7–

The Vibe

The vibe in a good club is viral and a good promoter can use that to take people beyond what they thought the night was going to be about.

(Male 32, 14 years' experience)

So far we have looked at the elements that combine to make clubbing such a hard-core leisure activity in terms of the sheer carnal and corporeal rush you experience when you're out on the razzle. In this chapter I want to examine the way in which this rush underpins the social practices of clubbing and makes those practices feel different from the ones people utilise in other public spaces. The social vibe found in clubs is the most important aspect of clubbing and if a club doesn't generate that vibe, then no matter who the DJ is, what the music's like, or how swanky the venue is, it will fail.

The social experience of going out and living it up with both strangers and mates was the aspect of clubbing most valued by my informants. There are two aspects to this experience: the first happens in the club itself; the second takes place at the all-back-to-mine gigs, which often follow on from and expand upon this initial immersion into the club space. In both cases the embodied rules of the habitus that usually govern and constrain our social lives are challenged. Through the adoption of alternative modes of social practice these changes allowed people to socialise in ways that often felt better, more natural and more satisfying than their other social encounters.

The sociality of clubbing is aspirational in that it grants people access to social experiences that more closely reflect their own ideal social models. As this informant explains: 'Clubbing offers you the chance to do the right thing by people, to treat them properly without having to worry about getting shafted or taken advantage of for behaving like that' (Female 41, 19 years' experience).

They get to experience their social selves and relate to other people in different ways and these alternative socio-sensual encounters can gradually become part of their everyday lives because they exist as a form of embodied knowledge that people take from clubbing. It is then up to them what they do with this knowledge. For my informants it was predominantly manifested in their relationships with their friends, which they felt had been changed for the better through clubbing together.

Party, Party

The party is the heart of clubbing. All the social interactions found in clubs can be found within common notions of what makes a good party: a welcoming friendly environment, a loosening up of social boundaries, a bit of intoxication to grease the party's wheels, laughter, smiles, flirtation, communication and inclusivity. That's the social basis of the party and it requires a certain level of mutual participation to succeed; everyone has to play by the social rules or else the party can't happen. This model of the party has existed far longer than clubbing and throughout the twentieth century it was intensified by the inclusion of drugs. The roaring 1920s roared with cocaine; the 1950s found speed; the 1960s weed and LSD; the 1970s went back to speed; the 1980s fell for cocaine and then Ecstasy arrived and became the drug of choice until the mid-1990s, after which cocaine and booze started to return. Now we have a whole medicine chest of intoxicants that can be used singularly or in combination, which feed into the construction of the party, intensifying it, accelerating it and imbuing it with a psychedelic edge. Yet it is the social model of the party that, in the West, has most often given these drugs a framework within which they can be used and allowed the experiences they offer to be shared with others. If you then add all the other elements of clubbing on top of that chemical intensification you end up with a space that feels very different from other spaces in people's lives. You create a hyper-reality, not in Eco's (1987) use of the term to label certain simulacra, but rather an environment that is experienced as a highly visceral, social and sensual reality that stands out in relation to their other social encounters. Goffman (1961: 75) described the party in these terms:

> So we find the euphoria function for a social occasion resides somewhere between little social difference and much social difference. A dissolution of some externally based social distance must be achieved, a penetration of ego-boundaries, but not to an extent that renders the participants fearful, threatened, or self-consciously concerned with what is happening socially. Too much potential loss and gain must be guarded against, as well as too little.

This model still basically holds true, but it must be amended to encompass the contemporary club space. In terms of clubbing you must add the sensual intensity we've been examining to the model offered by Goffman. This intensity plays a role in altering actual social relations within the space both amongst groups of friends and amongst strangers. We are examining a space where strangers surround punters, yet the way they experience these strangers is very different from the way they experience strangers in other public spaces. Clubs make sense of strangers by altering punters' emotional experience of those strangers and this social shift is exceptionally important. In statistical and demographic terms the crowd may not be a diverse melting pot though I have certainly seen clubs which fit this description particularly within the Asian club scene. Nevertheless clubs are predominantly made up of unknown faces and this simple fact generates the experience of social difference alluded to by Goffman.

We are taught from an early age to be wary of strangers because they are fraught with potential dangers. They are the potentially insane and dangerous demons of our social world: the paedophiles, the rapists, the serial killers, the thieves and the con men. Yet, this is the minority of people; the existence of whom deeply affects the way we encounter the majority. Within clubbing people's expectations are reversed; they expect strangers to be all right, to behave themselves; they are expected to be tolerant, chilled-out, smiley and charming. This expectation alters the way clubbers approach and interact with one another, which plays a hugely important role in turning these expectations into social realities. Clubs express the social aspirations of clubbers, not in terms of what they want to be in the social world, but rather how they want that social world to feel.

Strangers are sensual objects. Their presence plays a profound role in shaping the body of the city, which clubbing exists in opposition to. This opposition is not thought out as an idea; it is embodied as a particular way of inhabiting space that in itself has become habituated as a form of bodily technique. In the drug chapter, I examined the way ecstasy and other drugs could make people less fearful of the world around them while stressing that this fearfulness was not an idea, but a form of embodied tension that they had got used to over time. This is best illustrated by an informant's example:

> When I'm on the street, during the day, going somewhere, I'm always aware of the people around me, how close they are to me and if they start getting too close then my hand immediately goes to my purse to check it's safe. It's just something I've noticed myself doing. It's not that I'm really scared although I do find walking around scary at night, but even during the day I'm wary of people's intentions towards me. (Female 41, 19 years' experience)

This informant noticed her hand going to her purse, but the action was more of a reflex than a conscious decision: a bodily manifestation of her wariness. It was simply part of being in a city and seeing people through the eyes of that city. The intensity of the city, its bustle and hustle, is exciting and it infects the bodies of city dwellers with a particular state of tension that is sometimes valued and sometimes despised. It is a love/hate experience. The city can get on top of you, but its potential for excitement can also balance these negative experiences out. It is a world of social, emotional and sensual extremes that have become everyday and taken-for-granted forms of bodily practice. One informant suggested that:

I don't think human beings are designed by evolution to live in this type of city community where you have to share your space with thousands of people you don't know and there are points like on the tube where those people are all invading your body space. It's often very uncomfortable, but it's part of city life you get used to. Whereas, in a club everyone seems to share a similar mind set, a similar goal or theme, and it's a community simply because you've all chosen to share that for the night. (Female 32, 9 years' experience)

Following Damasio (1999), I believe that this 'similar mind set' arises out of a change in bodily practice, which shifts the 'proto-self' of punters from being inhabited by the body of the city to being inhabited by the body of the club. That change allows people to become part of the social realm of the party and relish that experience. The tube is a great example of the anti-club; it can certainly be uncomfortable, people avoid eye contact, they phase out and become as anonymous as possible, they rarely smile. People become objects in the city, by which I mean they become things to be negotiated, rather than engaged with. Think of all the times you've found yourself becoming irritated by other people, not because they are actively challenging you, but rather because they simply slow you down, get in your way, accidentally bump into you or even look at you in an odd way. All things that generally seem much less important or stressful in clubs. Any sense of empathy is obliterated and the person becomes an anger-producing object. In *The Science of Emotion* Randolph R. Cornelius (1995: 137) suggests that: 'Anger, for example, is a complex, social emotion as well as a basic emotion in that it arises when one person's plans or progress toward a goal are interrupted by another person's behaviour.'

Often, though, our goals are fairly diffuse anyway, but the sheer weight of human numbers in the city reduces our experience of people as people to be empathised with and enjoyed to people as objects, things to be traversed, avoided or irritated by. The body of the city is a defensive body, it is not a welcoming body, it does not want to be approached by strangers and it sends out visual cues to that effect: minimal eye contact, rarely smiling, feigning disinterest, sometimes rude and abrupt, bristling with tension. A simple physical lexicon that has profound effects upon the way the city is experienced at a socio-sensual level.

In clubs you are allowed to enjoy strangers, to talk bullshit to them, to watch them, to share their pleasure and enthusiasm. As one informant suggested:

Clubbing always feels like an incredibly sane reaction to city life because city living can get on top of you. It can tilt you towards seeing people in the worst way and clubbing seems to change the balance. A lot of the time you get to see people at their best. (Male 34, 16 years' experience)

Within a club crowd, strangers become fellow pleasure seekers, they are part and parcel of the pleasures of clubbing. If you can't change your perspective on them, from that of the outside world, you can't club because you will be constantly experiencing those crowds from a position of social and emotional distance. The changes in social practice found in clubs are incredibly simple, yet it takes a radical shift in a person's socio-sensual self to create them. The body of the city must be unravelled until people stop being perceived as impersonal objects because their pleasure and passion becomes so infectious that you want to empathise with them. Clubs allow you to engage with people in ways that would be unthinkable in other public spaces.

Participation

On his seventy-first birthday I took my Dad out to a club, a heaving sweaty sound clash where I was going to be the MC. Dad had no idea what to expect; I had no inkling of whether he was going to enjoy it or not and we'd told him that we'd take him home at any point if he wasn't having fun. At 3.00 a.m. he was still on the crowded dance floor, smiling away and grooving-on-down with my girlfriend whom he had been chaperoning while I dashed back and forth from the microphone to our table. Everyone was grinning at him; people would come up and give him a kiss or a hug; his head was steaming from the heat. It was a fabulous night and he partied like a pro, dancing away, chatting to people, saying he was 'in seventh heaven' and 'on cloud nine'.

My Dad had no previous experience of the contemporary club environment, yet his own mental model of how to behave at a party, which had been created in seemingly very different spaces, still allowed him to negotiate and enjoy the club experience, but it was his willingness to put that party model into action and to participate that made the real difference. As one informant suggested:

> People have to participate in the clubs and the crowds; participate and lend something of themselves to the social situation and the ones that do, well more often than not, they're the people who would lend themselves to any social situation, be it their Dad's re-marriage, Granny's birthday or whatever. They're the best ones; the ones you really want in a club, but I think you have to remember that there are always people who participate and there will always be people who are passengers. (Male 27, 10 years' experience)

My Dad summed it up when we were talking to him after our night out. He admitted that he had been a bit worried about going and he hadn't been sure what he was letting himself in for, but he had decided to go because 'it would be an experience' and that whatever happened he had already decided 'he'd stay until the end and make the best of it' and that's exactly what he did. Any opportunity to dance and he danced. If people came up to him he would smile and chat to them immediately. When he got a bit tired he'd just sit down, have a natter or simply watch the mayhem with a huge smile on his face until he was ready to get into the groove again. When the scantily clad girls came up to give him a kiss he'd pucker up with glee. He refused nothing and seized everything and with only two glasses of whiskey inside him he was certainly the soberest person at this party. As a fellow party goer commented to me:

> Is he your Dad?
> Yes.
> WOW I hope I can party like that when I'm his age; he's wild.
> Yes, he taught me every important thing I know.

The desire to participate and enjoy the night is the bedrock upon which the party state of mind is built. No one sets out to a club with the intention of having a shit time. Yet, there are barriers to the level of participation people can achieve. The sensual intensity of clubs is a seductive force that helps overcome these barriers and turns that intention into an embodied actuality. As my next informant suggests:

> People seem to think that they can buy a good night out. They expect to have it handed to them on a plate, just because they forked out twenty pounds to get through the door and they're paying way over the odds for their drinks. They think that they should be having a good time because they're spending money, but that's not the way it works; you've got to get-it-on in a club; you've got to make it succeed and if there isn't enough people pumping it out then clubs just fall on their arses. (Male 26, 8 years' experience)

Consumption must become production if a party is going to take off because parties must be rebuilt each night from the feet up. Punters must throw themselves into the thick of it and this process of sensual occupation gradually generates a shared 'proto-self' (Damasio 1999), which synchs their perspective upon the event. Many clubbers presume that it is the drugs that make the party and they undoubtedly have an important role to play, but as my next informant points out:

> The way I experience Ecstasy has definitely changed over time. I learnt to control it much more, which meant that it was never really the same, even after a couple of goes. It's still really enjoyable just not as intense. Occasionally you get a strong hit and people say: 'Oh these are amazing Es.' But it has far more to do with the mood you're in, in the first place. Certainly E can change your mood, but if there's stuff going on then it's not going to suddenly get rid of that. So if you're in a really good mood and happy and content and you're gagging for a party, then it's just an amazing rush, but if you're tired or ratty or anxious or you didn't really want to go out, then those feelings leak through into the experience and they can affect your ability to make the most of the night. So I would say that if you're counting on the drugs to ensure a good night, then you're on shaky ground. It has to come from you in the end, but if you're in the mood, then drugs

makes the whole thing easier to get into and even more intense. (Female 39, 9 years' experience)

Drugs are not enough to guarantee participation. Drugs shift the bodies and minds of punters, but if the insecurities and niggles of the outside world are too strong the drugs can't always cut through these pre-existing emotional states, which hold people back from participating in the event. This inhibits a sense of connection to the party that can make punters feel miserable and excluded. Some punters tend to blame everything, but themselves if they cannot connect to the space. The drugs, the crowd, the music, the club are all held responsible for a person's inability to participate in the party, occasionally this is the case mostly it is the punters themselves who have failed to leave their social insecurities and emotional baggage at the club door.

What you add to the space, the level to which you participate and how you participate, are the things that will really get you noticed in a club. As one informant put it:

> When you start getting recognised for your party talents, then that's the best bit. Suddenly you're getting invited out to nights because people know you can do it and you'll be an asset and make a fucking effort. They know that you'll go off and party regardless of the rest of the crowd. If someone puts me on their guest list, then they know they're going to get a player. It's free so I make an effort: I dress-up, I'll shave, pluck me eyebrows, shave my head and wear something wild and funky. I'll make an effort to look good and I don't mind doing that at all because it's fair, it's a trade off. That's all surface stuff though, window dressing if you like, the most important thing you can do is help create a good atmosphere. If you're all tarted up, but you're giving people attitude, then that's bollocks. I like to think I bring any attitude down because I won't let it wind me up or pander to it. I just party hard and I try and encourage other people to do the same. (Male 26, 8 years' experience)

Having seen this guy in action I can confirm that he was indeed a party asset and an excellent illustration of the fact that the party arises from people's determination to participate. In a club the desire to be amongst others, to share time and space with those others is one of the major allures of the event. Nobody is forced to be there, there is no obligation to club from outside of your own social circle and by choosing to club people decide to place themselves within a crowd. In one form or another they can either participate in that crowd or they can be 'passengers' who expect the party to provide them with more than they're prepared to give it. In terms of participation the most important element arises from carrying the *jouissance* of the party on the surface of the flesh; the party must be revealed; it cannot afford to be too cool, but must instead be hot, funky and passionate. It must become visible on the surface of flesh and that manifestation of exuberance links those individual party people together into a full on party crowd.

Courtesy

In the main, club nights are incredibly courteous, which is demonstrated in how people deal with one another when something goes wrong. Whether squeezing past each other, bumping into one another, colliding on the dance floor or simply catching each others' eyes, people respond differently to one another in the club space than when outside of that space. There is a startling difference between clubs now and clubs prior to the arrival of Ecstasy, as the next informant who had not lived in this country for over sixteen years and who I took to a club while he was here on holiday said:

> It's so different from how clubs used to be I couldn't get over it. It was far friendlier and everyone was so polite and laid-back. When I slammed into that guy on the dance floor, I mean I really collided with him, he just shrugged it off with a grin that would have been a fight when I used to club here, no doubt about it. This scene is much better; I had a really good time. (Male 45)

The club is a social swirl as it is grounded in the movement of people and bodies and that kinetic pulse manifests itself as an intrinsic part of the party's sociality. The message that you must be able to read from the club crowd is very simple: 'We're here, we're happy, we're having a time.' The core sociality of the party is grounded in pre-formed social groupings made up of your mates and acquaintances. They will provide the central social network and a deeper level of social interaction outside of which lies a room full of strangers but for a party to work these groups must communicate across their own boundaries, even if that level of commun-ication is fairly superficial. In fact superficial is the wrong word because it is so negatively loaded. In the club sense this surface-level communication is incredibly important because it underpins the shared nature of the event. A better word would be super-facial because social interactions arise out of the highly animated bodies and expressive faces of the club crowd who are pumping out that party vibe and revealing their enjoyment to the rest of the room.

Courtesy provides the framework within which this stranger-based commun-ication can operate without it pulling punters away from the kinaesthetic rush of the party itself. Conversation between strangers, except when they're chatting each other up, tends to be brief and shouted because of the noise there is little room for subtlety in people's way of speaking and to combat this effect the communicative qualities of the body comes to the fore. In club terms the way you say something, the physical stance that you say it from, is as important as the words themselves. The most important thing to communicate is your sense of being in the party. Often the words you use are pure blarney as they are simply an excuse to share a particular emotional charge with the world, which indicates that you and the person you're speaking to are part of something exhilarating, ecstatic and in social terms quite special. As one promoter said in relation to his own club nights:

> I think another way I'd try to describe a night-club is that they are the most excessively polite places you can ever go. People say please and thank you all the time. That's why we call ourselves 'Thankyou' because people are so polite and shit nights are the ones where people aren't polite, whether for reasons of snobbery or attitude, but when you get into a truly great night where there is no attitude, there is not only no attitude, but there's a desire to banish the idea of attitude completely and be really nice to everyone because they all deserve it and you make sure everyone's all right. (Male 32, 14 years' experience)

Attitude

I have placed this section here because it illustrates the opposite of courtesy. The term 'attitude' is most commonly used negatively. In its most basic form attitude simply means three things: hassling people, behaving violently and not showing any respect towards other clubbers. In its extended form it is used to denote spaces that either refused people entry or made them feel uncomfortable once they were inside. Clubs that have dress codes or other door restrictions are seen by some clubbers as having attitude, as are clubs that are inhospitable and unfriendly. Clubs that seem more interested in making money than looking after their punters will also be seen as having attitude. Attitude is basically anything that arises within the club that constrains people's ability to seize the event.

Clubs have social hierarchies; they are not completely egalitarian spaces in which everyone is equal. As one informant pointed out:

> There's a pecking order in clubs that's most noticeable on the guest list, who gets in free, who gets in cheap, who has to pay full price. They're all ways of ensuring you get the right crowd in who'll set the right tone. All clubbers know this. They've seen it in action on the door, but I think attitude arises when that hierarchy can't get over itself when it treats other clubbers with disdain, just because they're not part of that core social group that gives club its identity, then you get attitude. I think people accept there's a hierarchy; they just don't want their faces rubbed in it once they're actually in the club because they don't want to feel excluded. (Male 33, 17 years' experience)

Hierarchy doesn't disappear in clubs – it just becomes less important because if it becomes the focus of the night the vibe will remain muted and hostile, which is not the experience people desire from clubbing, even those who are part of the club's core crowd. However, people who complain about experiencing attitude a lot in clubs are sometimes just insecure. Clubs have their banter and their bouts of bitchiness and some people just can't cope with them. They immediately become defensive or upset, yet some club bitching can be funny; it is something you learn to deal with as you become more familiar with clubs. The overall vibe of the space puts intentionally vicious bitchiness into a different context from other spaces; it is seen as a glitch in the sociality of the night and clubbers treat it as such. So on one occasion I saw a woman dealing with some club bitchiness simply by pointing out that: 'Your friends can think what they want about me, but they can't insult me because I'm here to have a good time and nothing else really matters to me at this particular moment in time.'

She went onto have an exceptionally good time while the boys who'd been trying to drop snide little comments left early, sulking and whining because people had ignored their attempts to feel big and get noticed by putting other people down. She had defended her right to party and be left alone to party. She was in the right; the club space put her in the right because clubbers see attitude as being part of the everyday world, rather than part of clubs. As one informant pointed out: 'Clubs are supposed to be special; they have their own rules and when I see someone breaking those rules in a club I judge them far more harshly than I would outside of a club where you expect it more' (male 31, 14 years' experience).

One of the biggest causes of attitude in a club space is linked to the classificatory codes, which arose from the musical stylistic and identifiable labels that Sarah Thornton (1995) recognised and recounted in her work. The classificatory schema surrounding notions of 'subcultural capital' can skew clubbers' perspectives upon the event. If they are constantly trying to classify the event and to assess other people through those classifications, then they will never get round to just casting them all aside and participating in that night. In the last instance how you club is far more important than what you know about clubbing. I've met clubbers who wouldn't know a turntable from a pork chop, but it didn't stop them partying big style and getting themselves onto guest lists all over London, whereas you can pick up most of what Thornton defines as 'subcultural capital' from the clubbing media without ever learning how to really party. So 'subcultural capital' is often the very basis of attitude in clubs, it is used to create distance and generate difference to the point where it fragments the party.

More Smiles per Square Foot

The instant indicator that you're at a top night is the percentage of people who are smiling and clubs score mighty high up on the smileometer. The smile is the basic communicative currency of clubbing and in many cases sharing a smile with someone is the only communication that you'll have with them all night. It is interesting to note that in neuro-cognitive terms the actual physical act of smiling leads to the release of endorphins and a general lightening of your mood, regardless of your emotional state at the time, as shown by Ekman (1993). A smile helps construct and communicate a particular social buzz that is itself infectious. Like a yawn, a smile can unleash a mimetic, physical response, a synching of emotional perspective that tells you all you need to know about another's state of self. Smiling is also one of the few true human universals, even if the thing that elicits that smile is a cultural construction.

In terms of the party smiling plays two roles: it is an act of communication and it is also the actuality of being in clubs. It is why you're there, to experience the smile that rises deep from within your guts and explodes across your face. I have returned from clubs with my face aching from grinning for so long and this state wasn't necessarily drug induced; it arose from the social world that unfolds before you across the course of the club event. The deep voyeuristic pleasure of watching people seizing and wallowing in the frenzied excess of a top night; seeing bodies loosen and writhe; witnessing the bursts of laughter; the moments of surging madness that liberates the space and takes the club crowd 'further', to borrow Ken Kesey's use of the word from the famed Magic Bus. All these moments are grounded in the human warmth of the smile that lets you know that what you're doing is OK that you are being granted freedom by those around you and that all they want in return is a bit of respect for their own party shenanigans. People liberating people by granting a sense of informal social consent.

There are no guarantees attached to club tickets ensuring that this party sociality will always enter the building. What I am describing here is a core sociality that I witnessed repeatedly over the course of my fieldwork. It certainly wasn't contained in any particular style of club venue; no specific group had a monopoly over it; it could arise for a time and then evaporate; it wasn't always shared by all clubbers at all times; it could flicker across pockets of people or infiltrate the entire space; very occasionally it wouldn't arise at all and everyone would leave feeling let down. However, when it did hit it would taste like Utopia, not a permanent flavour just a lollipop sweetness that had to be re-licked over and over again, an experiential reality that at least for a short time re-enchants a socially jaded world. As an informant said:

> It's a place where you can smile at people without fear and that's great. Before I went clubbing I was very scared of smiling at people in the street in case they got the wrong idea and thought there was something, another message, than just simply smiling at someone. Then you go clubbing and everyone's just grinning and smiling at you and you can smile back and that's it. You're just smiling at each other for the pleasure of smiling. Then for me I noticed that I was just smiling more at people in general outside of clubs and they would more often than not smile back at me. It's such a nice experience to get this great, big grin back when you're in the middle of this grey city walking to work through the rain. It completely changes how you feel. I definitely learnt that from

clubbing. Yes it's harder to do outside clubs because you're sometimes not quite sure of the reaction, but I try and make myself do it because when you do get a response it's lovely. (Female 41, 19 years' experience)

The smile and the friendliness it communicates is absolutely essential in creating the club vibe. The desire to pull people into the space and to have them feel at ease may not be a clubbing universal because some clubs obviously fail in this elementary task. Take this informant's example of a bad club:

> In terms of the club environment the best thing about it is the lack of social pressure, nobody's expecting you to be anything other than a party animal. The clubs where you're expected to be something are the ones that have a strong image of themselves; they think they're so different and alternative. This is a perfect extension of the club ego gone wrong. One of the venues I used to go to went really wobbly over the last few months. Now it has an exclusive clientele in the worst sense of the word. For months they started enforcing an extremely dodgy dress code that they have only just started dropping in a desperate attempt to try and entice a happy smiley crowd back in, but I think it's too late. The DJs are diabolical. One time they played progressive dancy tunes. People would dance. There were no limits and that's what counted. Now it's all about how you look and the music is darkwave, goth stuff that is fine in blasts, but not all night because it's shite to dance to. I know the dealers there, nobody takes speed there anymore, they take pills, but they're listening to music, which is wholly un-pill orientated. It's whiny and depressing and because they're all pilled-up they get really mopey like a bunch of adolescents with acne. No one smiles and that immediately lets you know something's wrong with the night. When they do dance they dance in little cliquey circles and they won't split them so other people can join in, so you get this really arsey dance floor that's an absolute bastardisation of everything a dance floor should be. It's sad because it used to be a laugh. (Male 26, 8 years' experience)

My fieldwork didn't take me to any venues that resembled this place; maybe I was lucky, but I don't think so because my informants described the vast majority of clubs that they had attended in positive terms and the majority of those informants had been clubbing for years. The importance of the smile was demonstrated in all the different types of club I visited; it was essential for the creation of the club vibe. Without the smile there could be no process of seduction and clubs must be seductive; they must draw people in and take them to a point where they can seize the night.

Tolerance

Most clubbers see clubs as spaces of heightened tolerance, but in reality there are limits to what different styles of clubs will tolerate. In every case the least tolerable type of behaviour in clubs is violence and this was unacceptable in all the clubs I visited, but more than that it was viewed with a sense of disgust that clubbers didn't always experience in other environments. Take this example from one of my informants:

> Violence in clubs is pathetic, isn't it? It's not very common though. I mean I've been clubbing for what eight to nine years and I've only seen one real fight in a club; it made me feel sick. I've seen fights in pubs quite a few times and you just think: 'Oh shit here we go again.' You expect it more in a pub or even when you see people fighting on the street it's always nasty and horrible, but it's not such a shock, but seeing it in a club that was a shock. It's like: what the hell are you playing at? You're in a club, you idiots; people don't fight here. (Female 32, 9 years' experience)

The lack of violence in clubs when compared to other big social events is an absolutely critical part of the club experience because it stops the people in the crowd being scared of one another at a physical level. You may encounter a bit of club bitching or come across some attitude from other clubbers, which can adversely affect your night, but people don't expect this to lead to a fight. Clubbers have rejected violence; they don't want to be part of it and they don't respect it. This absence of violence or even the expectation that violence may occur underpinned the social changes that occur in clubs. One informant summed it up in these terms:

> As a man you're trained up like a fucking dog to have this relationship towards violence. It's always represented as the ultimate male thing; you're taught to respect it because it's a sign of strength. You've got Arnie and Brucie and Sly and now Vinnie Jones, for God's sake, and you're supposed to think: 'Oh I wish I was that tough, I wish I was that strong.' But I've stopped seeing it as strength, now I see it as a weakness because I've spent hundreds of nights out with gentle fucking people that don't want to hassle anyone. They just want to live and enjoy living and it's changed my entire attitude to violence. I just find it pathetic. Human beings were meant to be more than cruel, vicious shits and if we can't be then we're just bald monkeys with no fucking future. (Male 34, 17 years' experience)

Other types of behaviour that would be tolerated in clubs largely depended upon the style of club you were in. Some of the most tolerant spaces in clubland though had to be the fetish clubs where people could do what they liked to one another as long as everything was consensual and, as we have seen, people valued the sense of freedom that they were granted. This stress on open and honest consent created a social space in which people could cut through some of the complexities of social interaction because the right to ask and the right to refuse provided the boundaries within which communication took place.

Informality: The Script of the Party

> You could have a long conversation in the toilets with a woman who tells you that she's
> taken two 'E's, just been jilted by her boyfriend and is sleeping with his best friend for
> revenge, but ask her what she does for a living and she may well stop in mid-sentence
> at this insulting breach of etiquette. It is rude to puncture the bubble of an institution
> where fantasies of identity are a key pleasure. (Thornton 1995: 91)

Whether the above quote reveals a breach in someone's 'fantasy of identity' or
is simply a description of a punter's response to a particularly banal question is a
contentious point. Club identities aren't fantasies; they are just connected more to
the party than the outside world and they are as real if not more real than anything
punters create in that outside world. Club conversations can be seen as alternative
scripts; a concept defined by Bradd Shore (1996: 57) in these terms: 'Scripts are
standardized conversation templates for organizing interactions in well-defined
goal-orientated situations . . . Scripts are really ritualized conversations and are
pervasive in discourse.'

The 'goal' of a club conversation is often little more than to 'communicate for
the sheer joy of communicating'. Thornton simply went off script and classed her
informant's reticence as an indication of a fantasised identity. Her informant may
well have been spinning a tale, but tale spinning, bullshitting and talking blarney
are all part of the accepted clubbing script because the sensual act of communicating is more important than what is actually said. Most clubbers don't go out
partying so that they can spend all night talking about work to the extent that the
work conversation is seen as rather dull. If your work is all you've got to talk about
in a club then you can be viewed as rather one dimensional. Clubbers discuss their
leisure activities more than they discuss work; they talk about enjoying the party,
not enjoying the party, the people, other clubs, drugs, music and only later on if the
interaction continues long enough, which many don't, will people mention work.
As an informant suggested: 'In a good club people don't really judge each other in
terms of the life they lead outside the club. You judge people on how they club,
whether they can rock a night or whether they just stand around looking like a
prune that's the important thing' (Female 29, 13 years' experience).

The social hierarchies that exist outside of clubs do not disappear completely,
but they are relaxed once you've past through the club's doors. They become fluid
because they are no longer the central reference point in people's conversations as
they are replaced in that function by the immediacy of the party.

One of the most startling examples of this rejection of the world beyond the
club is found in clubbers' attitude to names. In the everyday world names are vital
and remembering someone's name is viewed as an important social act. In clubs,
however, names are of little importance, which increases the sense that they are

anonymous spaces that are detached from the rest of your life. It took me weeks to learn many of my informant's first names and months to catch their second. The whole notion of names defining part of someone's identity collapsed and people became that bloke from such and such a club or that woman in the gold sequins from wherever. What you remembered about people is whether or not they could party-hearty and you'd had a laugh with them.

When my girlfriend and I found out one of our clubbing buddies was in hospital we went along to visit him only to realise at reception that we didn't know his name, his address or his age. Yet, we still wanted to see him because, despite the seemingly fragile and anonymous nature of this relationship, we wanted to check out how he was doing because we had strong emotional memories of having such a bloody marvellous time with him and these made us care about him. (Luckily, the fab receptionist hunted him down for us so we got to see him.) This world without names is probably unparalleled outside of prison camps where it is used to dehumanise inmates, whereas in clubs it humanises people because they are judged on their actions alone.

In a club you are predominantly amongst strangers and so as an informant explained:

> Everything's really straightforward in a club there aren't long consequences about things, even if you misconstrue someone in a club you're probably not going to see them again. It's not ongoing; it's not going to affect your chances for promotion; it's not going to get back to someone so all your mates hate you. It's there; it happened; you didn't intend it to happen; you weren't trying to be rude, but in a club you just shrug it off and get back into the party and you hope the other person does the same. You are after all just two strangers; you didn't have any history up to that point; you're not going to have any after so it seems stupid to get upset. (Male 32, 14 years' experience)

The anonymity of clubs reduces the lines of communication that flow out from the party to other aspects of your life. Certainly gossip can pass between club crowds, but it is not going to get back to your boss, your parents or your colleagues and that grants a sense of heightened social freedom. The woman in Thornton's (1995) quote was using that freedom as she could happily tell a stranger intimate details of her life safe in the knowledge that this stranger wouldn't spill the beans. This sense of anonymity and intimacy allows people to reveal themselves to an extent that is usually reserved for the therapist's couch. There is an expectation that these people will listen without judging you because they have ceased at an emotional level to feel like strangers; they have instead become co-conspirators for a brief part of the night.

The important point to remember, then, is that the rules of clubbing exist outside of clubs; they are grounded in a particular social model of how to behave at a party, which are then intensified by the social, aesthetic and intoxicatory nature of the club event. This social model is aspirational in its content; it is the model of how people should behave on an informal basis when they leave the social hierarchies of the everyday world outside of the space. Obviously parties don't always succeed in this task, but because clubs as the contemporary home of the party offer a whole different set of participatory modes (dancing, smiling, chatting and watching) the party then provides the bulk of what is spoken about amongst strangers over the course of the night. This means the amount of baggage you have to bring in from the outside world in order to engage with the event is radically reduced. The most frequently asked question in clubland is: 'Are you having a good time?' Rather than: 'What's your name?' Or: 'Where do you work?'

Adventure

> I ended up naked and tied to a bed covered in Gladioli having my ass whipped by a woman I'd never met before. I hadn't set out with the intention of this happening, but at the time it felt like the right thing to do and in retrospect it was definitely the right thing to do. Some clubs have that adventurous feel like anything could happen and that's important to me. I want adventures and I'm open to them. You don't have to go to the Amazon to get them; you just have to get amongst adventurous people. (Male 34, 17 years' experience)

Clubbing is an adventure and this sense of adventure is important because it provides the impetus to explore clubland, to try new venues and meet new crowds. These adventures are sensual realities that can allow people to move beyond the bodily and classificatory constraints of the everyday world, but unlike Malbon (1999: 151) who suggests that 'rather than "resisting" notions of power which are acting upon them, individuals may actually be "resisting" other facets of *their own* identities'.

I see them as a way of expanding those identities and turning your dreams and aspirations into social realities: rather than resisting other aspects of people's lives they make sense of them. So in relation to work they become a reason for working, rather than the opposite of work. They validate work because that work provides the funding for these adventures as well as a point of sensual alterity that actually intensifies the club experience by providing a sensual counterpoint to those experiences. (One minute you're sitting on your arse bored or stressed; the next you're whooping-it-up with a room full of fellow funksters; the stress and boredom intensify the sense of release and fun.) The realm of clubs offers people the opportunity to explore their desires and uncover new aspects of their own selves by turning those often vague and rather disembodied desires into embodied experiences that occur in socially supportive spaces. People are pushing their own envelope; expanding upon the socio-sensual experience of occupying their own worlds and inscribing the knowledge of excitement and passion into their memories by moving beyond the constraints of their own self-consciousness and the restraints of the everyday gaze.

Meeting People in Clubs

It's similar emotionally to being in a football crowd. It's the same crowd psychology thing. When you're part of one body of people screaming goal or whatever you feel great because you're connected to those other people. It feels like that, it's that intense, but there's no enemy, no losers, we're going yes to ourselves and each other, not because our teams beaten another team. We're going: 'YES WE ARE US AND YES WE'RE TOGETHER.' It's a non-aggressive yesness. I think the essence of truly great clubbing is everyone scores a goal and nobody loses. (Male 32, 14 years' experience)

As I have shown, club crowds are predominantly made up of pre-formed social groups who must then allow the boundaries of those groups to become permeable if the club as a whole is going to create the requisite social vibe and reach the sort of social peak that my informant describes above. This process doesn't happen all at once; it must build incrementally over the course of the night, but as a number of informants pointed out the average club night is fairly long in relation to other shared leisure experiences.

Clubbing is a relatively long period of time to be with this many people. You go to a cinema or football match and it's ninety minutes in the main crowd part of the experience. Most other forms of entertainment seem to be about one-and-a-half to two hours long, but night-clubs go on all night. You're not the same person; you don't behave the same way all night; you don't usually go there and do six to seven hours of exactly the same thing. So there are points in the night when even though you know there's great music going on you might be resting and chatting at the bar or whatever and then you have those bits that are the peak of the dancing, say between two to three o'clock, and you're on the floor and you might lose it to the music, but that usually lasts about five minutes. The rest of the time you'll be dancing with people or going for a wander, chatting to your mates, watching, disco-napping, meeting new people, trying to score, attempting to get laid, whatever. It's all part of clubbing, which is really a range of things that all go into creating the whole night's experience. (Male 32, 14 years' experience)

The sheer length of time that you remain in clubs means that you have time to relax into it and gradually become part of the crowd on your own terms. Groups often stay together for the first hour or so while they settle in before beginning to explore the space especially in larger venues. In smaller clubs you are thrown into an instant physical relationship with everybody else. There are many ways of interacting in clubs and you can give something to the space without actually speaking to other people. I have seen groups that have stayed together all night, not really talking to other people, but nevertheless exhibiting their enjoyment and enthusiasm for the space to such a high degree that their actions are infectious to other punters. In this case they are displaying their allegiance to the party by dancing, laughing, smiling and generally having a time. Conversation is not the only form of communication that can gel a crowded room of clubbers into a party mass.

Arriving with a group also provides punters with an extra level of security; a social base that they can leave behind when they want to go off and explore and have an adventure safe in the knowledge that they can run back to their friends if it all goes pear-shaped. They can chat and dance with strangers, flirt with people, check out the different rooms and music.

When groups do begin to splinter and meet other people it tends to happen gradually. As one informant put it:

> My experience of what normally happens is that you meet someone, you're chatting to them at the bar, then one of your friends walks past and you say: 'Come and speak to this person they're lovely.' Then they either become part of your group of mates for the night and you grab in several people or else the opposite happens and two groups just collide and get on with it. It's about extending the boundaries of who are friends and who are strangers and the difference between the two of them. People you've never met before become people you'd treat as though they were at a wedding and you vaguely knew them and you can have safe eye contact with them and then you get your best mates for ever, the 'I love you friends' who are usually the ones you came with. Everything gets pushed out, so that as your personal space collapses, your public space gets bigger. (Male 32, 14 years' experience)

This makes a couple of points: it stresses the difference in intensity between the 'I love you friends' and the rest of the crowd and the wedding metaphor captures the social vibe particularly well. Crowds that haven't taken Ecstasy can still create this informal 'wedding' vibe because it is grounded in the idea of mutual celebration, rather than a being associated with a specific drug rush.

A lot of these meetings occur away from the noise of the main dance floor, at bars, in chill-out rooms, the toilets, in corridors, anywhere people don't have to bellow at the top of their voices to be heard. An informant told me that:

> I've met a lot of people in the loo or in the queue for the loo. In fact this is going to sound so sad, but what the hell, I've actually ended up queuing for the loo just because I fancied a chat. Sometimes I'll end up sharing makeup and I've met loads of people in the loo and some of them have gone onto become really good friends. I don't think men do that sort of thing in the loo. Do they? It's more of a woman thing, but it's really social. (Female 32, 9 years' experience)

Men don't spend a great deal of time talking to each other in the toilet; it happens occasionally, but it is not a major part of taking a piss and it is certainly not something that's worth queuing for.

The social interactions that make up this crowd sociality range from brief moments of silly banter to longer periods of getting to know people; how much those interactions can expand beyond the space of the club depends upon the depth of connection people make with one another. One informant described his social experience of clubbing in these terms:

> Once you come out of school or college, then most of the people you know probably come from those days. You hang out with people you know, people who you work with, the body of friends you grew up with throughout your life. Then you can go to a great night-club and you're suddenly friends with loads and loads of people you've never met before, just because you saw someone over a couple of weeks in the same club and you got chatting to them. A lot of the time you just have really great silly conversations with strangers and that's it, but sometimes it goes beyond that. You make key connections and you find your social group has massively expanded because you got to know one person well enough in a club that they've introduced you to their friends. (Male 32, 14 years' experience)

This informant stresses the way that clubs offer the opportunity to expand your social network beyond the people that you grew up around or went to school with. Clubs are points of collection that attract people from across the city and sometimes beyond; they are de-territorial zones in that they expand upon the sociality of the local and the biographical so that you get to meet people who you wouldn't normally come across.

Another point is held in the phrase 'key connections' because people tend to club in groups and a meeting between two individuals in each group can initiate a much larger set of social connections. The vast majority of social interactions in clubs will not be classed as 'key connections', but because we are talking about groups, rather than individuals, you don't actually have to make that many 'key connections' in order to alter the nature of your social network radically. A group of friends can club for months and just have a series of brief, funny and enjoyable social encounters that remain completely unconnected to one another, but once they've been around for a while and been seen around, then they increase the likelihood of making such a key connection, which can shift them into a larger set of interconnected social scenes that can expand beyond the club space and out into their everyday world.

You only have to look at the rise in phone chatlines, dating agencies and lonely hearts columns to realise how lonely people can become in the city and how difficult it can be to meet people from outside of your immediate experience of work life, home life and the social network held within your biography. As one informant explained:

I work in a small team predominantly consisting of women and I don't know how I would've met people otherwise. I was really lucky to meet somebody who I worked with that took me clubbing and opened up a whole new world. I've never met anybody in a pub. Don't go there to meet people you go with friends and I don't know how people meet other people in London. I knew one person when I arrived here. It's an entry into another world. I've never been to one club regularly, but I still meet the same people over and over again and you get to know them. Every guy I've dated I met while clubbing and I've also met them afterwards in clubs and bumped into people who I haven't seen for ages so for me it provided a social life. (Female 32, 9 years' experience)

Even when you don't meet anyone to talk to in a club, even when you spend the night just dancing, watching, listening and just being in the vibe, then the communicative physicality of clubbing, the phatic synching of emotional and social states still provides an intense social experience that draws people in and makes them part of the party. It provides an experience that is social, sensual and participatory; a combination that offers some level of social immersion, even if it doesn't always offer the long-term friendships that my informants have experienced.

Club crowds start to recognise each other just by sharing space or a particular club scene with one another. They begin to meet in other venues and at other nights; they become part of a diffuse social network that is grounded in the knowledge that they have shared good times with each other. This is an informal process based in having seen each other party, but as one informant suggested:

There's something special about watching people enjoy themselves. It's like you get to see them at their best. They're not being shitty to each other. They're just having their time and letting everyone else get on with it and when you do see somebody behaving like a twat in a club you see them at their very worst because if they're one of the wankers who can't hack it in a club, then what the fuck are they going to be like outside of a club. (Male 31, 17 years' experience)

On a personal note I came across some people over and over again while clubbing and although I can't claim to have got to know all of them well or that they have become close friends I saw enough of them to make me glad that they are out there doing their thing, living their lives, having their times, creating their worlds without seeming to screw anyone else over in the process. I am not trying to claim that clubs are some sort of perfect social world as there are always some people in any given club who can be rude, arrogant, mean-spirited and bitchy, but if they are not experienced as a minority, then the club cannot happen because the space will become socially toxic. I am simply pointing out that my own clubbing experiences and those of my informants have in the main been positive on both a social and personal level so the only conclusion I can draw is that clubs in their various guises grant more positive social experiences than negative ones, even if they will never be perfect.

All-Back-To-Mine

> For me the post-clubbing thing is also the clubbing thing. This flat's really well set up
> for after-parties. One of my mates monopolises the bath and people just get in and out
> of it with him. Everyone's E'd up. People talk; they do the music bit and it's about
> coming out at the other end of the experience closer to the people who you've shared it
> with and I think especially with the all-back-to-mine thing that's really important. You
> go out with a group, you pick some more people up along the way, then it's back to
> someone's flat and you've got absolute licence to tell them everything that's on your
> mind, you can be open with them. It's really passionate and really relaxed at the same
> time. (Male 32, 14 years' experience)

The all-back-to-mine aspect of clubbing is an important extension of the club
experience because it allows people to use the social-sensual and emotional states,
which were created through clubbing, in a more intimate setting. The chaotic world
of the club with its noise and its strangers is replaced by a more relaxed experience
shared with both old and potentially new friends. As one informant explained:

> I'd say socially what happens is clubbing and then post-club parties, which are the best
> place to make connections and are useful in all areas of your life, apart from just the
> socialising and entertainment aspect of it. The longer lasting relationships have tended
> to happen in those post-club parties while the shorter lived quick-fire hello in the street
> ones happened in clubs. (Female 29, 12 years' experience)

In social terms these all-back-to-mine sessions help deepen and intensify
people's relationships with their friends because the distractions of clubbing are left
behind. They are also playful: people gab, talk bullshit, laugh, get off with one
another, take more drugs and as one informant suggested:

> The post-party get together is important. It's often where the deepest friendships are
> formed or consolidated. You get to know more about people and, well, bond with them
> I suppose, but on a deeper level than in a club because it's easier to talk. They can be
> horny too especially when people are all loved-up and you get to snog or massage each
> other and fool around. I like that; it's really easy and laid-back and much less manic than
> when you're in an actual club. It's like two different experiences that go really well
> together. (Female 32, 9 years' experience)

The social and sensual slippage in people's behaviour, which marks clubs out
as radically different from other public space, is carried over into people's private
space, which changes both the way they communicate and what they communicate
about. Men in particular probably benefit more from this slippage because it allows

them to drop the bullshit and bravado that is an expected part of male conversation in other social settings where they focus on talking about stuff in general (politics, football, ideas, pussy), rather than communicating anything real about themselves. So conversations shift from good-humoured bullshit to moments of real truthfulness and introspection and then back to good old blarney when everyone's bored with being sensitive.

There is a laid-back and seductive feel to these gatherings; they are intimate and raucous and simultaneously serious and silly. Their importance is grounded in the social practices that arise out of the club gig, which provide the bedrock for an alternate mode of social experience that becomes embodied by these groups of friends over time. Until it gradually becomes the social model of practice that infuses these groups' relationships whenever they are together, regardless of whether they are drugged-up or sober. These events provide the bridge that allows the social knowledge gained through clubbing to begin to infiltrate clubbers' everyday world. We will explore this knowledge in more detail in the next chapter but at this juncture it is enough to point out that it represents a radical shift in people's lived social practice, which has generated a major shift in the socio-sensual landscape that underpins contemporary social life.

The Seductive Gaze

The theoretical framework that best explains the sociality of clubbing arises from Foucault's (1977) notion of the 'gaze'. I have referenced this gaze at a number of points throughout this work but in this section I want to explore it in greater detail in relation to the social changes that occur within clubs. The most concise definition of the gaze that I have come across was given by Chris Rojek (1995: 61) in his book *Decentring Leisure*: 'The basic idea is that our behaviour is regulated by the gaze of others and by the gaze of our own self-reflection. The eye controls order so that, at a glance, we can determine what the appropriate ways of behaving are for a given situation.'

Foucault theorised the 'gaze' as a force of surveillance and control. However, I would argue that in clubs the gaze gradually alters over the course of the night to become a liberating force. When Foucault speaks of the 'gaze' he views it as a disembodied force almost like a surveillance camera, but human vision is intimately linked to the emotional and embodied state of the human being who both gazes and is gazed at. At times people want to be seen, they want to be looked at and have their existence recognised by others and clubs allow them a space in which they can step forward and show themselves to the world without having to fear the oppressive weight of Foucault's 'gaze', which exerts a controlling and inhibiting effect upon them in other public spaces. Take this example from one of my informants:

I love to go to clubs because you can watch people and be watched. If you're in the street or a pub or something it's harder to look at people in case they catch your eye or get the wrong idea and when people look at you especially when they're not smiling that can feel quite threatening or make you feel a bit anxious, but in a club you can just watch people having a really good time and they can see you having fun and it never feels threatening. (Female 29, 10 years' experience)

In the public spaces of the city the gaze of others is avoided because it can be sensed as threatening, an invasion of people's anonymity as they negotiate this social realm. The simple act of catching someone's eye brings about an unwanted connection to the world of strangers. The gaze of the city is not only controlling, but it also makes people feel visible; it singles them out and penetrates the studied invisibility they attempt to maintain on the street especially when they move beyond their everyday routines and locales. Even those who deliberately stand out in crowds feel this gaze; they've just had more practice in dealing with it and the very fact they stand out can offer them some protection. People are suspicious of difference, but they also find it unnerving; the freakier you look the more unnerved people become. As my informant points out, this sense of becoming visible can be uncomfortable and threatening and she enjoys the freedom to watch and be watched in clubs. She becomes not only the object of the gaze, but also a gazer and this sense of reversal is important to her and clubbing as a whole because it allows her to connect with, rather than distance herself from, the club crowd.

The club gaze is not the disembodied surveillance of Foucault; it is an emotive force because it arises from within the radically altered emotional vibe of the club that has its own sensual parameters and social rules. The mechanism identified by Foucault still operates, but the gaze becomes seductive and subversive; it encourages the adoption and embodiment of the rules and behaviours of clubbing in opposition to those forced upon people in other aspects of their lives. An informant summed up clubbing experiences in these terms:

It's the freedom from having to think about how what you're doing is affecting other people that's a great freedom; you can dance really badly. You know in the cold light of day that you've looked really ugly in clubs, big eyes, gurning, looking stupid, but it's OK. (Male 32, 14 years' experience)

This sense of being less self-conscious is important in relation to the notion of the gaze because it reduces the force of self-reflection that provides the pathway via which the gaze becomes embodied. The club gaze rests upon surfaces; it cannot penetrate individuals or groups who because of intoxication or their own exuberant participation in the activities of clubbing have become less self-conscious about how they would look through the eyes of the everyday world. They expect to be judged by the rules of the club. When the gaze is experienced in a positive way, when the environment that it arises from and is embedded in allows seeing and being seen to be relished, then it underpins a slippage in the social rules and formalities that exist in the everyday world. The gaze becomes conspiratorial and reassuring. One female informant who loved to dress-up big style explained the difference like this:

> I used to get dressed-up and then get the tube and you'd feel people looking at you and occasionally they'd shout things out, you know insulting things, but often it was just the discomfort of being stared at that was worse. It made you feel vulnerable. It reminded you of how much you were standing out. Then you'd get into the club and people would still be looking at you, but it felt good. It was a completely different experience because the club felt supportive as they appreciated the effort you'd made.

There is a different set of expectations operating in clubs; they are spaces where you're supposed to be able to go wild. However, the extent to which punters can seize that opportunity is restricted by the rules of the particular club space they have entered. You can go wild, but you can't be violent, but as the vast majority of punters aren't in the club to be violent towards one another this behavioural constraint isn't registered as control or surveillance. The club gaze must be liberating and encouraging, it must bind people together, but how far people can then use this sense of informal social consent to allow themselves to go further in the space is regulated by a number of separate factors.

The first is their own sense of self-confidence, which will affect the way they experience and perceive of the space. You do see people in clubs looking uncomfortable and never fully engaging with the environment. However, people learn how to club over time; they become more confident and through experiencing these spaces they learn the extent to which they can modify their behaviour in relation to the social rules of the club space. This process makes clubs easier to occupy over time; the process of embodying the altered rules of the space becomes easier as people become more familiar with them.

The second factor was the one most directly related to Foucault's notion of the 'gaze' as it arose from the look of the crowd and the style of club that you see before you when you enter. This immediate assessment of the event will effect your own relationship to it. It tells you whether you're dressed appropriately, if this is your type of crowd and what sort of night you can expect. However, in the last instance, experiencing the social vibe of the club can void these assessments. If the club is rocking, if it possesses a positive and seductive gaze, then these potential fears about fitting in are replaced by the sense of being made welcome that is so important to the party in all its forms. The club gaze lets the body escape its everyday boundaries it becomes more visible and more expressive. You cannot be bullied into clubbing; clubs must seduce you and draw you in and that process of seduction is where their true social power lies.

Summary

The social model used in clubs is based on the social model of the party. This is enhanced and altered by the sensual intensity of clubbing that acts as a seductive force and binds the crowds together. The club experience is perceived as a radically different social experience by punters. The socio-sensual actuality of negotiating the everyday world is reversed, not as an idea, but as a deeply embodied social encounter that underpins people's passion for clubs. This alteration is a social process that must be recreated over the course of each club night. The idea behind clubbing is to have a good time, but what constitutes a good time in a club is grounded in a radical alteration in people's socio-sensual practice; they must move from one deeply embodied state to another deeply embodied state. This new state must then rise to the surface of the crowd's flesh; it must be made visible by their participation in the night. The club gaze must communicate the emotional reversal of the everyday gaze; it must be experienced in opposition to the controlling gaze of the everyday world; it cannot exert force, but must instead be seductive if it is to grant people the freedom they need to participate in the space.

Section II
Sensual Experiments in the Art of Being Human

–8–

Knowledge in the Flesh

The body believes in what it plays at: it weeps if it mimes grief. It does not represent what it performs, it does not memorize the past, it enacts the past bringing it back to life. What is 'learned by body' is not something that one has, like knowledge that can be brandished, but something that one is.

(Bourdieu 1990: 73)

So far we've been looking at the differences between clubs and the everyday world that surrounds those clubs. Now I want to examine the ways in which those club experiences move beyond the club space itself and filter out into that everyday world. This has been attempted before, but not altogether successfully because academics have tried to turn clubbing into other forms of knowledge. Redhead et al. (1993) tried to politicise clubbing as a form of resistance, which just doesn't hold up in the long term. Thornton (1995) simply turned it into a field of consumption, which virtually ignores the experience itself. Malbon (1999) focused on the experience, but couldn't move beyond the club space.

My informants were adamant that clubbing had exerted a powerful influence on their lives and that this influence didn't just evaporate once the party was over. I began to look for a framework that could account for this belief and reveal how the experience of clubbing could be viewed as a form of transferable knowledge. The knowledge generated by clubbing is created when people move from one socio-sensual state to another. This experiential shift expands the parameters of clubbers' sensual landscape and moves them beyond their own habituated social practices, emotional boundaries, fears, insecurities and their ingrained perceptions of the world in which they are immersed. This is knowledge lived, rather than knowledge to be brandished. It doesn't just vanish when people leave the club space but rather it becomes entrenched in the body over time and re-orientates the body's relationship to the everyday world at certain levels. This is not a simple process; it happens incrementally; it can collapse at any point and the everyday world acts as an opposing force that continuously discounts the veracity of the club experience. In this chapter, I want to explore some of the social, biological and cognitive frameworks that underpin the existence of this knowledge so we can examine the ways in which clubbing exerts a wider influence on people's lives once the drugs have worn off, the dancing's over and the hangovers have faded.

Habitus

Although Bourdieu (1977, 1990) identified the existence of the habitus he made no attempt to uncover its bodily foundations or the cognitive mechanisms that allowed it to exert such a powerful affect on people's lives. His definition grew out of the work of Marcel Mauss, a brilliant French sociologist, who showed us that the body is a cultural product, which is shaped and constructed by the society in which it is immersed as shown in the following:

> Native women adopted a peculiar gait . . . that was acquired in youth, a loose-jointed swinging of the hips that looks ungainly to us, but was admired by the Maori. Mothers drilled their daughters in this accomplishment, termed *onioni*, and I have heard a mother say to her girl: '*Ha! Kaore koe e onioni*' ('you are not doing the *onioni*') when the young one was neglecting to practise the gait. (Mauss 1979: 102)

Cultures have different bodily techniques and habits that are transmitted both overtly through instruction, as above, and more covertly via the adoption, often through the process of mimesis, of particular physical habits. For Mauss (1979) the various bodily techniques employed by any particular culture played a role in constructing that culture's habitus. Bourdieu (1977, 1990) expanded upon Mauss's (1979) idea of the habitus by relating the bodily realm, discussed by Mauss, to the ideological structures of a culture. In his formulation habitus was an aspect of the body of social relations and cultural practice that was grounded in the unchallenged taken-for-granted ideas of a society.

The notion of habitus is in itself fairly diffuse and hard to pin down. It is part of the fabric of a culture but it is rarely articulated by that culture. It is lived more than it is expressed and it is held within the way people occupy space; the way they interact socially; their physical stance within the world. A society's habitus is the physical and emotional manifestation of that society's rules and ideological perspectives, which have been embodied by both individuals and groups. It is the bodily actuality of gender relations, class relations, points of reciprocity and morality.

The habitus of a culture is a deeply emotional construct although very little work has explored this particular element of it. The simplest example of this aspect of the habitus in action would be the feeling of guilt. We feel guilt when we have broken one of the rules of our own society but, more surprisingly, we can still feel guilt when we've broken one of our society's social rules, even when we no longer agree at an ideological level with that rule. Take this example given by one female informant when we ended up discussing her ideas about sex:

> In my head I know that sex is nothing to be ashamed of, that my sexuality is my own that the only morality, which I believe in, in relation to sex, is based in open and honest

consent between people. It's taken me a long time to make that idea an actuality though because, even though it was what I believed and what I'd tell you, it wasn't always what I felt and it's taken a lot longer for those feelings to catch up with my ideas.

Can you give me an example?

Anal sex is probably the best example. I really enjoy it now, but I used to be really squeamish about it. I used to feel dirty and a bit slutty and feel a bit uncomfortable with the whole thing, even though I knew that there was nothing wrong with it. I knew it wasn't immoral, but for a long time it still felt sort of immoral. I felt like a dirty girl, which had its own thrill, but was also really dull because those feelings didn't match my ideas and that was frustrating. I felt like I was betraying myself as I don't think sex is dirty and now I just fuck how I want and the sense of guilt's gone. I've done it enough to experience it positively; it feels good. My partner and I enjoy it; he doesn't think it's dirty or weird or anything, so I feel comfortable with it. I know it's not wrong in my head and my gut feelings have stopped trying to disagree with me.

This quotation illustrates the relationship between the body and the social ideas that surround it. On one side we have anal sex as a social taboo, a dirty, immoral thing, which reflects certain ideas about the person engaged in it. On the other side we have anal sex as a sexual practice that feels good and takes place consensually and is just another variation in people's ongoing sexual practice. My informant could change her ideas about anal sex but it took far longer to disentangle herself from the gut feeling, which the habitus imposed upon her as a form of sensual morality that suffused her flesh. This bodily morality subverted her ideas about sex, it kept churning away in her stomach insisting that: 'Nice girls don't butt fuck.' It was only through positive experiences that her ideas could once again be made to match her feelings. This example reveals the extent to which social ideas infiltrate people's physical being. They reside within them as physical, mental and emotional constructs and that simply changing your ideas on a certain subject is often only the first step in a process of change, which must eventually become embodied as a new sensually assured ideology.

Bourdieu makes a link between the forms of bodily techniques and bodily practice, which a society instils into its occupants and that society's ideological perspectives, which become embodied as both individual and group forms of practice. In Bourdieu's (1990: 53) own terms:

The conditionings associated with a particular class of conditions of existence produce *habitus*, systems of durable, transposable dispositions, structured structures predisposed to function as structuring structures, that is, as principles which generate and organize practices and representations that can be objectively adapted to their outcomes without presupposing a conscious aiming at ends or an express mastery of the operations necessary in order to attain them.

Basically, then, you're taught to have a particular sensual, social and emotional relationship to the world through the imposition of particular practices (ways of doing things). So, for example, it is perfectly acceptable for a kid to cry, but not so acceptable for an adult, particularly a man to cry. Not all societies react this way; I saw men cry in Egypt when a song moved them, but they cried in a masculine way because their society has taught them how to cry in a masculine way, rather than simply denying them the capacity to cry.

These bodily phenomena are part of people's sensed experience of being-in-the-world that carries within them connections to their society's system of belief. So in the Kabyle society, examined by Bourdieu, ideas about masculinity were manifested as a particularly manly set of bodily practices. As Bourdieu (1990: 70) explains:

> In the use of the mouth: a man should eat with his whole mouth, wholeheartedly, and not, like women, just with the lips, that is, half-heartedly, with reservation and restraint . . . Then in rhythm: a man of honour must eat neither too quickly, with greed or gluttony, nor too slowly-either way is a concession to nature.

Through the adoption of these bodily practices men learn to behave like men, to both experience themselves as men and to express their masculinity to others. Women's bodily practice in Kabyle society is constructed in opposition to men, which creates two alternate forms of body, two ways of being-in-the-world that, in this specific example, mirrors this society's ideas about gender. These bodies subsequently underpin and naturalise a whole series of beliefs, signs and ideological perspectives pertaining to gender because they allow them to be lived as practice.

All societies create these bodily forms. The factors that determine their structure will reflect the hierarchy of the society, its economic disparities, notions of religious faith and other structures of distinction, which operate in the social realm. For the sake of clarity I've used the term habitus, throughout this book, but we must realise that in contemporary terms we are actually talking about 'habiti', multiple variations of the habitus, which reflect class distinctions, ethnicity, gender and age. However, I use the term 'habitus' because the socio-sensual experiences offered in the club environment throw the habitus into relief and make its 'structuring structure' visible regardless of which particular habitus a person possesses.

The next aspect of the habitus that Bourdieu examines is the way that these lived practices possess a logic all of their own. This logic isn't necessarily a rational form of logic; rather it is a sensual, social and emotional logic that runs through different modes of practice and, as Bourdieu (1990: 92) points out:

> The idea of practical logic, a 'logic in itself', without conscious reflection or logical control, is a contradiction in terms, which defies logical logic. This paradoxical logic is

that of all practice, or rather all practical sense . . . This logic which, like all practical logics, can only be grasped in action, in the temporal movement that disguises it by detemporalizing it, sets the analyst a difficult problem, which can only be solved by recourse to a theory of theoretical logic and practical logic. The professional dealers in *logos* want practice to express something that can be experienced in discourse, preferably logical.

The problem then is that when someone like me tries to make sense of practice there will be a tendency to make those practices seem too tidy and logical because that is what is demanded of them if you're going to turn them into a book and sound clever. Clubbing isn't logical but then neither is the everyday world. The habitus simply makes one feel more logical or correct than the other by imbuing it with a sense of social and moral worth, which it denies club life. What we are looking at in clubbing, then, is a disruption of the habitus, which has its own social and experiential logic that is largely derived from the difference between the social logic, which governs certain aspects of leisure time and the logic of everyday time. The logic of clubbing practice is radically different from the logic of everyday practice. It exists in opposition to this practice and in opposition to the sensual parameters that the habitus imposes.

One of the problems with Bourdieu's theory is its inability to explain change. The bodily structures of habitus would seem to exert such a level of sub-conscious control over people that it roots them consistently into a specific set of taken-for-granted assumptions, which govern their social encounters. Yet, in the club environment people valued the fact that they interacted with people differently. The taken-for-granted ideas that governed these interactions were radically altered usually for the better in that people displayed a more positive and open attitude to these encounters. So to return to Bourdieu's ideas about the logic of practice, bodies are remade and in the course of that remaking the logic, which normally governs their individual and social actions, is weakened and becomes fluid.

The connection between body and culture is not as all-pervasive and concrete as Bourdieu suggests, because it is open to the power of seduction. The sensual potential of the flesh is open to manipulation; it can be seduced beyond the sensual and emotional parameters of the habitus. So that the habitus ceases to be lived as a taken-for-granted framework because people adopt alternative practices. However, because we are talking about a practice and a counter practice we should be wary of viewing these bodily constructions as resistant ideologies. Clubbing can be experienced as an act of resistance by some clubbers, but for others the same or very similar experiences were the reward they gave themselves for being part of the system of capitalism, the rock-star model of success, cocaine, champagne and 'birds in designer dresses'. Both perspectives are founded upon the sense that clubs feel radically different from other social spaces and house an altered realm of bodily practice, which takes you beyond the experiential confines of the everyday world.

Example 1

This example is of taken from Collin's (1997) excellent book, about the history of Ecstasy and clubs, *Altered States*. I chose it because it comes from the beginning of Ecstasy use in this country before the drug had gained a history and a context that has tempered the way people speak about its effects. As such, it captures the mutational power of the drug and the experience of shedding the bodily framework of the habitus, which allows people to glimpse the world from an alternate sensual perspective.

> Well I had a little magic tablet mate, and I fucking just fwooor . . . it was a yellow burger and it tasted like pepper and it fucking knocked me. I'd heard all about Ecstasy, I'm getting a guy coming up to me, used to be one of my close pub mates, who's now wearing an orange fucking shirt, a Smiley bandanna, only got half his teeth in his head, telling me how much of a good time he's had down King's Cross. I'm thinking, three months ago you were down . . . with me at the Thomas A'Beckett getting lagging, I wondered why I hadn't seen you for a little while. I remember this yellow burger, I took it, I walked around, and then I got this feeling from the tip of my toes to the top of my head – like this burning rocket fuel – and I got scared because I wasn't used to the buzz, three pints of lager I could handle but an E, I didn't have a clue . . . I remember literally running to a wall, and it had nothing to hang on to, and I just slid slowly down. I was running round this fucking place with my shirt inside out, shouting 'I'm on one!' because I'd fathomed it out, and everybody was shouting 'mental!' and clapping their hands – I fucking loved it man! This girl came up to me and said: 'Wouldn't it be good if the whole world was on E?' She was sweating it, I was pissing sweat – I didn't know what was going on – and all I could think of was: 'Yeah, you're so right love.' And this is so unlike me. I came out of there in the morning, and I just sat in a car in Peckham all day, just watching people – I was just karma'd, I couldn't believe what had happened to my body. I've got a big blue lion tattooed on my arm, and MFC on my arm, like a mug – I used to go to Millwall when it was the Den – I had to spit at a pig, I had to call a guy a Paki because monkey see, monkey do; it was Neanderthal man going down the Den, it was programmed. E changed my life completely – if I saw you walking down the street and you were from north London and I was from south London we would supposedly have to have a scuffle, which is bollocks, but we all lived by that, we didn't know no better. You couldn't get east, south, west and north London kids in the same warehouse without having a fight – you're fucking asking for miracles to happen, and you didn't get miracles in the eighties – but you did with the miracle drug. (Collins 1997: 121–2)

The Ecstasy and the 'set and setting' of the club environment generated a socio-sensual state from within which this guy's past ideas became disembodied and emotionally untenable. He had slipped out of the body that kept those ideas locked into the flesh and he could no longer relate to them. The everyday world would deny this powerful and positive experience any meaning because it took a drug to bring this revelation about, but it was obviously so intense that it challenged this man's entire perception of himself and his world and changed his life. Through dislodging the structuring logic of the habitus from his body and so moving beyond its 'programming' he reconstructed the socio-sensual connection between himself and his world and subsequently the ideas he had about that world. However, the everyday habitus is not so easily escaped; it will return to suffuse the body with old habits, postures and emotional responses, which arise out of the social world that surrounds you. It is only through altering this social world that the insights offered by the Ecstasy experience can be sustained, but as clubbing itself offers an alternative social arena, which developed its own social codes and structures based around such experiences it can help sustain these new perspectives.

The History of the Habitus

The work of Norbert Elias (1998) offers a more historical perspective on the construction and maintenance of the habitus. Elias examines the gradual process of creating 'civilised bodies' and his work charts the shift between the largely unregulated and uncontrolled body of the Middle Ages, which freely expressed its 'drives', 'desires' and 'violence' to the controlled and mannered body of the Renaissance period and beyond, which structured the habitus of our contemporary world. His basic thesis is that the body has been subject to ever-greater degrees of social control in terms of the embodied limits imposed upon our more emotional and carnal feelings. As Elias (1998: 49) explains:

> constraints through others from a variety of angles are converted into self-restraints . . . the more animalic human activities are progressively thrust behind the scenes of men's communal social life and invested with feelings of shame . . . the regulation of the whole instinctual and affective life by self-control becomes more and more stable, more even and more all-embracing.

The civilising process altered the way in which people experienced themselves and both perceived and related to others. It had both positive and negative attributes. Positive because it generated a more ordered and less violent society, as Shilling (1993: 154) suggests in relation to Elias's work: 'In contrast to the violence and lack of prohibitions on behaviour which characterized the Middle Ages, the Renaissance onwards witnessed a long-term trend towards greater demands on emotional control and the rise of differentiated codes of body management.

(Even now we are more physically and emotionally reserved than our counter-parts from the Middle Ages.) Negative because it leaves us with a problem, as Elias (1998b: 236) points out:

> If one wanted to try to reduce the key problem of any civilising process to its simplest formula, then it could be said to be the problem of how people can manage to satisfy their elementary animalic needs in their life together . . .

This creates a situation where:

> The battlefield is . . . moved within . . . the drives, the passionate affects, that can no longer directly manifest themselves in the relationships *between* people, often struggle no less violently *within* the individual against this supervising part of himself. (Elias 1982: 242)

So, we have a situation where our bodies and emotions have become so ordered through both external and internal constraints that we are not given any social space in which we can express our desires. Instead they stew in our guts and make our sensual engagement with the world feel stale and constricted. We become discontented with that world and distanced from the institutions that control it. An experience that was summed up beautifully by Octave Mirbeau (1989: 50) in *The Torture Garden*:

> You're obliged to pretend respect for people and institutions you think absurd. You live attached in a cowardly fashion to moral and social conventions you despise, condemn, and know lack all foundation. It is that permanent contradiction between your ideas and desires and all the dead formalities and vain pretences of your civilization which makes you sad, troubled and unbalanced. In that intolerable conflict you lose all joy of life and all feeling of personality, because at every moment they suppress and restrain and check the free play of your powers. That's the poisoned and mortal wound of the civilized world.

Elias (1983: 111) suggests that this process has profoundly effected the way in which we interact with people because it: 'enforces a curbing of the affects in favour of calculated and finely shaded behaviour in dealing with people'.

Socialising became a more complex activity because of the imposition of codes of practice that made us more self-conscious and aware of appearances, which in turn made us more reserved or calculating.

As direct displays of emotional violence and passion became less acceptable people became more Machiavellian in their social negotiations, which allowed them alternative ways to unleash their emotions that are more guarded but no less painful for the recipient. This side of the 'civilising process' results in viciousness and cruelty becoming covert and controlled, rather than disappearing completely. They become 'head games', rather than bodily confrontations. The office bully, being a primary example, can wage psychological war on people for years. My informants did not refer to the everyday world as a 'civilised' world, but rather a world of 'petty power games' and 'bullshit office politics'. Instead of the visible immediacy and carnality of violence these more covert forms of power play impact in the same ways as water torture: a constant drip, drip, drip, the effects of which increase in severity over time.

Nevertheless, I would largely agree with Elias's perspective that the body has become more controlled and regulated in the modern world and this process is important in understanding the club experience. We saw, in the last chapter, how the social rules of clubbing challenge these controls. The sensual framework that the civilising process imposed upon us via the habitus is disembodied and replaced with a far more carnal and expressive experience of self, which revitalises our occupation of the world by making it feel less stale. We are relocated in that world on an alternate sensual plane, which has generated its own codes of social behaviour. Elias recognised the importance of leisure in allowing people to move beyond the bodily restraints of the everyday world long before we became a fully fledged leisure culture: 'The quest for excitement . . . in our leisure activities is complementary to the control and restraint of overt emotionality in our ordinary life. One cannot understand one without the other' (Elias 1986: 66).

The lack of violence found in clubs is one of the most important elements; it arises out of the civilising process, but also allows club crowds to move beyond its constraints because it allows people to let themselves go and reveal themselves in an alternative social form. This in turn expands upon that civilising process because we are able to experiment with intense experiences of sensual pleasure (drugs), emotional expression (dancing) and social expression (sexual display and dressing-up) without these experiences becoming antisocial. Instead they become the platform out of which arises novel social groupings set within alternative sensual frameworks. Clubs exist at the edge of both the civilising process and the habitus. They house and express a social ideal based in a desire to be with people while experiencing a sense of liberation as to how you can interact with those people and present yourself to that crowd. Simply being allowed to occupy an 'uncivilised' body for a night: to grin like a fool; to laugh too loud; to sweat it out on the dance floor; to flirt outrageously; talk well-meaning shite to strangers; feel sexual, carnal and exhilarated. All these experiences create a sensual alternative to the internal and external constrictions upon our sociality, which operate in the everyday world. Living-it-large allows us to temporarily move beyond the taken-for-granted assumptions, which suffuse our social life with fear and insecurity, but it counts for nothing unless you can take some of that knowledge back out into the world beyond clubs.

Individual Bodies

Bourdieu's (1977, 1990) and Elias's (1978) theories allow us to look at the social frameworks that are altered via clubbing. Now I want to examine the way clubbing affects the individuals who make up the crowd. Again I was faced with the problem of finding a framework upon which I could map these effects because clubbing influences people in subtle and slippery ways. I ended up turning to neuro-cognitive studies and particularly the work of Damasio (1994) in *Descartes' Error and the Feeling of What Happens* and LeDoux (1999) in *The Emotional Brain* in order to find such a framework.

Damasio (1999) explores the relationship between the body, the emotions and consciousness and as I was dealing with a social space in which altered states of consciousness play an important role it felt pertinent to have a theory of consciousness to refer to. We have to be careful when dealing with the notion of altered states of consciousness because they have often been imbued with a pseudo-spiritual reverence, which detracts from the fact that, in this instance, we're talking about people getting out of their boxes and having a laugh. All drugs alter consciousness including alcohol and cigarettes, however it was the psychedelics, especially LSD, which turned even radical altered states of consciousness into a mass, leisure option. Although some of the ideology that surrounded acid when it first appeared now seems dated and rather naïve because it insisted on a quasi-spiritual, rather than social interpretation of the experience.

Most theories of altered states focus on them as purely mental phenomena, but Damasio's work allows us to develop an alternate approach to both their causes and their potential impact. Damasio has developed a more embodied model of consciousness. He makes a strong case for the bodily basis of consciousness via a structure he calls the 'proto-self', which is the map of the body held in mind that provides the embodied framework for how we consciously apperceive the world. The 'proto-self' is a glutinous, fleshy and emotive structure that constitutes our perception of the world from the bottom up by generating a framework of sensory data, which subsequently structures our thoughts about that world. However, we are not conscious of the 'proto-self'; rather, it exerts its strongest influences unconsciously, which is why you can find yourself feeling sad, happy or manic without really knowing why you are experiencing these states. The brain processes the world in two ways, as explained by LeDoux (1999: 272): 'This influence of memory on perceptions is an example of what cognitive scientists sometimes call top-down processing, which contrasts with the build-up of perceptions from sensory processing, known as bottom-up processing.'

The idea of bottom-up processing is important because it allows us to view the fleshy dynamics of clubbing as a form of sensual expansion that has escaped the control of the habitus and allows us to glimpse alternative relationships between ourselves and the ideological realm created by culture. That culture attempts to control both forms of processing. It controls the symbolic realm, which we perceive from the top-down through its manipulation of signs and the bodily realm of bottom-up processing through the habitus, so moulding these alternative modes of perception together into a unified cultural whole.

It is my contention, and I go beyond Damasio's (1999) thesis at this point, that the 'proto-self' is the biological mechanism that supports the habitus. It allows the body to be constructed by society and underpins our perception of that social world, so binding us into the practices through which we negotiate it. Clubbing alters that 'proto-self' and therefore the habitus and allows us to become conscious of our world in a different way. However, this is clubbing we are talking about, not some great spiritual awakening, so most people take these shifts in perception with a pinch of salt. Their impact is limited by the restraints of the everyday world that dismisses them as silly and irrational. Nevertheless I did detect certain emotional modalities that seemed to resist the everyday world by refusing to take it and its structures of belief seriously and all cultures want to be taken seriously. People had begun to find their culture funnier and more absurd; they were increasingly dismissive of the claims it made, its social and moral pronouncements, its deter-mination to continue to behave as if people still believed in it. They had embodied alternative experiences, which made the claims of culture sensually untenable. They didn't want to fight that culture, they were happy to use its structure to get what they needed, they simply wanted it to leave them alone so they could get on with living their own lives through their own socio-sensual networks and beliefs. They had altered the body through which they perceived their culture and had become conscious of it in a different way.

Emotional Memory

Clubbing impacts upon people's emotional memory systems. The memory of clubbing is not so much the memory of facts about clubbing, but rather an emotional modality that shapes people's relationship to the world at an unconscious level. This is most simply illustrated by recourse to the work of Swiss physician Edouard Claparede. As LeDoux (1999) recounts, Claparede was presented with a case of extreme amnesia: a female patient who would completely forget who Claparede was or having ever met him before. On one visit to her, he approached her and held out his hand and as she took it he pricked her with a concealed pin after which he left the patient. When he returned she could not remember his name or ever having met him before, but she would not shake his hand and backed away from him. Although she could not consciously remember him her previous response of being pricked by the pin remained as an emotional memory of their earlier encounter and this shaped her bodily and proxemic posture and emotional attitude towards him. LeDoux (1999: 181) summarises this situation in these terms:

> It now seems that Claparede was seeing the operation of two different memory systems in his patient – one involved in forming memories of experiences and making those memories available for conscious recollection at some later time, and another operating outside of consciousness and controlling behaviour without explicit awareness of past learning.

The action of this amnesiac patient reveals this dual memory system, but we must be wary when applying the existence of these systems of gaining knowledge to clubbing. Clubbers have both types of memory system operating, although the high levels of intoxication found in clubs can make the memories of the explicit, conscious system of recollection hard to recall, which brings to mind the old adage: 'If you can remember the sixties you weren't really there.'

Just as the bodily techniques of clubbing can become embodied over time so too can the socio-emotional memory of clubbing. The memory of clubbing is the emotional memory of having felt good and intensely alive, it is the smile that sweeps across the face of clubbers when you mention clubbing and drugging, even when they haven't done it for a few years. On a social level you can view clubbing as Claparede in reverse – rather than being pricked by the pins of others, people are instead connected to those others, especially their friends, by the sheer intensity of the pleasure they have shared that binds them together at a bodily level.

As Claparede shows this emotional memory generates unconscious effects and relationships with the world, which structure the way people encounter that world at an emotional level. This unconscious, emotional reaction is important as it is the initial bodily structure of knowledge that will further structure our subsequent factual knowledge. This is because they carry within them the emotional memory of people's previous encounters with the 'objects' of their world, which orientates their physical and emotional posture toward these 'objects' via these unconscious bodily mechanisms.

Emotions connect us to the world at a visceral level; the emotional response we have to an 'object' situates that 'object' in our mind and imbues it with the sense of urgency and immediacy, which will structure our reaction to it. It foregrounds the 'object' and 'flavours' our experience of it by making it part of our body and hence part of the mind. As LeDoux (1999: 19) suggests: 'Emotions easily bump mundane events out of awareness, but nonemotional events . . . do not so easily displace emotions from the mental spotlight – wishing that anxiety or depression would go away is usually not enough.' We always have an emotional connection to the world; the extent to which we experience an object in mind depends upon the emotional intensity that it invokes.

Damasio (1999: 52) also examines background emotions:

A special word about background emotions is needed, at this point because the label and the concept are not a part of traditional discussions on emotion. When we sense that a person is 'tense' or 'edgy,' 'discouraged' or 'enthusiastic,' 'down' or 'cheerful,' without a single word having been spoken to translate any of those possible states, we are detecting background emotions. We detect background emotions by subtle details of body posture, speed and contour of movements, minimal changes in the amount and speed of eye movements, and the degree of contraction of facial muscles.

The inducers of background emotions are usually internal. The process of regulating life itself can cause background emotions but so can continued processes of mental conflict, overt or covert, as they lead to sustained satisfaction or inhibition of drives and motivations.

Background emotions arise from both the biological regulation of life and our ideas about the world, which is the way in which we mull it over in our minds and experience our relationship to it. As Damasio points out, this internal process of reflection is itself reflected upon the body; it becomes part of the body's 'object' nature in the world that can be 'read' by others. This is probably what is behind such informant statements as:

You can spot a clubber; there's a definite recognition thing there and it's not just what they wear or anything because I've met people through work that I thought clubbed and then found out I was right. I don't know there's something about them. You can recognise it: big, sparkly, inquisitive eyes that look alive, the way they are with people, there's something. (Female 32, 9 years' experience)

This recognition was picking out some of the background emotions and bodily postures created by the practice of clubbing that people had embodied to the point that they utilised them within their everyday worlds. (Although you can also spot a clubber because they look so wasted on Monday morning.) These bodily postures are most evident when you watch groups of clubbers socialise with one another and even strangers. They are used to being amongst strangers and their emotional memory of strangers is generally positive. Obviously the social context plays an important role in either liberating or constraining the body through which they socialise; they will be more wary on the street or at work than at home or a party. They are more likely to greet you with a smile than a scowl because they are used to smiling at strangers. They have embodied an informal mode of socialising in public: a social body that exudes an enthusiasm for socialising. Other forms of emotional interaction can destroy this body; if they come across brutality and cruelty it can be erased altogether. If it isn't erased, though, it is strengthened and built on until it becomes the dominant mode of social practice through which people socialise, even when away from clubs.

Another major element of these club-generated memories is the sense of having lived. As one informant suggested:

No one wants to think that they live a boring life, do they? Especially when you're young. I think that's one of the major appeals of clubs; they let you experience passion. You don't feel like life's boring when you're in a club and that experience is open to anyone with the money really. You can be really normal in other ways and still have a life that feels exciting because you've got this hardcore playground to hang out in. (Male 27, 10 years' experience)

This sense that life is exciting becomes part of people's emotional memory and subsequently part of the way they occupy that world. They expect to enjoy life and they know that in order to do that they have to get out there and create their own pleasure. They don't expect pleasure to come to them; they do not see pleasure as a right; they realise that they have to make their own fun in this world.

Gaining access to and modifying your emotional memory system is an extremely difficult thing to achieve. It is an exceptionally powerful and enduring part of your sensual landscape. Whereas, Freudian therapy can take twenty years to impact upon it, a pill can temporarily rewrite it in twenty minutes and allow you to both experience and socialise through this novel emotional state for five to ten hours. One informant who'd had a rough childhood culminating in two suicide attempts by the time she was seventeen was adamant that Ecstasy had saved her, even though she was just as adamant that she'd gone too far with it and nearly screwed herself up. She made a couple of interesting observations. Firstly, she suggested that taking Ecstasy had allowed her to get over her fear and mistrust of others and build a social life for herself through clubbing. Secondly, she said that:

When I'm on E I find that I can look at my problems in a different way. They don't overwhelm me. I can be on a dance floor and I can just let them float through my head and look at them without getting all fucked-up by them. They feel different and that means I can look at them and try and work them out because they're not on top of me. (Female 34)

The Ecstasy gave her a break from the emotional posture that her memories generated; she could gain some emotional distance between herself and her problems, which allowed her to look at them without being overwhelmed by them. This is one of the most positive and potentially dangerous aspects of drug use. You can look at your own life in a different way, but you can also end up trying to hide behind the drugs because they are the only thing that allows you to cope with your own emotions. The impact of drugs on the emotional memory system is only of any real use if it feeds into social systems that allow the existence of this new emotional framework to continue bearing fruit once the drugs have worn off.

Embodied Metaphors

So far we've looked at the mechanisms by which clubbing can shift people beyond the habitus and beyond some aspects of the civilising process. We've also seen how these shifts affect individual consciousness and people's emotional memory system. The last area of theory, I want to explore, is the ways in which these changes begin to generate alternate forms of linguistic and symbolic knowledge.

One of the problems of understanding clubbing arises from the fact that it is quite difficult to articulate the experiences it generates. (If you don't believe me try explaining what a trip feels like to somebody.) LeDoux (1999: 99) suggests that: 'I am very fond of the idea that the emotional brain and the "word brain" might be operating in parallel but using different codes and thus are not necessarily able to communicate with each other.'

The language of feelings and emotions operates differently from the language held within signs. We can understand a sign despite its arbitrary nature because it refers to a thing, so we learn that a cow is a cow. However, the language of feelings and emotions can only be understood empathetically. Sad is not a thing, it is a complex bodily state and if we had been freaky enough to have never been sad we would never truly understand what sadness was. When we speak of sadness we speak of being 'down', 'low' or 'heavy' and these words actually mirror the sensation of sadness.

In *Metaphors We Live By,* George Lakoff and Mark Johnson (1981) explored the way that metaphors organised human speech and ideas by creating systems of coherence amongst disparate ideas. For example, they looked at orientational metaphors such as 'I'm feeling up today' as a way of describing happiness and concluded that such metaphors have an embodied and experiential basis that grants them saliency. So 'feeling up' is happy while 'feeling down' is sad. However, the same up/down orientation also encompasses a number of other experiences. So power is perceived as 'up' while weakness is seen as being 'down'. Morality is 'high minded' while immorality is 'low down'. They claimed that: 'In actuality we feel that no metaphor can ever be comprehended or even adequately represented independent of its experiential basis' (Lakoff and Johnson 1981: 19).

Clubbing by introducing people to new sensations creates new embodied metaphors and changes language. Many of these terms like 'getting high' or 'coming down' are founded upon the same bodily metaphors discussed by Lakoff and Johnson. The majority of metaphors, examined by Lakoff and Johnson, are derived from simple physical and spatial experiences (standing, lying, moving, and so on) in contrast the metaphors of clubbing evolve out of a radically altered body. The phrase 'feel the rush' doesn't mean you're running for a bus; rather, it captures the physical sensation of your body changing under the influence of Ecstasy. E rushes through your system in waves, saturating the body, shifting the mind, unravelling the flesh, altering perception, until it stops rushing and you get the loved-up vibe you were chasing. So although we are familiar with the word rush, its meaning has changed because its sensual structure has been fundamentally modified.

The language of clubbing often refers to a sense of moving beyond the mundane. People talk about freedom, liberation, abandonment, getting out of it, going mental and living-it-large. Even the terms shitfaced, bollocksed and messy aren't necessarily negative because they all refer to states of self that are no longer trapped within the confines of the everyday. Critics of clubbing are quick to classify this sense of moving beyond as escapism and dismiss this alternative socio-sensual reality as false. However, it is just as easy to classify it as an expansion of that everyday reality through which people begin to understand that the socio-sensual limits of that reality are as arbitrary as culture itself. (The first thing you learn studying anthropology is that there is a multitude of cultures and that none are any more real than the others.)

Others metaphors, like 'trippy' refer to complex sensations that lie beyond everyday bodily knowledge. I have heard people use 'trippy' to describe artworks, television programmes and social situations. This label gives them a frame of reference through which people can comprehend these diverse phenomena. However, it goes deeper than acting as a simple linguistic referent particularly in social terms because you can find yourself using the same social and emotional strategies, which get you through a trip to both comprehend and deal with the situation that you're in. If you are a seasoned tripper you become used to the world looking, feeling and behaving in odd and bizarre ways and you've learnt to handle these experiences, to control your reactions to them, to turn them into positive states. (Or else you've at least learned to run away screaming and hide under the bed, which can be a surprisingly useful survival strategy.) What you've learnt is how to control the often extreme emotional states that tripping can induce; you learn to find things funny, rather than threatening; you learn to go with the flow because once you've taken a trip there is no going back for the next six to twelve hours. You also learn how to deal with other people when you're in this state.

The same can be said for the loved-up vibe of Ecstasy. It isn't an ordinary experience. It doesn't refer to the conventional usage of the term love, but rather a particular social state, which has no real counterpart in the everyday world. The phrase loved-up captures a whole gamut of interrelated experiences relating to your sense of self and that self's relationship to others. The same can be said for feeling coked-up, speedy or stoned. These complex embodied models act as alternative points of reference or to use Lakoff's term 'ICM' (Idealised Cognitive Model) from *Women, Fire and Dangerous Things* (1987).

An ICM is a form of social template that combines mental, physical and emotional schema through which knowledge of the world is mediated. A job interview would be a good example of an everyday ICM because it has a particular social, emotional and bodily structure that frames our behaviour because we know how we should act, talk, sit and so forth during one. We also use the job interview model of presentation and behaviour to negotiate other social occasions when somebody has power over us and we want to impress them – such as going to court.

Once you've been loved-up and shared that sensation with others it becomes a new ICM in the sense that it becomes the embodied model of how you want your relationships with other people to be articulated and feel at a sensual and emotional level. You obviously can't do it all the time, but the model remains as something that you can strive for especially with your mates. The sense of emotional depth in those relationships, the intensity of the experiences you share and the way you relate to one another all become alternate co-ordinates within the frame of reference that encompasses your social world.

Example 2

The following example shows how the social body formed through clubbing can provide the basis for an new ICM, which underpins a shift in people's experience of their own social world:

> The first time I took speed was the first time in my life that I felt truly confident. I remember it was 'pink champagne', lovely whizz, and I couldn't shut up. Before that I was very shy, very quiet and I remember that for the next few days I was thinking: 'That's how it feels to be confident and that's what I need to do. I need to learn how to feel that way without the drugs.' What's been really nice is that in terms of slowing down over the last few months I recognise there are other things that I have learnt about having a good time, which I've managed to carry over from partying without the drugs being present. Very positive on the whole. (Female 32, 9 years' experience)

This woman's experience of confidence made the idea of confidence more tangible to her. It gave her a model through which she could comprehend confidence, which became something she had experienced as a social actuality. She had given herself an embodied and experiential basis from where she could view her shyness as only one possible social state. This experience was physical and emotional in that amphetamine changes the body and this change subsequently alters a person's emotions in relation to the 'set and setting' of the environment in which it occurred. It was through this novel body and novel emotional state that she began to socialise and experience a sense of confidence. Clubbing as a non-everyday and non-mundane sensual practice grants people access to alternative embodied states that alter their experience of inhabiting their world.

The same informant continued in answer to my question: 'Has clubbing changed the way you interact with people?'

Something has. The classic example is me going on a course for work. I have to go on these courses and I used to hate them. I didn't know anybody and I'd feel like I had to make conversation with people. I dreaded the breaks and the lunchtimes wondering: Where you were going to be? Had you met anybody to be friends with? Are you going to sit and be the sad one on your own? Now I went on a week's course recently and it's not even that I found one person to link to, which is what I would've done before. I didn't do that at all. I just happily bounced around and met loads and loads of people and every break and every lunchtime I'd find someone else to spend my time with and so at the end of the course I'd met most of the people there. That's really different to how I used to be. It was a far clubbier way of interacting.

We have here a model of social interaction that has no specific label in language. It is a socio-sensual practice that was discovered through clubbing and then shifted beyond the club arena. Note my informant does not mention the phrase 'loved-up', so it is not that intense club experience that she is referring to – rather the clubbing model of social interaction gave her a more general prototype for her social relations in the outside world. Her experience is derived from a number of bodily and emotional relationships with other people that she feels has been changed through clubbing.

We should also note that my informant's behaviour on these courses was not due to her taking drugs and in response to my question: 'Your job must teach you to interact with people though?' She replied:

Yes obviously that and age makes a difference, but I'd already been in the job four years before I started doing the clubbing and drugging thing, rather than just boozing and dancing and I hadn't developed the confidence I've now got from the job alone. Certainly, now at work I'm being asked to apply for the team-leader post and three to four years ago I would never have dreamt of doing that and they wouldn't have thought of asking me.

My informant's experience had changed her bodily and emotional response to other people. Through clubbing she had experienced and practised a new ideal of social interaction. Note the term 'bounced around' – it gives an upbeat impression of the way in which she approached people and the body through which she made that approach. Bouncing around certainly doesn't sound in the least bit shy or threatening and it reveals a certain enthusiasm for socialising, which is far removed from the withdrawn physicality often associated with shyness. My informant had recognised and transferred an embodied state, which was initially created through drugs into her sober work world. It had given her something to work towards: a socio-sensual and emotional model that she would eventually carry beyond clubs without the use of any drugs. This model was a hybrid in that it was neither the full social rush of clubbing or her previous everyday persona, but rather a bodily practice, a learnt technique, which allowed her to occupy a social space and relate to other people in that space in a different way.

Summary

In this chapter we have examined the bodily frameworks that enable us to classify clubbing as a form of social and individual knowledge, which can move beyond clubs. Through clubbing people experience new socio-sensual models, these models are embodied over time as practices and gradually slip back in into the everyday lives of clubbers particularly amongst people who have clubbed together. These practices have a harder time surviving outside of these friendship networks. However, clubbers create further socio-sensual models, hybrids, based on their clubbing practices as they negotiate their way through their own social realm. They use the social, sensual and emotional knowledge uncovered via clubbing to generate a new bodily posture that re-orientates their relationship to and perspective upon the world that lies beyond clubs.

–9–

Sensual Experiments in the
Art of Being Human

Clubbing is a bit like taking psychedelic drugs. It's not the same thing, but psychedelics are powerful tools, once you've taken them they affect you for the rest of your life. The rest of your life you know that there is something else, another type of experience out there. You've walked over the meadow and you know what the other side feels like. What you make of it after that is up to you, but it does stay with you. Clubbing's like that; it lets you know that there is another way of having a good time with people, something more intense. (Male 32, 14 years' experience)

In the last chapter, we looked at the social and bodily systems that generate and structure our sensual experience of the world. In this chapter, I want to examine the way in which shifts in this field of socio-sensual practice manifest themselves as new knowledge in people's lives by creating alternative practices and perspectives upon those lives.

Abandonment

Clubbing taught me about the joy of abandonment. Abandoning yourself to the whole thing. It's quite a young lifestyle as well; it's still developing. (Female 32, 9 years' experience)

What is a lifestyle of abandonment? What does it mean? Abandonment came up again and again in the interviews as being a positive experience that was valued by participants. However, there were degrees of abandonment; it was rarely a case of absolute abandonment and when it was it usually meant that things were about to get or had got a bit messy. Even then, when this sense of abandonment was derived from excessive and total intoxication people still found things to value in the experience.

I will explore three types of abandonment that are intimately linked to one another; they play into each other and intensify the others' presence. Abandonment is a potent experience; it is a particular style of being in the world that is intimately linked to the moment in which it occurs. To abandon yourself is to cast off both past and future and to reside absolutely in the present; you're not thinking about yesterday or worrying about tomorrow; you are seizing pleasure right there and right then. The world outside of this space and time diminishes to the point of non-existence. One male informant summed it up like this: 'When you're in the thick of a really rocking night the world outside the club doors ceases to exist. It has no real relevance because you're just focused on the party and having a good time.'

The idea of living for the moment is obviously not new, but the experience of living in the moment was not an easy thing to accomplish for many people. Clubbing changed that by creating intense passionate and socially charged environments that taught people 'the joys of abandonment'. In the process people's perception of what constituted pleasure changed; it was intensified and socialized into an alternative form; its distractions were reduced to a minimum. Sensual hedonism became more hedonistic for more people because it found a home and ceased to be the preserve of the hyper-rich and decadent. For some of my informants this search for pleasure has become a total lifestyle, for others it is a hobby. As one informant pointed out:

> What a lot of people fail to realise about all the clubbing and drugging is that it's simply a leisure option nowadays, whether you get off on it or not is just a matter of personal taste, some people like golf, some like football, some like antiques fairs or going to the theatre, some people like skydiving, others like drugging and dancing. It's just a way of enjoying themselves with their mates. I know people who have arranged their whole lives around it because it's their favourite thing to do. Then there are the ones who dabble and just get out there when it's convenient because they've got other stuff they want to do as well. I also know people who arranged their whole life so they could spend the majority of their time scuba diving. I don't see the difference, except the law keeps insisting one's valid and one's not. It is bollocks; people will have their pleasure. Clubbing's often called escapist, but why is it any more escapist than reading alone in your room or pouring over your stamp collection or listening to classical music. No one ever claims that these are escapist, do they? They're just hobbies, things that people enjoy, a way of passing time between birth and death. (Male 27, 10 years' experience)

In terms of clubbing abandonment arises in a number of ways.

1. Physical Abandonment

The joy of giving yourself to the music, the dancing, the swirl of the crowd. The physicality of clubbing is fluid, expressive and super charged: the body in sublime sensual motion. However, most of the time we are really talking about a relative state of physical abandonment set within the sociality of the club; the joy of watching people loosen up, shedding the muscular habits of the everyday world, bodies becoming expressive and sensuous, pleasure dripping off the crowd, the grins, the laughter. Most importantly the dancing that carries its own meaning. To dance is to physically occupy a meaningful time and meaningful space that is the secret of dance. That's why every culture dances.

2. Emotional Abandonment

For many people in clubs the emotional insecurities of the everyday world evaporate to a degree. People become more expressive and they communicate with a heightened intensity, but that communication is predominantly physical or blarney based. It is about 'communicating for the sheer joy of communicating'. It is rarely opinionated or particularly deep in terms of ideas; it is far too noisy most of the time for intellectual games. It is a raw form of emotional communication; it is celebratory. As one informant so succinctly put it:

> You're allowed to be happy in clubs; you don't have to explain why you're happy; you don't have to justify it; you can just be happy. People don't expect you to be happy in life in general; they don't trust it; misery grants you a lot more kudos. If you're happy people think there's something wrong with you; you must be naive, but that's rubbish. Things aren't perfect, but in comparison to much of the rest of the world we're pampered in the West, but if you actually dare to claim that we are lucky people treat you like a freak because it challenges the excuses they use to justify their own failures and their own misery, but in a club you can be happy. It's actually expected of you; it's the one place where being a miserable git is considered ridiculous, rather than meaningful. (Female 41, 19 years' experience)

Why would people value a space in which you can simply express happiness? The answer lies in the connection between the body and the emotions. The feeling of an emotional response is intimately linked to how that emotion is expressed on a physical level. As Merleau-Ponty suggests: 'The gesture *does not make me think* of anger, it is anger itself' (1994: 184). In terms of the club environment you are in a space that is physically more expressive than other spaces. You can express your emotions through your body and this physical intensity deepens the experience of the emotion. You can express your happiness in a club; you don't have to constrain its appearance, so you are allowed to relish it to its maximum potential through that expressive body.

Another informant suggested that:

> Clubs and E have made me more emotionally expressive. I ran up to G, one night, threw my arms around him and was saying: 'Oh hello darling, how are you? God it's good to see you.' And I had never done that before. I know it sounds a bit 'lovey', but I really like G so why shouldn't I tell an old friend how good it is to see him? Why shouldn't I

be enthusiastic about that friendship? It's the truth and the smile I got in return suggested he felt the same. You get to celebrate your friends and be open with them. (Female 32, 9 years' experience)

Again we're talking about a relative abandonment with, as we saw in the section on Ecstasy, people making a strong distinction between friends and strangers in terms of the meaning they attach to the encounter.

The physical intensification and sense of emotional abandonment that people experience in clubs, allows those emotions to be savoured within an expanded body. You can express an almost insane level of happiness in clubs to a degree that would be unthinkable in other public spaces. This capacity to express your feelings through your body intensifies them; the emotional intensity of this deep happiness is not just a drug phenomenon but a form of bodily wisdom that is crushed by the gaze in other social situations. People's understanding of pleasure is altered at a corporeal level as the bodily constraints of the everyday world are challenged; pleasure gains a new physical and psychological form that becomes the embodied model against which other pleasures are compared.

3. Social Abandonment

Whether living-it-up with friends or talking animatedly to strangers club's house an informal breed of social encounter, wherein at least a portion of the fear, anxiety and mistrust that often suffuses social relations is abandoned. In the best clubs the crowds forget to judge one another because they're too busy having a laugh. As one informant explained:

You meet someone in a club and you realise that they are a bit of a laugh and you'll talk to them all night and have a laugh with them and there's nothing else involved, just enjoying people. It taught society how to get on at the end of the day. Not everyone, there's always some deadheaded arseholes in any club, but for the majority clubs are a place in the middle where they can meet. (Male 28, 12 years' experience)

The informality of clubs, combined with the intention to simply enjoy yourself and other people for the night, creates this sense of clubs being 'places in the middle' where you can learn to get on with people. We take the act of socialising for granted in many ways, but like any other skill it improves with practice and clubs are good spaces to practice and gain confidence because people's actions in clubs have a minimal impact on other areas of their lives, which makes them a distinct social arena.

People abandon a lot of their social reserve in a club, as we saw in the section on the club gaze; they get off on the crowds and enjoy them; they relish the sensation of being part of that crowd. They experience it positively and that allows them to go further, to become bigger and more expressive, to be less self-conscious and scared.

The three forms of abandonment that I laid out above are fluid; they combine and dissolve into and through one another, changing tempo, offering different forms of intensity, suffusing the night as a whole, rather than existing as a single onanistic peak. They manifest themselves in chance meetings, wonderful visions, hysterical laughter, moments of introspection, bizarre conversations, sudden rushes of beauty, discovering fabulous people, seeing a club go off before your eyes. It is the actuality of movement, the burn of your own and your friends' excitement, the allure of bodies writhing on a beat. Its immediacy is one of its most powerful and ethereal qualities. However, as one informant suggested:

> One minute you're there, absolutely in the thick of it, rushing on a tune or talking ten-to-the-dozen with someone or just watching everything go off, feeling fucking magnificent, then the next second you're wondering whether you've got enough milk in the fridge so you can have a nice cup of tea when you get home. It's funny to go from absolute Waaah to utter mundanity in a split second, but fuck it, I like it. It adds to the whole thing, keeps it in perspective, stops you turning into a toad-licking crustie. (Male 31, 11 years' experience)

So clubbing is not a single constant state it is a series of states that range from the sublime to the ridiculous. It is, however, a technique of the body, a skill you can learn, a physical and mental stance towards pleasure. To experience it you have to throw yourself in headfirst. You have to overcome distance and seize the potential for pleasure that the space offers. One particularly full-on, gurning-to-the-max Australian, clubbing household who were interviewed for BBC 2's Choice World Clubbing put it like this: 'This house's attitude towards clubbing: go hard or go home because you're here for a good time, not a long time.'

Abandonment is a hobby, a leisure option, one amongst many. Like many other hobbies it can become people's central passion, sometimes for a couple of years, sometimes, as in the case of my informants, longer. For some people clubbing defines them in the world both to themselves and others. Its sensual intensity allows them to feel different from others; they are not mundane, not like the rest of the population because they have tasted the full intensity of the club gig; they have had those conspiratorial experiences where their existence shifted gear and the pleasure of living burnt deep within their flesh. People who haven't done the drugging, dancing, getting-on-down thing may well view it as false or escapist, but for clubbers it is the people who have never tried it that don't have a clue how to live. In clubbers' eyes they are the unimaginative ones that believe the intensity of life is set within specific unchallenged parameters, rather than being a fluid and permeable property of the flesh. Something that can be changed at will. As one informant said:

What was pleasure thirty years ago for most people? Sitting around a pub chatting, a weeks holiday in Bognor Regis in the rain, maybe a disco full of drunks on Saturday night, smoking a bit of spliff as a wild and special treat. Obviously for a few it's always been more than that, but not for the many. Well that's changing, now pleasure is two weeks in Ibiza splattered out of your conch, round the world air tickets, a psychedelic sunrise, fucking on drugs. In Britain our very notion of what constitutes pleasure has radically changed; it's all about a shift in intensity and a change in morality, the way the world feels has changed. To be honest I think we're still getting used to it; we haven't fully learnt how to cope with it yet. (Male 34, 16 years' experience)

Another put it this way:

Well take weddings, they're something that has happened for hundreds of years. Couple of hundred years ago the prime focus was the religious ceremony. Then, I don't know, half way through the last century the focus became the meal and speeches. It was about communication and eating as a social event. Recently I was one of the DJs at a very posh wedding on a Saturday night. Rich folk, professionals and there was the ceremony, then speeches and food. We happened to have a bag of Es on us, mentioned this to a couple of people and woomf they were gone like locusts had struck. Then we started playing the tunes and the party really started to kick-off, everyone started dancing, the E was obviously kicking in and we had a fucking great night. It made the wedding in many ways; it was the icing on the cake, the big finale. Nowadays even old people understand that dancing and partying is the thing that brings people together. It's not the religion or the food; they are no longer the peak moment for most people at a wedding, particularly the younger ones. It's been usurped by music and dancing and whenever possible a few drugs that's become the benchmark of a good time for more and more people; it's the thing they compare other experiences against. (Male 32, 14 years' experience)

The British perspective upon what counts as pleasure is changing; our experiences and our notions of pleasure have shifted for an ever-growing percentage of the population. The combination of factors you find in clubs, the people, the music, the drugs, the sex, the dancing, offers a set of potentials each with the ability to give pleasure. They are the basic elements in an on-going socio-sensual activity that is anchored in the idea of 'having a laugh with your mates'. It is more accurate to look at these club potentials, these disparate phenomena housed in a single space as things to be shared; it is through sharing them that people experience the most pleasure. This is hedonism as a social, rather than an individual force; it is grounded in the connectivity that arises within the club between friends and strangers alike. It is a sociality that arises from an extreme state of sensual intensity. That's why

Ecstasy was so important in altering our perspective on what makes a good night out, it changed the social experience of that night.

In the initial period of clubbing the sociality frames and serves the sensual, which makes it accessible; later as clubbers continue to club the sensual begins to serve the social, which becomes the major focus of the experience. Most importantly, this sensuality becomes a tool for altering and intensifying particular sets of social relationships. My informants all agreed on one thing: after years in clubs getting drugged-up, dancing like 'nutters', sucking on tune after immaculate tune, the thing that they ended up valuing most was the people who they'd shared it all with.

The Gender Blender

In Bourdieu's (1990) work on Kabyle society one of the main indicators of the structuring force of the habitus was the difference between the bodily practices of women and men. Their bodies were structured in opposition to one another and this structuring had profound social effects by naturalising all the subsequent conceptual levels of gender difference in Kabyle society. These differences exist in all societies including our own. However, clubbing temporarily shatters these bodily codes in that the clubbing body is not so much a gendered body, but a Dionysian body. In Malbon's (1999) work he discusses the idea that clubs are a potential space of liberation for women. He notes that women both enjoy the lack of sexual pressure in clubs and that they can get to be sexual for themselves, both statements with which I would agree. However, I would contend that by focusing on women he has skewed the object of study because clubbing liberates the bodies of both men and women and it is this shared liberatory practice that produces the club as a whole. So men are just as liberated and can get to experience their bodies in very different ways in club as much as women can.

One of the most important elements in this shift in bodily practice relates to intoxication. As we saw in the section on alcohol, in the drugs chapter, women's drinking was always viewed in a far harsher light than men's were. This created a gender disparity within the field of intoxication: men and women drank differently and women were supposed to remain more sober and in control than men as befitted their status as the carriers of virtue in society. (See: Gefou-Madianou 1992 and Maryon Macdonald 1994 for further discussion.) Then Ecstasy appeared and it equalised this disparity in intoxicated states by generating a shared Dionysian body that was removed from the social models that surrounded alcohol. Suddenly men and women were both getting completely out-of-it around one another, but they were doing so in a radically different way than they would have done using alcohol, because alcohol intoxication had been encultured over the years to reflect the gender differences of the everyday world. Getting drunk was imbued with the logic of practice, which suffused the wider world of gender relations; dropping an E wasn't.

The early days of rave produced two sets of Dionysian bodies: male and female, but both were grounded in the reduction of social fear and insecurity, which in turn underpinned a novel form of social practice. A sense of sensual equality marked clubs out as different from other social spaces. Everyone was on one and they all presumed they were sharing a particular emotional buzz. Men ceased to be 'from Mars', women ceased to be 'from Venus'; instead they had landed on planet Ecstasy, which swallowed the presumption of gender difference whole. This shift wasn't grounded in the dissipation of desire between the sexes: people were getting too hot and sweaty to not feel like fucking. It was a communicative shift: women and men started to talk more, to share the dance floor, to enjoy each other's company, to feel less threatened by one another.

The presumptions of feminism that men always possessed power over women hid the actual shyness and insecurity that many men experienced when they spoke to women. Firstly, because those men didn't know what to say to women, having predominantly experienced male company when they were completely wasted. Secondly, because the women presumed that the men were trying to chat them up. Friendly banter was always a loaded exercise because communication was perceived as sexual communication, as if that was all that women and men could ever have in common. However, under the influence of Ecstasy the presumption that sex was the only reason that people would want to talk to the opposite sex diminished. They began 'communicating for the sheer joy of communicating.' As one informant explained:

> One night this guy walked over and just said: 'I just wanted to tell you how gorgeous you look.' And that didn't feel like a come-on and later I met him and his girlfriend, so it hadn't been a come-on at all. It was just a lovely thing to have said to you. If a guy starts talking to me and he doesn't come across as having an ulterior motive, then I am quite happy to chat to him and I don't worry about it at all. You get more astute over time at working out what people's motives are. A lot of it's non-verbal; it's their body language; you can tell if someone's trying to pick you up or whether they're just having a good time and they want to chat to someone. (Female 32, 9 years' experience)

This ability to approach people and just compliment them or chat with them arises from the emotional rush of Ecstasy, its 'social exuberance' as one informant called it, and as this woman suggests, body language plays an important role in that communication and the body language of the Ecstasy user is very different from the body language of a drinker. The same informant continued:

> I think the E experience has shifted and maybe even confused some of the relations between women and men in clubs because the being friendly thing, well when does that

move into something else, when does it become being seduced? You can think a guy's just being friendly, whereas the guy thinks his friendliness is a come-on to you and vice versa. That's part of the difficulty when everyone's E'd up, then everyone's a lot more friendly and I think clubbing's muddied the water because when a guy used to come up to you, you used to presume he was trying to pick you up and so your reaction would be solely based on whether you fancied him or not and I used to be wary of giving out the wrong signals by being friendly to a guy I'd met in case he thought I fancied him. You could just smile at some guys and they'd follow you around all night like a dog and that's changed, which is great. Once men could appreciate that a woman being nice to them doesn't necessarily mean they want to shag them, then clubs got a lot better, but now people don't know when it is the case. I think people need to be much more obvious and straightforward in clubs when they're making a move. I don't mind men being direct as long as they're not rude and can take no for an answer without getting all arsey and sulky like little boys.

This shift in relations, the sudden increased friendliness in clubs spaces between women and men changed the way they communicated and blurred the traditional rules of seduction. People still ended up in bed with each other, but clubs ceased to feel like 'cattle markets' for women because men had begun to participate more intensely in clubs and weren't just standing around drinking and trying to pluck up the courage to chat someone up. Yet, as this informant suggests, it also led to some confusion, a blurring of signals and counter signals from within the sensually altered bodies of E'd up punters. This is interesting in light of the rules of engagement that exist in the fetish club scene where being candid about your desires and intentions is one way of dealing with the increased sexual rush of the space. This straightforward sociality only works because it occurs in a space where the right to ask and the right to refuse are both accepted practices.

This altered social experience between women and men has had a profound effect on gender relations even away from clubs. It accelerated the sense of social equality between women and men, which the ideas of feminism had been promoting because men and women embodied new social practices that turned those ideas into sensual realities. Through sharing these extreme sensual states women and men began to share the same Dionysian body and the same emotional rushes. They were equal, but equality didn't mean that sex, desire and seduction had to be eviscerated from their relationships; it just meant that it ceased to be the sole basis of those relationships during the leisure hours of the night. As the Ecstasy scene receded to be replaced by other styles of club, the crowds who had shared that experience continued to reproduce the style of communication they had experienced on Ecstasy. It became part of people's knowledge of how to behave in clubs and beyond. The drug that my female informants mistrusted most in terms of how it made men behave towards women was alcohol:

Clubs get that cattle-market feel back when there are too many drunks. I think the laddy thing takes over. When will guys learn that women want men, not lads? I think it's the booze they drink to get some courage up, but they have to drink so much before they've got the bottle to talk to you that they're just drooling by the time they get round to it. Whereas with E or even coke and speed they seem to be able to get the confidence they need to approach you without turning into complete dicks. (Female 29, 11 years' experience)

Women's attitudes towards booze has itself changed, they are drinking more and at least part of that shift is due to the fact that women and men have got used to being heavily intoxicated around one another. So the gender divide that stressed female propriety over male drunkenness has itself collapsed, which means that whatever the drug there is still a sense of mutuality between the crowds; women can cane it like men cane it. One informant summed it up like this: 'I want to be somewhere where men and women don't have to behave differently that's my utopia and I'm not interested in clubs when women and men can't just do the same things' (male 32, 14 years' experience).

Chemical Intimacy

The visceral nature of clubbing, its physical, emotional and social potentials, has altered the way in which people socialise by changing the practices through which that socialisation occurs. This is particularly evident in a crowd of E'd up clubbers, but this stranger-based experience is not the facet of clubbing that seems to be valued in the long term by clubbers; instead it is the way in which the experiences offered by clubs reverberate within the social groups who share them that has the strongest and most lasting effect. Getting drugged-up with your friends is 'a great way to spend your time' and the Class A drugs intensify this experience beyond the limits of what is achievable on alcohol, which was for so long the only way to share an intoxicated state with your friends. As a female informant said: 'There's nothing like going out and popping an E with someone to cement a friendship.'

As we have seen, the effects of the club drugs expand the time people spend together, the energy available to them and the way they interact. These three aspects of drug use are important for users whether they occur in clubs or beyond at an 'all-back-to-mine' gig. In some cases taking drugs with your friends at someone's house can begin to replace clubbing as a way of socialising the drug hit. As one informant explained:

The last E I had was just with a couple of friends round at their place. It was lovely, we just lolled around, talking, giggling. It was very intimate and relaxed, gentle in comparison to being in a club. I felt really close to them. I mean they're my friends so I am close to them, but it's just good to experience that sort of strong connection to them. It reminds you how amazing they are; it stops you taking them for granted. (Female 30, 11 years' experience)

This experience of not taking your friends for granted is extremely important. When drugs are taken in a quieter environment you focus on the people you're with. You have long, intimate and sometimes bizarre conversations as the drugs facilitate the process of making odd connections between ideas. As one informant said:

Clubbers talk about different things, sometimes it's really stupid mad bullshit, but that's not the end of it; they're not scared to talk about their feelings, their dreams. They're less frightened of expressing themselves, but when they do they're not so precious about them; they can often see the funny side as well, even when they're being serious about something. They don't get so serious that they can't laugh about it at some point. I think that's really healthy. (Female 32, 9 years' experience)

This particular style of intimacy is both intense and frivolous and arises from a certain social contract that exists between drug users. You can get confused on drugs, your emotions can swing between extremes, but clubbers have developed a particular style of social practice that keeps this side of drugs to a minimum. People don't want to be the downer on the night. As one informant explained:

In clubs you start by talking about clubbing and then conversations go off on a tangent, some of it's social chit chat, then people tell antics and club stories that's more the type of thing you talk about with strangers. I don't want to get too deep or serious with people; I get enough of that at work. Sometime you talk to boyfriends about where you're at and where you're going because it's a bit easier to do when you're chilled-out, but otherwise not too deep.

A social contract is formed between people sharing drugs. They've taken the drugs to have fun so even when conversations turn intense that sense of having fun still infiltrates them. Sometimes that humour can get very dark and warped but it is still there. This style of social interaction is difficult to imagine unless you've had it. It is intimate, open, honest and funny; one minute you're talking about something serious and important to you; the next you've dissolved into a fit of giggles; it has its own rhythms and logic. It is the social practice of intoxication. The psychedelics and Ecstasy can leave you emotionally fragile and vulnerable; drug teams are supportive because they recognise this aspect of the experience. However, if people consistently fall apart on drugs but still insist on taking them they will find themselves left out because they are downers on the nights. Experienced drug users expect each other to be fairly self-reliant on drugs, to be able to cope with their effects and not behave like a lightweight. They expect one another to contribute to the experience, rather than detract from it, and they respect this ability. This tends to bring out the best in people; they want to 'keep things sweet'; they don't want to bitch and whine all night; they avoid moaning and try to remain positive, so that they can control the emotional alterations initiated by the drugs.

The sharing of drug states is one of the primary motivations for taking drugs; taking them on your own just isn't the same; they are predominately social tools. However, as we have seen not all drugs give access to the same types of experience. In my experience sharing Ecstasy or the psychedelics with people changes the interpersonal dynamic of the group far more radically than the accelerants because they bring about more intense psychophysical alterations in people's sense of self and other. One informant gave a detailed description of the social differences he perceived between drugs and why he valued these states:

> The phrase I'd use is chemical overlap. When you're on cocaine your ego expands to the point where it covers several people around you. When you're on E you just feel that everyone else's ego has expanded into you. There's a chemical overlap, instead of being rigid lines between what's me and what isn't me they extend into each other and you get an overlap and you find this space that's still at bit of you, but it's also both of us as well. Normally you get that with loving intimate relationships, but the drugs can do that, but in a different way. (Male 32, 14 years' experience)

This quote reveals a particular perspective upon the notion of intimacy. When he speaks of overlap he is suggesting a particular kind of relationship, a connection that is felt at an emotional level. It is not reliant upon sharing words or opinions but is about feeling another's presence and a connection to them, which is grounded in sharing and enjoying that presence without feeling as if you're under any pressure to articulate it. It is like touching somebody without actually touching. Touch has an immediate presence, it is profoundly intimate in a way that words can rarely match. This informant's notion of overlap, the way the ego expands or contracts in relation to various drugs is a physical sensation that other users report and I can confirm through my own experiences. He goes on:

> Even when you're with someone who you're intimate with you can still be conscious of yourself. Truly great intimate moments are when you're practically as one. One of the great signs of intimacy is to be able to be completely silent around one another without there being any pressure to talk or interact or without being uncomfortable with the silence. There's no pressure of communication and being drugged-up there is no pressure of communication because you can be utterly insular about dancing or just watching the people around you or you can be really social about it. It's about not having to follow particular social conventions and doing things that you wouldn't otherwise do. There's a lack of self-censorship; you cease to self-censor and I think that's a very healthy thing for most people.

The idea of a 'loving intimate relationship' and the ability to be silent with someone without feeling uncomfortable suggests the experience is felt as a high degree of intimacy. The sort of intimacy that arises from long-term relationships with people where you don't feel as if you have to put on a show, but can simply be yourself. When this experience is had with strangers it is wonderful. As the following informant explained:

> In terms of making mates it often doesn't go beyond the club with complete strangers. Sometimes you're making contact while dancing and moving around and you get to enjoy the presence of another person and it can make you curious so you can end up talking to them. I also really enjoy the anonymous element sometimes. I used to club completely on my own and feel really good things with other people and not exchange a word and just leave it as history when I left. I think that sort of contact is excellent; really feeling closer to people and yet not doing the business or taking it further. It's just a little gift that the night gives you. (Female 30, 12 years' experience)

However, this feeling can evaporate once you part; it has an effect on the way you perceive people, but if that form of perception isn't backed up by your other encounters with people in the world it can begin to be treated with suspicion. However, when you have these experiences with friends, then they become part of your ongoing shared social history. They take place within a social framework and play a role in revitalising and intensifying that framework. This is particularly interesting in the light of the following assertions by an informant:

> I don't think I'd be so cool about being single if I didn't get to have these really intense experiences with my friends. We're a tight-knit group. We have a good time together and it's not all drugging and clubbing. That's just one side of our friendship, but you form strong emotional bonds with the people you take drugs with regularly. They help take that friendship to a different level. I think I touch my friends more now and that's important. I'd hate to have to go through life without being able to touch people. I think E's changed that between friends. You never used to see gangs of tough-looking guys with their arms round each other, did you? I'm not saying I want to remain single forever, but when you're having this good a time it doesn't seem so important to find a partner. (Female 29, 12 years' experience)

The number of single people in our society is growing rapidly. A report by National Statistics (Social trends 33 2003) revealed a 50 per cent rise in the number of people living alone over the last thirty years. They also reported that the average age of marriage had risen to almost thirty-five amongst men and thirty-two for women. There is obviously a series of factors at work that are leading to these phenomena. These shifts have brought about a change in our perspective upon and experience of friendship. Its importance is growing with the rise in single people and the growing nomadism of our population. People are living further away from their family and the friends they grew up with and they have had to create new relationships, which are imbued with a high degree of emotional depth to fill this social vacuum. Although we must remember that many of these people value their single lifestyle because it grants them a certain amount of freedom.

However, being single is one thing, but these people don't want to be alone. These changes have put an extra emphasis on the importance of friendship as the core social relationship in people's lives particularly in terms of how long it remains as such. They want those friendships to contain a depth of intimacy that makes them analogous to the emotional depth shared with family or lovers because of the sense of emotional support that carries. They are not trying to replace family or lovers – just to create new styles of social relationship within their friendship networks. The drugging, clubbing, all-back-to-mine experience expands the sensual parameters of those relationships. This shift arises from the embodied states that clubbing underpins and manifests itself as a form of sensual slippage between people. It can become fairly extreme giggly group sex for the sheer fun of it or it can remain at a more muted level, just having someone wrapped in your arms, stroking their hair, kissing, massaging them while other people talk and laugh around you. It is about sharing a level of intimacy that moves beyond the traditional boundaries of friendship. One informant explained how she had ended up spending the night sharing her mate's boyfriend after a night clubbing: 'We were just playing around snogging and laughing. We didn't shag. It was just something to do, a way of spending time together, which meant that I didn't have to be left out, which would have happened in the past.'

Another club team I spent time with had begun by dropping Ecstasy in clubs, but now moved between clubbing and throwing parties at home with a few close friends where they'd pop some pills and just share the rush with one another. They'd strip off or dress-up (dragging the men up was a popular game), dance, massage each other, find ways to excite the senses, show off their bodies and get sexy; it was just laid-back sensual fun. This group was a close knit and supportive bunch of mates who shared a high degree of trust and openness and they were well aware of the role played by Ecstasy in deepening their relationships and allowing them to experiment with the parameters of friendship. They still valued clubbing but their clubbing practice was also subtly changing: they began dressing-up more, wearing more revealing costumes, using the freedom offered by clubs to its maximum potential.

One group had taken this experience to the next level. These friends had not only sensualised, but also sexualised their relationships with one another and they provided a particularly revealing model of how this process began:

It began once we got back from our club nights. We'd all be in a really good mood and still full of drugs. We just started playing around with one another. The Ecstasy gave you the confidence and made it seem less odd, it's a gentle drug too. We started getting off with each other; it wasn't serious. It didn't happen all at once, it was a gradual thing. It sometimes felt a bit funny; I'd be all over some girl while my partner would be wrapped round another of my friends. It felt naughty, but that just added to it. It was fun to find yourself with a woman on each arm kissing, joking around, chatting, jumping in and out of the shower, getting naked, there was no pressure. We weren't going anywhere in particular; it just developed its own momentum. Not everyone joined in; it wasn't expected; it was just going on if you fancied it. Then we started throwing parties at my place just for my friends, sometimes just a couple of people at others more of us. We had sex with another couple of mates; it was odd, exciting, but it was relaxed. We just took it easy, if it got a bit weird we'd stop and talk about it, then start again. A week or so later we met up and laughed about it. We'd all enjoyed it so we carried on, then more friends came round and we all ended up in the shower; one of the women starting grabbing willies; it took off from there. We were all drug fucked so Mr Droopy would come and go as the night progressed, but it just didn't matter, it was hysterical, but horny. I felt like I was living somebody else's life, but I wasn't it was mine and it felt excellent. It doesn't happen all the time – just say one night over the course of an occasional long weekend. It definitely grew out of the parties and the Ecstasy was important; I don't think I could have done it without the E. It just felt like a natural progression, an extension of the feelings that the drug offers and the way it makes you behave around your friends. I couldn't do the hardcore orgy thing; I think it would be too serious. This is so laid-back it's almost silly. You've got nothing to prove to anyone because they're all your friends. It's just a different way of having a good time with them, an extension of our experiences together. (Male 30, 12 years' experience)

This is an extreme example of a usually more muted phenomenon; it arises from within the sensual states offered by clubbing and as such differs from the sex club scene. It is a particular form of chemical intimacy and, as the informant above points out, it didn't start life as an idea, no one decided to throw a sex party, it arose out of cluster of sensual states that related to how individuals felt and interacted with one another. This is interesting when we relate it back to both Mauss's (1979) and Bourdieu's (1977, 1990) notion of habitus. Mauss identified the bodily element of habitus: the way in which society creates particular bodily practices and particular sensual parameters within relationships. Bourdieu expanded upon this idea and began to identify the relationship between that bodily construction and the ideas held by cultural groups through examining the way in which this physicality makes those ideas tangible as a visceral, physical and emotional form. We can see that the socio-sensual states found in clubs have altered these bodily boundaries. The body has become a plaything, it has gained a certain fluidity by being introduced to a heightened sensual world and subsequently the moral and social sensibilities of my informants have been altered via these shared experiences.

However, another informant revealed one potential downside of this chemical intimacy:

> I used to live in a house with six other people, we were best friends, did everything together, lived, worked, partied and we caned it for about four years and it was all right for a long time, but eventually it all got too weird and too intense. Incestuous if you know what I mean. We were never apart and all these tensions started to build up and the drugs magnified them. We were fucked-up constantly. We were getting paranoid and it just got really claustrophobic. We lost the ability to talk things through and in the end we had this really nasty split up and now a few years later there's still a lot of animosity associated with it. So although I think drugs can change the way you relate to people for the better I still think you have to be careful and give each other space to breathe. You have to have sober time in there and another outlet otherwise it can spin out of control, but then again that can happen to people's relationships even without any drugs, can't it? You meet some couples in particular who just seem to play stupid little power games with one another; they fuck with each other's heads and you don't really know why they're together because they seem to cause each other more pain than anything else. So maybe the drugs just magnify it and bring it all to a head. (Female 34, 18 years' experience)

So these intense levels of chemical intimacy can have a down side to them if people aren't careful. They can create relationships that are too reliant upon drugs and too introverted to the point where they become stagnant and destructive. However, as this informant points out, this may well be a property of certain relationships, rather than necessarily a property of the drugs. The inclusion of drugs simply intensifies the whole social cycle and exaggerates the internal dynamic of the relationship. People can engage in such behaviour and fail to recognise these social patterns without drugs and problems can arise in relationships just because people spend too long around one another without a break. The other groups I spoke to did not live together; they met up a few times a week, but also had very distinct and separate lives at other points. They got together for a good time, rather than living together and that stopped it all becoming too 'incestuous' and 'claustrophobic'. More importantly they didn't need to be completely out-of-it to enjoy each other's company and they were aware that they had changed over time. As one informant explained:

> My group of friends are all quite aware when we're slipping into repetition and everybody starts breaking out and escaping a bit; they get a bit of space from one another. Everyone is now aware that we've changed. We want different things so when we throw another party we'll have to take that into consideration, but we're changing as a group and I haven't really experienced that as a group before, all slightly making things change, instead of having to leave the group in order to move on. Which is great because we're developing together. (Female 30, 11 years' experience)

Sensual Morality

> You know when somebody doesn't club they have a different idea of morality. In some ways clubbers have their own morality, which is just as valid and people seem to be more open minded and tolerant, not tolerant that doesn't really come into it they just give each other the space to be themselves. (Female 32, 9 years' experience)

The morality of clubbing is not really articulated as a set of ideas. It is a morality that is derived from the socio-sensual practice of clubbing. It is more a moral sensibility than a moral philosophy. Certain moral perspectives that exist in the everyday world such as people's attitude towards sex and drugs are gradually challenged through the practices of clubbing. The Protestant-Christian moral stance that still suffuses our culture's perspective upon bodily pleasure can only condemn clubbing. Yet clubbing is so social and pleasurable that this condemnation is seen as a complete ridiculous by clubbers. They begin to disembody that morality and create alternatives. However, clubbers rarely shout their opposition to these everyday moral perspectives, instead they just challenge them through practice.

There is a moral tension between the everyday world and the world of clubs, which is particularly in evidence in the press. Celebrities are caught snorting coke and the press still attempts to impose a moral perspective upon the story, despite the fact that cocaine is endemic in the world of celebrities. Most clubbers would just laugh and suggest they would be surprised if the person involved hadn't snorted coke. Drugs are mainstream but illegal and so they generate a moral hypocrisy that is largely class based. (Nothing new there then.) In many ways we are refusing to recognise that we have become a nation of drug users, be it booze or cocaine, and this head-in-the-sand strategy creates its own problems because it imposes an outdated moral framework onto the social reality that exists in Britain today. We are a leisure culture and our attitude to and experience of pleasure has gone beyond the moral guidelines that traditionally surrounded pleasure and so made them obsolete. People are left to create their own moral frameworks because they have rejected a morality that simply denies their experiences any worth whatsoever. In the main they are doing a damned good job and if I had to sum up the basic, moral position of my informants it would be a belief that people should be allowed to do whatever they like as long as they don't harm others.

This is more of a process of sensual deproblematisation than a countermorality. So, for example, in the everyday world sex is still linked to the moral frameworks of the past (if you don't believe me check out the morning TV discussion shows) whereas my informants treated it as a sensual adventure. As this informant illustrated:

> My man and I sat down and wrote out a list of all the things we'd like to do sexually and even included some things we weren't sure about like water-sports, just so we'd give

them a go and we've been working our way through it. It's great, we've discovered a lot. Having a list and just trusting one another and being really honest about our experiences opens up a whole world. It's about experiencing these things and that list grants me a lot of freedom. It's like giving myself permission to experiment and I'm finding I'm pushing myself further sexually, just to see how far I can go, how much I can feel. (Female 28, 9 years' experience)

This informant was traversing the sexual morality of the everyday world within a relationship that had a high degree of trust and honesty about sex. Sex ceases to be soiled by immorality and becomes a species of sensual knowledge, rather like drugs that could be experimented with in order to intensify and alter the sensual parameters of this couple's sexual practices. So water-sports cease to be a problem, there's nothing immoral about them, they are simply a sensual possibility that you may or may not find enjoyable and you'll only find that out by trying them. People's attitudes towards sex have been gradually changing for years; sex is spoken about in different ways now than it was even twenty years ago, but all this 'speaking' of sex has the effect of making sex justify itself, as Foucault (1977) pointed out. This couple's relationship was not so much based on making sex 'speak', but was more in line with Elizabeth Grosz's (1995: 227) suggestion in *Space, Time and Perversion:*

> Rather, it is a refusal to link sexual pleasure with the struggle for freedom, the refusal to validate sexuality in terms of a greater cause or a higher purpose (whether political, spiritual, or reproductive), the desire to enjoy, to experience, to make pleasure for its own sake, for where it takes us, for how it changes and makes us, to see it as one but not the only trajectory or direction in the lives of sexed bodies.

My informants are not 'speaking' sex, they are simply getting on with it and by doing so they cut through the world of discourse and replace it with actual sensual practice. They challenged the morality through which the everyday world attempts to classify and label sexual practices as good or bad because as a shared sensual adventure sexual acts became 'moral' through the level of consent, honesty and trust, which suffused their relationship. My informants' sense of sharing a mutual adventure reflects back on the notion of gender equality arising in relation to sensual practice and nullifies the presumption of domination or submission, which exists in a great deal of the discourse and rhetoric that surrounds sex.

Sensual practice creates an alternative experiential platform from where the moral discourses of the everyday world can be viewed from a contrary perspective. People distance themselves from that discourse at a sensual level and that discourse ceases to 'stick' to their bodies with the same emotional force. Clubbing has played a huge role in granting people access to this level of sensual alterity that begins to manifest itself as a moral sensibility because that alterity is grounded in the social practices that arise from clubbing. The sexual experiment, set out above, grew out of the socio-sensual practices of clubbing and the levels of intimacy and trust that people experience through sharing drugs with one another. This creates a new idealised cognitive model which is a mental template based on past experience that underpins a social framework through which other sensual practices can be explored.

The sensual intensity experienced via the bodily practices of clubbing can change people's own relationship to their bodies as they begin to understand that this sensual realm can be explored like any other realm of knowledge. Clubbing can initiate this shift in perspective by deepening people's experience of the ecstatic and Dionysian rush of this sensual realm. As one informant suggested: 'Most people's morality is simply mental laziness; anything that defines how you could be living abdicates you from the responsibility of deciding how you should be living' (male 32, 14 years' experience).

Summary

Clubs offer an alternative socio-sensual environment that is grounded in a process of radical sensual intensification, which underpins an alternative set of social experiences that feel very different from the everyday social practice lodged in the habitus of our culture. Over time these experiences have become democratised, they have become mainstream. The percentage of young people in this country who have encountered them is growing rapidly as is the amount of people who have continued clubbing and made it part of their adult lives. Clubs have initiated a process of sensual change largely bereft of a specific overarching ideology and these changes are part on an on-going process that is still being worked out on the ground. Different groups use this sensual shift in different ways, they mould these experiences into a social form that suits their needs and desires. They are felt most intensely within the social relationships that make up an important part of the experience of clubbing. Whether interacting with strangers or hanging out with friends the sensual charge of clubbing reverberates within and radically alters the form and depth of these social encounters. This can be a problematic process, it has its dangers, but it also has its rewards and my informants viewed those rewards as worth the potential risks they were taking.

The bodily techniques people encounter via clubbing can escape the confines of the club space and can be woven into people's social practice in the everyday world. They grant them new perspectives upon that world that challenges the embodied logic of the habitus. This is particularly evident in notions of intimacy, gender relations and a shift in people's moral perspective upon sensual pleasure. All these things are not entirely down to clubbing they are also part of the social changes occurring in the wider everyday world. Clubbing simply provided an arena that allowed these wider ideas to become experienced as socio-sensual actualities. They were embodied and this process of embodiment created its own logic of practice that in turn generated a wider shift in social perspective amongst clubbers.

–10–

Back into the World

People often say that this or that person has not yet found himself. But the self is not something one finds, it is something one creates.

(Thomas Szasz 1973)

The trouble with the rat race is that even if you win, you're still a rat.

(Lily Tomlin)

In this chapter, I want to expand further outwards from clubs to look at the relationship between the altered body created via clubbing and some of the ideas that structure our culture's beliefs and values. These ideological and symbolic frameworks are re-experienced and reassessed by clubbing because the habitus through which we encounter and understand them is challenged. This shift generates novel emotional experiences and perspectives that grant people access to alternative practices through which they can explore these symbolic frameworks at an embodied level. This is not necessarily an act of resistance because some of the ideas such as self-identity and the notion of freedom, which people are exploring through these altered practices, are already part of our own culture's ideological framework. However, although they exist as ideas they have yet to be fully manifested as social practices and this creates a schism between the body and culture. Clubbing is testing the limits of contemporary ideology, it is making demands upon it and revealing its shortcomings because it creates social bodies that have developed their own 'habiti', which allow people to socially and sensually underwrite the possibility of experiencing these ideological forms as shared practices.

Identity

The creation of identity has become a complex phenomenon in the contemporary world. Shilling (1993: 181) suggests that:

In traditional societies, identities were received automatically through ritual practices which connected people and their bodies to the reproduction of long established social positions. High modernity, though, makes self-identity *deliberative* (Lyotard 1984). The self is no longer seen as a homogeneous, stable core which resides within the individual (Shils 1981). Instead, identities are formed reflexively through the asking of questions and the continual reordering of self-narratives which have at their centre a concern with the body (Giddens 1991). Self identity and the body become 'reflexively organized projects' which have to be sculpted from the complex plurality of choices offered by high modernity without moral guidance as to which should be selected.

The question 'who the hell am I' has gained unprecedented prominence within our culture. The idea of being yourself, being different from others, being unique plays a hugely important role within contemporary Western ideology. Identity used to be inextricably linked to a culture's social and symbolic frameworks. It was given to us. The symbolic order mirrored the social hierarchy and for the vast majority of people their place and classification within that system was set at birth. Self-identity was not really an issue; people were of course different, but that difference did not underpin the idea of choice and movement or the opportunity to mould yourself into an individual who created their own social and symbolic allegiances and defined themselves as a singular entity that they themselves had created. This is why Lyotard (1984) called identity 'deliberative'; you have to work it out for yourself from within a shifting field of possible symbols, ideological perspectives and social allegiances. We believe in individuality as an idea, but we have never really been taught how to be individuals because the practices and social frameworks that could cater for a society of individuals still largely evade us.

The tension that exists between the individual and the wider social world, that split between 'being and nothingness' explored by Sartre (1993), creates points of confusion in terms of the actual practice of being an individual. Where are you yourself? At work? At home? In your shed? Well you are yourself all the time because that self is actually comprised of selves, 'multiple drafts' (Dennett 1993), held together through the body by which they are lived. This is the stabilising power of Damasio's 'proto-self'; it is the body that links these alternative selves, alternative narratives and alternative modes of social presentation together into an enduring self-image. As Damasio (1999: 225) explains:

> The rich imaginings of our mind do prepare "multiple drafts" for our organism's life script – to place the idea in the framework proposed by Daniel Dennett. Yet, the shadows of the deeply biological core self and the autobiographical self that grows under its influence constantly propitiate the selection of "drafts" that accord with a single unified self.

These selves are labelled in two ways either internally by the individual or externally by the social world. We have seen that many of the external labels such as job, class and even names, that Sartre (1993) identified as being antithetical to individuality, have much less force in clubs, which already makes clubs one step removed from the surrounding social world on a symbolic level.

There are moments when we feel more like ourselves and, as we have seen, clubbing offers such an experience for many people. The body of clubbing has shifted beyond the social and emotional constraints of the habitus and become more expressive. It has become part of a social world that has its own rules surrounding that expressivity. People's work-selves and home-selves are replaced by a leisure-self and as Paul Willis (1990: 15) points out in relation to this world of leisure:

> In many ways 'leisure' is now a wholly inadequate term to encompass these meanings. It simply cannot contain or invoke the sense of the massive symbolic investment now placed in free time and the ways in which it is used to explore transitional stages in growing older and to make and internalize new identities.

The process of internalising new identities is not simply symbolic; it arises from creating and experiencing new practices through which people negotiate their social realm and there is a recognisable pattern that captured many of my informants' experiences of clubbing and its impact on their own sense of identity. This pattern also explains the way in which the club scene has changed over the years. It started out as raves and people were simply ravers, but over the years it gradually splintered into a myriad of different forms, partly for commercial purposes, but also because people wanted to mark themselves out from the mass of clubbers. (See Thornton 1995 for a more in-depth discussion of this process.) People's initial identification with a group of clubbers through the classifications of music, fashion, ethnicity, sexual orientation and class is often only a symbolic catalyst; the first step in redefining the self and it has its limits, as Cas Wouters explains:

> There is a greater tendency amongst these emancipatory generations to seek individual self-fulfilment and self-realisation in groups or in social movements. In that respect the strongly individualistic tendencies one encounters here have a very different character from that presented by political or cultural liberalism. [And therefore] . . . the restraints which life in groups imposes on the individuals are apt to thwart again and again the imaginary hopes for individual freedom. (In Gleichmann 1977: 444)

However, Wouter's presumes that these groups are formed to create shared identities and so mirror the structure of a cultural grouping. He doesn't contemplate the creation of informal social groupings that have no shared symbolic allegiances or ideological frameworks, but only shared practices which make them capable of supporting higher levels of individual expression and experimentation. Many of my informants started out in particular styles of club, but had gradually moved on from being part of a recognised scene to inhabiting smaller groups in which they felt they could be themselves, as one informant explained: 'Clubs allow you to experience unity, to celebrate it, to have respect for it. However, this is a unity that is amplified through individuality' (Male 33, 20 years' experience).

They gradually refined their experience of clubbing until symbolic allegiances were replaced by experiential criteria. The party became more important than the labels and my informants began to express more and more of themselves and display less and less devotion to these symbolic codes. In its most extreme manifestation this leads to club spaces in which nobody looks like anybody else, so identifying with a particular style was all but impossible. Such a night is focused around the expression of individuality in any way people damned well please. The only expectation the night and the people make of you is that you will make an effort to make the party. How you choose to express yourself is your business and the rules of presentation that operate in the wider social sphere are shattered. These practices generate a space in which people can be themselves in a crowd and they can subsequently build upon this feeling to explore that self and try out new variations based upon novel presentations. The question of: 'Who am I?' ceases to be an existential problem because it becomes a social experiment based in creative practices that move the ontological or hidden-self to the surface of the body where it can be revealed.

These experiences are accumulative, they build within the body as people gain more confidence in clubs; how far this window of opportunity is pushed depends upon the clubbers themselves. For some the sense of alterity uncovered through the practice of clubbing is different enough to satisfy their desires. For others that sense of alterity becomes a point of departure from the constraints of the everyday world, which allows them to not only experience a feeling of liberation, but to also develop upon and explore the properties of this liberated-self and so expand upon the sensual and expressive parameters of their identity. The construction of identity becomes an ongoing creative project aimed towards the creation of a sense of personal and social authenticity. The identities created are fluid, rather than fixed, in that they are grounded in practices, rather than signs. As such, they are founded upon experiences and the creation of emotional and sensual narratives memorialised through the body. Their final resting place is within that body, within its emotional memory system, its social reality and its practices. Identity is gradually created from the bottom up, rather than the top down and these seductive narratives begin to suffuse a person's being and generate a framework of corporeal and visceral knowledge that becomes a lived posture in the world.

Capitalism and Consumption

Clubbing's relationship to capitalism and the consumer realm is interesting for a number of reasons. It is, of course, an arena of consumption, but it is what is actually consumed that makes it intriguing because clubbers walk away from a club night with only their experiences, memories, stories and hangovers to show for all the money they've spent. The tautological reality that lies behind this 'experiential consumption' (Malbon 1999) is that in the last instance it is the clubbers themselves who have created these experiences, they must produce the club and make the night happen and they are being forced to pay through their noses for that privilege. Paying a great deal of money to get into a club in no way guarantees a good time; in fact it simply increases the chance that you'll walk away feeling ripped off because you expect too much from the club and too little from yourself.

Thornton (1995) points out that clubbing is set within the system of symbolic capitalism so that people use it to mark themselves out and generate their 'subcultural capital'. However, this wasn't clubbing's most important role for my informants. The growing role of 'experiential consumption' in contemporary consumption, which covers clubbing as well as such activities as holidays, sports, drug taking, prostitution and gambling indicates a shift away from signs in favour of experiences.

Contemporary capitalism has seized the realm of signs and made it its own. Baudrillard (1998) suggested that semiotics was contemporary capitalism and it has created a surfeit of signs, which provide the major markers when creating social distinctions and group identities. We are supposed to believe that the objects and goods we buy will mark us out as individuals – that they have social worth – and marketing has become inextricably linked to the notion of lifestyle. Companies want us to identify with their goods and imbue them with this worth, but this symbolic realm is inherently transient because it is set within the changing world of fashion.

All cultures create symbolic frameworks in the form of totems, social hierarchies, rituals, system of gender and religions. However, these structures are granted their power via the subcutaneous force of the habitus, which imbues them with a taken-for-granted status that suffuses the flesh at an emotional level and invests those frameworks with an embodied depth. The signs created by consumer goods create only temporary and fleeting allegiances, which make them an ethereal codification of the social realm. One minute you're in, the next you're out and this slipperiness largely precludes any sense of stability or permanency. What I am suggesting is a schism between body and sign; a growing sense of disorientation grounded in the accelerated disintegration of the sign world, recognised by post-modern theorists such a Lyotard (1984) and Baudrillard (1998) amongst others.

However, the process of 'experiential consumption' creates another option that resists the overloading and subsequent disintegration of the sign world through practice. It is the body, rather than the world of signs, which becomes the final site of individual and group authenticity as people attempt to inscribe a socio-sensual narrative into their flesh. Rather than defining themselves through signs they define themselves through actions, moments, memories, stories and experiences, which make up the actual practice of inhabiting their world at a corporeal level. Consumption is at least partially rejected in favour of production as people's devotion to that little Versace number is replaced by an allegiance to what they actually got up to while wearing it. 'Experiential consumption' is a growing feature of our consumer world because shopping for symbolic capital simply isn't a potent and rewarding enough experience to allow people to embody their own culture in a meaningful way.

Shopping has given way to grazing in the contemporary world, it has become bovine in that people just wander through it spending their money on what happens to be there, rather than on things that they really truly want. One informant suggested that:

A lot of how we're taught to live is basically Pavlovian; we're taught to consume. Too often we press the bell and things arrive without no real effort or thought on our part, but the best pleasures are hard won and challenging; you have to put a lot into them; simple consumption isn't satisfying enough. (Male 32, 14 years' experience)

With the rise of the disposable income shopping moved from being analogous to hunting, where people saved up for special things that they felt real satisfaction from buying, to a gatherer activity, where people just graze on whatever's there. (Except in the case of bargain hunters who get to feel like they scored a point or two over the world of consumption.) Consumption is becoming boring; it is just not a big enough rush, its satisfactions are being eroded and consumers themselves are gradually questioning the whole realm. (However, its demise is a long, long way off because becoming bored with it is itself a luxury created through experiencing a surfeit.)

Experiential consumers are not predominantly seeking to surround themselves with the symbolic accoutrements of capital although experiential consumption cannot escape this realm entirely because of its all pervasive grip upon modern culture. They want to create a life that feels passionate and exciting, they want to immerse themselves in extreme experiences, social networks and sensual groupings that reflect and fulfil their own desires. They want to feel the world and through that feeling construct a body that knows it has lived. Imagine for a moment the legendary moment of death when your whole life flashes before your eyes. Experiential consumers want that flashback to be filled with experiences, rather than objects, with people, rather than things because the symbolic world of contemporary consumption cannot ensure that this near death encounter will be a rush, rather than an Ikea dominated whimper.

This form of consumption is only now becoming a large-scale possibility because the body itself has been freed from the constraints of the habitus that closed off the sensual realm through moral frameworks. The advent of drugs, travel, extreme sports, and so on, has heralded new bodily potentials, new degrees of experience that have altered the way we perceive of pleasure. It is the social aspect of clubbing that stands out in this realm of experience because people are buying a particular social encounter: a certain way of interacting with people that allows them to savour others and enjoy their presence. In the face of our fragmented communities these spaces provide the foundation for social experiences that temporarily transcend the urban environment. Clubbers are buying little more than a space and a sound-system when they club because it is up to them to create this vibe for themselves. A free party is the only radical option and they were largely hunted down and destroyed early on in the game. As Vaneigem (1983: 7) suggests 'Illicit pleasures are banned until they become profitable.'

Clubbers, then, are creating a meaningful body in the face of a symbolic world that is choking on its own excesses. Advertisers are increasingly attempting to access the realm of the body to grant worth to their products. Game consoles exhort you to play-more; pasta-sauces have adverts set in clubs as do many other products; ice cream tries to pass itself off as the seven deadly sins; biscuit manufacturers resort to philosophical treaties to justify having a break from the grindstone and energy drinks promise to 'give you wings' (and so get you high), even if you'll never fly as high on them as you will on cocaine. Advertisers, as usual, are ahead of the game by offering a vicarious link to the fleshy world of passionate experience through their products. Advertisers prey on people's dreams, desires and aspirations and link them to products that can never play a role in fulfilling them. They must increasingly try to insert their products into the sensually amplified body of leisure and avoid association with the 'stale bodies', which exist at the centre of culture. They are attempting to hijack the flesh to make themselves part of a world that only humans can create and people don't need anything, but each other to create it. It is not enough that we recognise a logo – we must somehow be persuaded to live that logo by associating it with the things we really enjoy. They face a problem though because wearing Nike doesn't mean you'll ever know what sport feels like and it is up to the individual to fulfil the claims made, by the advertisers, by getting off their arses and creating those experiences for themselves. The body is granting meaning to the sign and not vice-versa and I certainly met clubbers who recognised this and decided that they didn't need those signs after all. As one informant revealed when describing what she thought could ever replace clubbing in her life:

> There's religion and dangerous sports. I can't do religion, but I'm learning how to rock climb and that's an interesting culture, there are lots of people I meet who are clubbers and thrill seekers. A life without passion, a life of complete sedateness and normality that would destroy me. I would rather be dead and buried as far as I'm concerned. So if anything replaces clubbing it would be have to be passionate, some kind of extreme sport

or travelling or real love, nothing else really appeals. I don't want to end up just watching telly and going to work and filling my flat with things that just gather dust. (Female 32, 9 years' experience)

So consumer goods are reduced to 'things that gather dust', whilst experience is seen as a goal in itself, which possesses the capacity to suffuse a life with passion and worth.

Freedom

Through entering clubs people experience a sense of freedom, but we must be careful when dealing with the notion of freedom in relation to the club environment, as one promoter explained to me early on during this study:

I don't think people who are working all week and go out on the weekend, meet a mate in a pub, have a few beers, go to a club, have a few more drinks and whatever drug is available and then get a cab home, I don't think they see it in terms of freedom. It's part of getting nutted. It's a basic sense of freedom, but I don't think they would write it down as freedom. They don't realise it's something they can do with their time and their life, but they wouldn't label it as freedom. They would label it as getting NUTTED. A sense of not worrying about things and when you're standing in the middle of a dance floor sweating your arse off that's how you feel. (Male 27, 11 years' experience)

The freedom found in clubs is more akin to 'letting your hair down' than an act of revolutionary resistance, yet people value this experience, they desire it. So when we speak of freedom in clubs we must think of it as a sensual state that arises from a liberated body and an altered style of social interaction. However, even this temporary sense of freedom can alter people's perspectives on their own lives and allow them to embody the idea of freedom that is part of our culture's ideological make up.

In *Fear of Freedom*, Erich Fromm (1991) makes a distinction between the notions of 'freedom from' and 'freedom to'. 'Freedom from' relates to the process of political change, the overcoming of tyranny. 'Freedom to' is a more subtle construct – it relates to people's ability to actually recognise and seize the freedoms they have won, but that the habitus of their own culture may still conceal from view by keeping them outside of practice. As Fromm (1991: 217) suggests:

Modern man seems, if anything, to have too many wishes and his only problem seems to be that, although he knows what he wants, he cannot have it. All our energy is spent for the purpose of getting what we want, and most people never question the premise of this activity: that they know their true wants. They do not stop to think whether the aims they are pursuing are something they themselves want.

At an ideological level the Western world prides itself on the levels of freedom enjoyed by its people, but Bourdieu (1977, 1990) has shown us how the bodies of those people carry within them the sensual and ideological limits of that society and they are predisposed to reconstruct the social world in which they are immersed. As he explains:

> The habitus, a product of history, produces individual and collective practices-more history-in accordance with the schemes generated by history. It ensures the active presence of past experiences, which, deposited in each organism in the form of schemes of perception, thought and action, tend to guarantee the 'correctness' of practices and their constancy over time, more reliably than all formal rules and explicit norms. (Bourdieu 1990: 54)

The shift in habitus that can arise from clubbing alters people's perception of what they actually want from the world. They glimpse alternative 'wants' and so re-order their perception of self in relation to these newly discovered 'wants', rather than in relation to the wants, desires and socially sanctioned trajectories, which reside in the habitus. These new 'wants' are in themselves socio-sensual modalities in that they arise out of the knowledge of how people want their worlds, their relationships, their jobs and their lives to feel at an embodied level. My informants had then set about creating worlds that fulfilled these 'wants' and desires even when away from clubs. These new 'wants' are resisted by the everyday world. Consumer capitalism is built upon its ability to create consumer desires; it must induce a constant state of discontentment that keeps us buying ever more stuff in an attempt to satiate our consumer hunger. If we were to reject this hunger and replace it with alternative desires, then the whole edifice would begin to collapse. There is a tension at play between individual desires and the concerns of our culture as that culture must instil its needs into each generation. Hence, Westerners are taught to want consumer goods at earlier and earlier stages in their lives. However, clubbing generates social 'wants' as much as consumer 'wants' and it allows people to focus on the primacy of social practice as a source of pleasure, enjoyment and fulfilment, rather than the symbolic realm of consumption. It is not that clubbers abandon consumption after all clubs are arenas of consumption in themselves. It is more that they develop new desires that are not necessarily consumer based because they arise from alternative forms of social practice that allow them to explore new social modalities out of which they derive a sense of satisfaction and meaning from people, rather than things.

The dog-eat-dog ideology of capitalism, which generates an embodied metaphor that structures the way we perceive of our relationship to each other is challenged. The everyday world dismisses these new social desires and ICMs by labelling them escapist, naïve and immature because they challenge the preferred social model that dominates capitalism; namely the model of an individual striving for wealth, success and fame, which isolates the individual and sets them against others. However, if we are not free to create our own models of social practice, then we will never experience freedom. Instead we will always be trapped within the metaphors of capitalism that stress the primacy of acquisition over shared social experience.

At an Alternative Miss World event that I attended, the contestants were asked what they would do for the world if they were crowned. The clubby crowd erupted *en masse* and demanded: 'free drugs and sex on the streets'. They weren't joking. Although we possess 'freedom from' we are only just beginning to comprehend 'freedom to' because that 'freedom to' is a social practice, rather than a political ideology.

We live in and are increasingly dominated by a hyper-rationalised world in which our allegiance to the notion of reason and reasonable behaviour has begun to move beyond a stress on the antisocial to become part of the fabric of our lives and the contemporary habitus. Bourdieu (1998: 90–1) suggests that:

> This makes the progress of reason without doubt go hand in hand with the development of highly rationalized forms of domination . . . it also creates a situation in which sociology, alone in a position to bring these mechanisms to light, must choose, now more than ever, between putting its rational instruments of knowledge at the service of an increasingly rational domination, or rationally analyzing domination and especially the contribution that rational knowledge can make to domination.

Clubbing exists outside of this framework of rational control and domination, which views its sensual intensity as a health risk. This rational authority could never understand how staying up all night, taking drugs, dancing, laughing and falling about with your friends could possibly relate to the rationalised body they want to dominate the modern world. Clubbing is too risky, too messy and disordered to be granted anything other than aberrant status. However, as one informant suggested: 'Clubbing's quite an animal experience, quite carnal, but in the best possible sense in that it's physical and intense, but it's the more positive side of that animal experience. It's not violence. It's just people trying to enjoy themselves and share that with other people' (male 34, 17 years' experience).

Obviously the use of the term 'animal' is loaded, but the point this informant is trying to make is that this animal body can be unleashed within social frameworks that have been constructed to cater for its existence. Dance clubs, sex clubs, dress-up clubs, drug clubs and even fight clubs structure our carnality and socialise it. The everyday rational world may never understand why you need to dance until you drop, fuck in public, dress-up as a go-go dancer or imbibe copious amounts of drugs with other people, but in terms of actually experiencing the 'freedom to' live our lives beyond the internal and external constraints that operate in the social sphere they appear to be both increasingly popular and important experiences for many people, despite the health risks involved. A desire to live temporarily overcomes the fear of death stressed by medical authorities and the notion that longevity is a goal in itself is abandoned.

The sense of freedom found in club spaces is created through shared consent: a determination to let people do what they want as long as they don't hurt anyone else. It is not a political ideology but a social practice that tests the limits of our presumed freedoms. It is not antisocial but hyper-social in that it moves beyond the social constraints that order the 'acceptable' world and replaces them with an alternative sociality grounded in passion, which challenges the taken-for-granted beliefs that underpin the whole notion of acceptability.

For example, in the sex club scene the notion that monogamy is the only moral framework for a relationship is scorned. (Although I've never heard anyone on that scene belittle the notion of love.) These clubbers refuse to believe that people should treat each other as possessions, so denying those possessions a sensual life of their own. They also happily admit that moving beyond monogamy isn't an easy thing to do and suggest that both partners can only achieve this movement if there are high levels of trust and emotional maturity in the relationship. Jealousies must be combated, insecurities faced and fear confronted in order to create a new model for sexual relationships in which desire is unshackled from its internal emotional constraints and the cultural weight of sexual monogamy, especially in marriage.

The shared environment of the sex club allowed people to create a social framework that could cope with sharing sexual partners. Everyone knew the rules, there were no false expectations raised when having sex with other people; you weren't trying to make them your partner – you simply wanted to make them cum. You could enjoy watching your partner having sex with other people; you could savour their pleasure because the social expectations housed within the space reassured you and helped hold any negative emotions in check. You were granting them their sexual freedom and this deeply embodied freedom resonates more potently than the idea of freedom that operates within the sphere of Western ideology. 'Freedom to' can only exist as a social practice; the claim to freedom held within Western ideology is being tested on the ground and these practices of freedom are often met with resistance by the authorities, which appeal to rationality and morality to control this liberation of desire.

Meaning in a Meaningless World

People have developed a healthy disrespect towards the old institutions; they see politics as sleazy; they don't believe in God; they feel like capitalism's corrupt and playing them for fools; they're losing their respect for authority. (Male 34, 17 years' experience)

The perspective articulated above is a particularly concise version of a wider view that is best seen as a sense of disillusionment towards 'old institutions', which generates a certain confusion or uncertainty akin to a loss of faith in people's lives. Shilling (1993: 180) suggests that: 'There has been a massive shrinkage of space occupied by religious authorities in modernity. This has undermined the ability of societies to provide people with meaning systems which allow them to deal with death.'

He continues by claiming that high modernity or postmodernity, call it what you will, has:

> Swept away '*all* traditional types of social order, in quite unprecedented fashion' (Giddens 1990: 4). High modernity has radicalized these changes even further in terms of the sheer pace of change, the scope of change and the nature of modern institutions. By undermining traditional meaning systems, the conditions of high modernity stimulate within people a heightened reflexivity about life, meaning and death. (Shilling 1993: 181)

Shilling's assertion allows us to locate clubbing in a world in which problems of meaning have increased and become imbued with a 'heightened reflexivity'. Clubbing is one example of a field of practice in which problems of meaning are being reconfigured in such a way that, rather than remaining ideological or exist-ential problems, they become bodily negotiations with the world.

The basic distinction I am making here is between meaning that is embedded in the ideas, ideologies and symbols of culture and meaningfulness that arises from the emotional and embodied connections people make between themselves and their worlds. There is obviously an overlap between these two systems since ideo-logical beliefs must be embodied if they are to gain any emotional force in the world. Yet, as LeDoux (1999: 19) explains: 'connections from the emotional systems to the cognitive systems are stronger than connections from the cognitive systems to the emotional systems.'

The process of embodying ideas will be virtually impossible if there is no emot-ional connection to those ideas that grants them a sensual life.

A whole meaning industry has been generated through consumer symbols, self-help books, new-age spiritual beliefs, single-issue political movements and self-care regimes that in turn gives rise to a plethora of often conflicting ideological perspectives themselves open to the vagaries of fashion. As the symbolic and ideological world becomes more and more transient people are attempting to immerse themselves into the world in ways that suffuse their bodies with a sense of meaningfulness. Meaning is a property of the body more than it is a property of words or ideas, it is a posture in the world, a sensual orientation that permeates the symbolic and grants it a fleshy and emotive third dimension.

The body of clubbing is lived as meaningful in two ways. Firstly, it feels more passionate, alive and social than the constricted, urbanised body through which people live their everyday lives. Secondly, it allows people to experience a sense of self that, as we have seen, fulfils some of the ideological beliefs of our own culture that have yet to develop into fully fledged social practices in that culture's everyday manifestation. This sense of socio-sensual location in the world creates a particular co-ordinate within a person's embodied map of their own passage through that world, which exists outside of the bodily constraints of the Apollonian habitus in terms of its lived intensity. This sensual co-ordinate must be brought into alignment with people's other experiences of their world that form further co-ordinates in that sensual map. These alternate realms of practice are gradually woven together to create a sensual landscape, which provides an embodied back-drop out of which people's perspective upon their own lived relationship to their world will arise and be suffused with meaning.

You can draw an analogy here to the world of ritual practice. In many rituals the socio-sensual world of participants is intensified and moved beyond their everyday experience of the world. This socio-sensual shift grants people access to the divine; it allows them to embody that divine world and experience it as a sensual reality that refreshes the lived power of the cosmological and moral world that surrounds the ritual. However, in a world that has largely abandoned religion and stresses the importance of the individual this intensified body has become a secular construct that manifests itself as a leisure option, which can allow people to embody the social and symbolic allegiances that they themselves have created. In social terms it isn't culture that is refreshed through clubbing, but rather the friendship networks through which people club and their own occupation of the world. Ritual shows us that these extreme bodies have played a role in constructing and consolidating the meaning of cultural and cosmological worlds for many thousands of years by providing the social mechanism through which they could be embodied. Clubbing plays a similar role, but in a radically altered social and cultural setting that denies this intense body any meaning or social worth. However, these extreme bodies can still provide access to a lived sense of meaningfulness on a much smaller social scale by creating experiences that move people beyond the sterile body of the everyday world and suffusing their lives with a sense of passion.

Problems can arise for clubbers when clubbing is the only meaningful co-ordinate in that landscape. Then their relationship to the space and the drugs can become desperate because it is all they have in their lives that feels right. However, for my informants the altered social practices, styles of communication and modes of participation, which they had learnt through clubbing had moved beyond clubs and played an important role in allowing them to create further points of connection to the world. It had pervaded their relationships, their work lives and their per-spectives upon the world. It had created new desires and new 'wants', which re-orientated their relationships to the ideological frameworks in which they were immersed. The most important element of this process was the continued focus upon the primacy of the social to grant their lives meaning, rather than continually judging themselves in relation to the symbolic realm of culture. One informant summed up this shift when I asked him what he thought the meaning of life was: 'The meaning of life, well I'd say that it lay somewhere between sociality and creativity. They're the things that feel most meaningful to me anyway' (Male 31, 13 years' experience).

This is the meaningfulness of practice of continually striving to create a life from the bottom up, rather than clinging to the top-down processing imposed by culture. It is not based on an allegiance to any particular ideological or symbolic framework to grant the world meaning; these are of secondary importance. Neither does it completely preclude culture, people just engage with it from a sensual viewpoint that isn't completely enclosed by it because they have experienced alternative practices that have thrown its taken-for-granted status into relief.

One female informant explained her attitude to work in these terms:

> Well money's ceased to be the be all and end all of work for me. Obviously I need enough to live on, but I wouldn't necessarily take a job that paid more money if I didn't think that the people and the atmosphere would be all right that's more important than the money. After all you spend a long time at work so I want to work somewhere that I can actually enjoy that time and I get on with the people I'm working with and work on things that I can get interested in and excited about.

Now compare this to Paul Willis's (1990: 16) assertion that: 'In the world of work, the managerial and public world of formal relations, people are treated like objects.'

My informant no longer wants her work life to immerse her in a hierarchy that treats her as an object and demands that she treats others in a similar way. She wants her work to be socially fulfilling, rather than working and then trying to seize a social life for herself at the weekend. Another informant suggested that: 'Having known the degree of pleasure that you can experience in this world. It changes the way you approach work' (Male 32, 16 years' experience).

It changes our perception of work because it challenges the social practices that underpin the cultural iconography and hierarchical determinism of the workspace. People want to draw the sense of social satisfaction they encounter through clubbing back into that space. They are happy to work – they are just tired of the division between their work and leisure worlds and the cultural emphasis placed upon the worth and importance of work in relation to that leisure.

This shift in perspective upon work is not simply a product of clubbing. There is a wider social perspective that 'there must be something besides work', which arises out of the feeling of 'staleness' that is part of the highly controlled body of work. The perspective of clubbers comes from the other end of the physical spectrum from within a body that has tasted the socio-sensual liberation of clubbing and they view work from the perspective of that experience. This body is imbued with a sense of meaningfulness that is partially derived from having participated in the experience of clubbing. The starting points of reassessing work may be different, but the results are similar – changing career, downsizing, self-employment in order to make work more personally, socially and creatively satisfying.

Money ceases to be an end in itself; it becomes a creative tool that will allow people to build their own world and they want that world to feel radically different from their current everyday experience. They want to move beyond the socio-sensual boundaries that underpin the limits of this experience and relate to the world sensuously, rather than symbolically to become participants, rather than passengers, active agents, rather than voyeurs.

Shilling (1993) asserts that the body has become a project in the modern world and I would expand upon this idea by suggesting that the body has become the site of meaningfulness in that world. People's lived bodily practice generates and constrains their sense of both individual and social authenticity in the face of the contemporary world's ideological confusion. The altered sensual parameters discovered through the practices of clubbing expand upon this process by opening up realms of socio-sensual experience, which feel more deeply embodied and authentic than other aspects of people's lives. The subsequent sense of meaningfulness that people derive from these experiences is created from the 'bottom up' so that it suffuses participant's emotional memories. They create practices and bodies that anchor them in the world at a social and corporeal level and this point of anchorage offers a sense of social, sensual and emotional assurance in the face of the world's ideological and symbolic confusion.

As the power of religion wanes our perspective upon life and death is altered. People no longer think they will enter the eternity of either heaven or hell and life is seen as being finite, which alters our perspective upon both the future and the present. They want to live now, in the present, they want to seize life and savour it whenever possible because they know they're going to be a long time dead. The death of God has entirely altered people's relationship to the world at an embodied level. The practices that orientated them towards a religious eternity have lost their power to create meaning and grant succour to people in times of pain and hardship. Real people and real pleasure are replacing God because they provide lived and tangible points of connection to the world out of which a lived sense of meaningfulness arises. Yet, we live in a culture that is deeply suspicious of pleasure and refuses to grant it any real social worth. It discounts pleasure as escapist, immoral and unworthy of serious attention, it refuses to recognise that God has gone and that people feel its absence and they are attempting to live their lives without that

God. It is religion that is escapist because it refuses to allow humans to stand on their own two feet and live entirely human lives in all their confusion, doubt and impermanence. This is not an easy transition to make; religious practice played a huge role in structuring the Western habitus and replacing it with alternative practices that carry the same sort of social and moral power is a complex social problem.

People are creating their own altered habitus, rather than simply accepting the habitus of the culture in which they are embedded. This sensual freedom challenges and partially erases the body transmitted to them by culture, but that culture will resist this transference of sensual allegiances and attempt to re-impose itself, even when people are seeking ways to fulfil that culture's own ideological premises. As this sensual slippage is based on practices it is only through the continued creation of alternative practices that it can sustain its existence within the body.

–11–

Conclusion

To say yes to life is no longer a dream imprisoned in endless sleep awaiting one millenarian night. The economic priority is ceding to the primacy of desires for life. Slowly now, then faster, round me, round every individual in search of autonomy, whirls the collective life-force's shuttlecock, weaving the old world's winding sheet.

(Vaneigem 1983: 39)

Throughout Western history the urges, desires and passions of the flesh have been treated with suspicion. Subsequently the social and moral frameworks that surrounded the body stressed discipline and constraint suffusing that body with a moral depth, which made it a unique social object that was ordered internally by the habitus and externally by the gaze. As the power of Protestant-Christian morality receded it was replaced by a new philosophy of health, which translated that older morality into the rationalised scientific language of the twentieth century. The body remained problematic within this new medical cosmology of restraint that denied sensual excess any value or worth.

As the 'civilising process' imposed new internal and external constraints upon our bodies people began to feel stale and monochromatic, drained of passion, trapped within the physical boundaries of the habitus and denied any form of social expression. Despite our culture's wealth, its security, its claims to individualism and freedom, people still felt discontented. In comparison to the rest of the world Westerners were lucky but they didn't feel it. They perceived themselves as trapped, rather than liberated, a mode of perception that arose from their own stifled flesh and manifested itself as a nagging urge for more. Although people did not want to return to violence to grant their lives passion, they did want a way of challenging the sense of constraint they felt within their own bodies. Waves of experimentation during which the dominant habitus was challenged came and went. The arrival of cocaine in the 1920s, dope in the 1950s and LSD in the 1960s all generated novel periods of socio-sensual experimentation that caused the moral panics of their times. Each of these waves was bigger than the last and eventually Ecstasy took these bodily extremes beyond the confines of the bohemian world and out into the mainstream because it was such a profoundly social drug that could be easily incorporated into the increasingly important sphere of leisure. All over the country

Cinderella-Rockafellas died a swift death and rave swept through both the suburbs and the cities. The flesh had slipped its leash and hedonism was the order of the day and in the process dancing became acceptable again particularly for men, which in turn changed the music we listened to and the way we experienced it. The boundaries of the night were expanded and people got use to seeing the sun rising to the beat of a pumping tune. They felt alive in a way that their own supposedly freedom-loving culture could not fulfil.

A new perspective upon pleasure arose from those beginnings and novel social experiments created new spaces in which those pleasures could be shared. The drugs changed, the music changed, styles of clubbing came and went, but the party continued. The realm of intense socio-sensual practice was democratised and seized back from the rich and the titled who had guarded it as their own particular social preserve hidden behind a veil of hypocrisy that condemned with one hand and voraciously seized with the other. This was the aristocratic realm of elaborate royal parties, courtly intrigues, wealthy libertines and perverse bishops who were all safely hidden from the public gaze that controlled the rest of the populace. Their power and wealth brought them the invisibility to indulge in the same fleshy, carnal and supposedly immoral pleasures that they condemned in the poor.

People began to invest ever more of themselves into their pleasures, including their money, their time and their sense of self. They cast off the Victorian frigidity and moral hypocrisy that had kept pleasure beyond reach. The cat was out of the bag; pleasure was not immoral – in fact it felt meaningful, it added something to their lives, it revitalised them by shattering the social and bodily constraints that ordered their everyday existence. They experienced new emotions, discovered new ways of communicating with one another and realised that the body could feel more than they had ever been led to believe. These socio-sensual experiments aren't always pretty: people fuck-up, lives are shattered, mistakes are made as the process of learning about the social and individual nature of these pleasures are explored. The medical, legal and governmental establishment offered no guidance, just moral condemnation and the taint of irrationality, they wished that the body would behave and climb back into the shackles from which it had escaped.

We have had to discover the limits of these pleasures for ourselves, their dangers, their pitfalls, their traps and their downsides. We have learnt from the mistakes of the past so that we have largely rejected the esoteric interpretations of the hippies, the nihilism of punk, even the initial hedonistic fervour that rave unleashed. We have become pragmatic about our pleasures and in the process their importance has grown; they have become normalised and mainstream, even if the powers-that-be remain resolute in their refusal to recognise this simple fact. Taking drugs, dancing all night, wearing rubber knickers, getting spanked, having sex with strangers, beering-it-up and swinging in the suburbs have all become part of an alternate definition of us. This is a sensual definition grounded in practice rather than ideology; it doesn't resist, but rather ignores. It is a naughty, giggly, chaotic world that nevertheless underpins a radical shift in the sensual fabric of this country.

The nature of hedonism has changed; pleasure in itself is not the greatest good, instead sharing pleasure with others has replaced that individualistic stance. We have moved from the private furtive pleasures of wanking to the public shared realm of the orgy. Through clubs, through the Internet and through word of mouth we have begun to realise that a pleasure shared is a pleasure intensified; it draws people together and creates novel social groupings grounded in the morality of consent.

The search for and sharing of sensual pleasure is rarely granted any value as an activity in our culture because it involves people in practices such as drinking, drugging, sex and even certain forms of music and dancing, which all lie outside of its rational and moral framework. The fact that sharing pleasure is a powerful social force that binds people together has been largely ignored in favour of a condemnation of the activities that make up that pleasure itself. Clubs allow people to access the social in a way that doesn't exist anywhere else in our culture, which in itself makes them important because we exist in a society in which the experience of community is crumbling.

Capitalism does not need society, it does not need the family and it does not need friendship because all it needs is consumers. So it attempts to persuade us that it alone can fulfil our needs and desires by filling our lives with things that can be bought, rather than people who usually come free in monetary terms, but are expensive in terms of a social investment. Objects are sanitary and uncomplicated, they link us to the world vicariously, they don't turn up drunk at two o'clock in the morning, they don't make demands upon us and they don't need a shoulder to cry on, frustrate us, confuse us, flirt with our girlfriends or drive us mad. As the civilising process exerts its rational, emotionless and frigid power over the contemporary world we are becoming less and less able to deal with the emotional chaos that is part of human relations. (Hence pet lovers and collectors.) We are beginning to treat people as objects and expecting them to behave like objects. Clubbing on the other hand is the benign face of human passion; a sensually extreme, messy and uncomplicated environment based on everybody having a laugh. It allows us to enjoy strangers and relish our friends because we see them at their best and it creates a social experience wherein the majority of people are trying to get along with one another by actively being friendly. People are no longer expected to live the sanitised life of an object.

The shared pleasures of clubbing generated a sensual backdrop that radically altered the way we socialised, related to and communicated with one another. The drugs diminished clubbers' sense of fear, insecurity and self-consciousness to the point where they were able to socialise with each other in ways that matched their aspirations as to how their social relations should feel. The club environment managed to turn this aspirational ideal into practice. This is most obvious within the club space itself, but the social practice of clubbing managed to spread beyond clubs and out into our everyday lives.

In the process it remoulded the bodies connection to the culture in which it was embedded and introduced a fluidity into that relationship. This impacted on people's sociality in two ways. Firstly, it allowed them to turn pre-existing ideas into actual social practices as in the case of gender relations. Secondly, it allowed people to move beyond the embodied constraints of the habitus and forge new perspectives on what they wanted from their world. This was neither resistance nor capitulation, but an ongoing process of socially creative experimentation, which created alternates modes of socio-sensual knowledge that impacted on people's lives to differing degrees.

It was never enough to simply club because the gap between the club world and the everyday world simply left people feeling somewhat schizophrenic, which produced disillusionment and cynicism. Instead that gap had to be bridged and clubbers became more pragmatic, developing the capacity to move between extremes, rather than getting bogged down in the middle ground where the everyday habitus could re-establish its hold upon them. They learnt to play the social games of the everyday world and how to cast them aside when they became bored with them. They developed two bodies and two modes of socialising that were grounded in those bodies. They became less reliant on drugs because they had sufficiently embodied the knowledge found in clubs to be able to re-create it when sober (well soberish anyway).

Most importantly they had learned to value people, not as an abstract humanitarian ideal, but as a lived practice. It was their people, rather than the signs, symbols and trinkets of capitalism, the mythological realm of Gods or the obtuse realities of political ideology that grounded them into the world and granted it meaning. The revitalisation of this primary social knowledge within the lives of clubbers is such a simple and important part of the clubbing process that it is easy to miss. We are supposed to value people, but as the stress we place on the ideal of the individual grows we can begin to treat them as obstacles to our own individuality and our own freedom. We focus on the way they constrain our lives, rather than liberate our lives through their mutual support and consent. However, when those people have themselves abandoned the moral and social structures of our culture in order to create new ones based in novel shared practices they cease to impose that culture's constraints.

The friendship networks I encountered amongst clubbers, when I was researching this book, did not rely on a shared identity, a shared style or a shared allegiance to particular ideals. Instead they were grounded in a virtually shared body as each member possessed the embodied memory of all the passionate, wild, wonderful times they'd shared together. The people who made up these groups were individualistic, they accepted difference and they were held together by social codes that granted one another the freedom to change simply by refusing to label one another in the first place. The groups lacked hierarchies or leaders. People could wear what they liked, behave how they liked as long as they weren't vicious or vindictive and they expected each other to treat new arrivals and strangers with the same respect. They could tell each other anything; there was no game playing or point scoring; they were open and straightforward people, which made them damn fine company. I came across this style of social interaction again and again and it always felt radically different from the social frameworks I encountered in the everyday world. These social practices have often been overlooked in examinations of clubbing. They have been seen as a side effect of Ecstasy, rather than a series of bodily techniques, which people learn and take away from clubs. However, they provide a foundation for the knowledge discovered through clubbing and a pathway down which it can flow. This experiment has gone global and each culture it touches will change and use the altered body of clubbing as a socio-sensual framework in which people can engage with their own specific social needs. The historically constituted and heavily encultured bodies of the past are being erased and new practices and perspectives are emerging out of that erasure. It is this process that has allowed me to perceive of clubbing as a sensual experiment in the art of being human.

Glossary

All-back-to-mine: A post-club get together at a fellow partygoer's house.

Asian beats: Dance music that blends Asian and Western musical styles.

Ballistic: Intense, passionate.

Bass-bins: Big powerful bass speakers.

Beering: Out on the ale.

Big-looks: Extreme dressing-up.

Blarney: Talking for the sheer fun of it.

Blasted: Got intoxicated.

Bliss, blissful: State of extreme happiness, contentment and immersion into the world, a peak experience often associated with dancing while on drugs.

Blistered: Used to describe the effects of taking too much amphetamine, a state of agitation and tension.

Blowjob: Oral sex.

Bollocksed: Highly intoxicated, exhausted.

Boogie, boogying: Dancing

Booty, shake your booty: Term for someone's bottom, also sexual slang and term to describe dancing.

Buzz: Used to describe the sense of sociality and excitement that suffuses a club.

Cane, caned: Taking a great deal of drugs over an extended period of time.

Chilled out, chill out, chilling out: Relaxed, but not slumped, calm, contemplative at ease.

Ciderdelic: Rural party crews using a mixture of cider and mushrooms. The eco alternative.

Clangers: A happy family of woollen puppets who live on a faraway planet; they dance, eat soup and gain wisdom from a metal chicken.

Class A: The most illegal drugs or generic term for all illegal drugs. Speed is Class B. Marijuana is Class C.

Cock-strap: Leather straps worn around the base of the penis and scrotum – highly recommended.

Coke, coked-up: Term for cocaine and being under the influence of cocaine.

Come down: When the effects of the drugs sadly start to wear off.

Come on: An attempt at seduction, signalling sexual interest.

Coming up: The transition from sobriety to a state of Ecstasy or LSD intoxication.

Crashed, crash out: Had enough, slumped, asleep.

Crustie: Traveller, free spirit, fond of dogs.

Cum: Orgasm.

Cut a rug: Dance.

Deadheaded: Unimaginative, scared and suspicious.

Disco-napping: Falling asleep for a brief part of the party, then waking up and starting again.

Dominatrix, dom: A woman who wields the whip in an S&M relationship.

Double barrels: Simultaneous vaginal and anal penetration.

Downer: Feeling miserable or people who make you miserable.

Drag-queen: Big theatrical transvestite.

Drum 'n' bass: Dance music, originally **jungle**, heavy bass, multiple drum riffs and rhythms.

Dub: Style of music often with a heavy bass line that existed before clubbing in its contemporary form, often associated with Rastafarian culture.

Dungeon: Space in fetish clubs set aside for S&M play.

Ecstasy: Methylenedioxymethamphetamine, MDMA. Drug with strong euphoric effects.

Feel the rush, rush: The sensation of coming up on drugs, also excitement.

Feely: The way people touch each other and relate to each other on Ecstasy, relaxed, gentle, social interactions.

Flog, flog your body: In this usage the passionate bodily participation in dance.

Freaked out: Upset, confused.

Fuck-me pumps: High heeled very stylish and sexy shoes, look great, often hurt like hell to wear.

Funk, funky: Musical style, something good, interesting, enjoyable.

Funksters: Funky people.

Gab, gabbing: Informal chatting.

Gagging-for-it: An intense desire to party, have sex, enjoy yourself.

Garage: Musical style, two-step beat and also **speed garage** a very different style – fast relentless beats.

Givin'-it-some, vent: A high degree of participation, not holding back.

Goofing off: Playful behaviour.

Grooving-on-down: Dancing

Gurning: Ecstasy users can grind their teeth as tension concentrates in the jaw, looks like they are pulling faces, not an altogether attractive look.

Hardcore: Extreme.

Hard-on: Erection.

Heebie-jeebies: Panic, paranoia, unease.

Hip-hop: Black American musical style and lifestyle with its own codes of honour and respect also associated with graffiti art, lyrical poetry and linguistic dexterity.

Honk, honk down: Snorting drugs especially cocaine and Ecstasy.

House: Musical style, euphoric, Ecstasy-inspired dance music, also **hard house** and handbag house.

Kick back: In this usage relaxed, also a bribe.

Kitty-suit: Cat costume.

Jouissance: French term meaning little orgasm.

Jungle: Black British musical style, pre-cursor of drum 'n' bass.

Knackered: Tired.

Lagging, getting lagging: On the lager with your mates.

Laid: Having sex.

Laid-back: Relaxed.

Large, living-it-large: Enjoying the good times, expansiveness, moving beyond the mundane.

Lightweight: Someone who finishes partying early, can't handle their drugs.

Look: As in 'having a look' – a very individual style of dressing.

Loon: Lunatic.

Losing it: Confusion caused by over intoxication.

Love librarians: Glamorous, bespectacled, sexy women.

Loved-up: Friendly, passionate, gentle loving feelings associated with Ecstasy use.

Mashed: Heavy intoxication.

Max: Maximum, the limit, all the way.

MC: Master of ceremonies, DJ, rapper.

Media flu: Monday morning hangover especially associated with the media's use of cocaine.

Messy: Out of control, losing your dignity, being sick.

Mr Droopy: A flaccid penis.

Naughty: In this usage engaging in activities that the everyday world may disapprove of, but which people enjoy.

Neck: Drink, swallow.

Necking: Kissing

Nose around: See what's going on.

Nutted: Intoxicated, free from worries.

Nutters: Mad people.

On-one: Taking a tablet of Ecstasy, also enthusiasm, enjoyment, a sense of seizing an experience to the fullest possible level.

Out-of-it: Freed from worries, relaxed body, stripped of petty concerns, also heavily intoxicated.

Out-of-your-box, head, gourd, brains: Intoxicated.

Party animal: Someone who loves to party and parties hard.

Party-hearty: Partying with gusto.

Party liability: Someone who spoils other people's nights.

Party pooper: Someone who resolutely refuses to have a good time.

Party-posse: Group of friends who party together.

Pear-shaped: When things go wrong, derived from a particular body shape.

Pill, pilled-up: Ecstasy tablet, having taken Ecstasy.

Pissed, pissed-up: Drunk.

Posse: Group of friends who party together.

Prime love: Penis.

Puking: Vomiting.

On-the-pull: Finding a sexual partner, trying to find a sexual partner.

Punters: The people who make up the club crowd.

Rumpy-pumpy: Sex.

Rush, feel the rush: The sensation of coming up on drugs, also excitement.

Screwed: Messed up, destroyed.

S&M: Sadomasochistic sexual practices.

Scagging around: Listless and unglamorous behaviour.

Score: Buying drugs or getting laid.

Shag: Engaging in vigorous sex.

Shagged out: Tired

Shapeless casuals: Well worn in old clothes, worn only for comfort, style free zone.

Shitfaced: Intoxicated, not always negative.

Skanking: Dance style, associated with Dub, laid-back, stoned way of moving.

Skinning up: Rolling a joint.

Skunk, skunkweed: Very potent marijuana.

Snorting: Imbibing drugs through your nose.

Sound clash: Two sound systems battling for musical supremacy.

Speed: Amphetamines.

Speedy: The experience of being on amphetamines.

Splattered, splattered out your conch: Highly intoxicated sometimes positive.

Spliff: Marijuana, a drug cigarette.

Stash: Store of drugs.

Stoned: High on dope.

Stoner zombie: Someone who is constantly and heavily intoxicated on marijuana.

Strutting: Being visible and on display.

Sub-Bass: A modern acoustic technique for amplifying and enhancing the visceral force of a bass beat.

Super-facial: Animated and expressive body language.

Techno: Music, heavily electronic, fast repetitive beats.

Tiddle: A small amount.

Toad-licking crustie: Derogatory, someone who's taken too many drugs, reference to imbibing the psychedelic bodily secretions of some amphibians.

Top: Someone who controls an S&M scene.

Trance: Music with new-age psychedelic influences, repetitive beats, so that people can trance out and reach states of bliss.

Tranny: Transvestite.

Trip, trippy, tripped out: Pertaining to LSD, also metaphorical for something reminiscent of the LSD experience, often visual.

Trolleyed: Highly intoxicated.

Tunes: Music.

Up for it: Ready and eager to party.

Wasted: Over intoxicated, tired.

Weed: Marijuana.

Whizz: Amphetamine.

Whooping-it-up: Partying hard, enjoying yourself.

Bibliography

Alvarez, A. (1996), *Night: An Exploration of Night Life, Night Language, Sleep and Dreams,* London: Vintage.

Bataille, G. (1985), *Visions of Excess Selected Writings 1927-1939,* ed. Stoekl A., trans. Stoekl, A., Lovitt, C. R. and Leslie Jr., D. M, Minneapolis: University of Minnesota Press.

Baudrillard, J. (1998), *The Consumer Society: Myths and Structures (Theory, Culture and Society),* trans. Turner, C., London: Sage Publications.

Blake, W. (1978), *The Marriage of Heaven and Hell, Proverbs of Hell, introduced and ed. Bronowski, J., Middlesex: Penguin.*

Bourdieu, P. (1977), *Outline of a Theory of Practice,* trans. Nice, R., Cambridge: Cambridge University Press.

—— (1990), *The Logic of Practice,* trans. Nice, R., Cambridge: Polity Press.

—— (1998), *Practical Reason on the Theory of Action,* Cambridge: Polity Press.

Collin, M. (1997), *Altered State: The Story of Ecstasy Culture and Acid House,* London: Serpent's Tail.

Cornelius, R. R. (1995), *The Science of Emotion: Research and Tradition in the Psychology of Emotion,* New Jersey: Prentice Hall.

Damasio, A. (1994), *Descartes' Error: Emotion, Reason, and the Human Brain,* New York: Grosset/Putnam.

—— (1999), *The Feeling of What Happens: Body and Emotion in the Making of Consciousness,* London: William Heinemann.

Dennett, D. C. (1993), *Consciousness Explained,* London: Penguin Books.

Eco, Umberto (1987), *Travels in Hyperreality: Essays,* trans. Weaver, W., London: Picador.

Ekman, Paul (1993), 'Facial Expression and Emotion', *American Psychologist,* 48(4): 384–92.

Elias, N. (1978), *The Civilising Process Vol 1: The History Of Manners,* trans. Jephcott, E., Oxford: Blackwell.

—— (1982), *The Civilising Process Vol 2: State Formation and Civilisation,* Oxford: Blackwell.

—— Dunning, E. (1986), *Quest For Excitement: Sports and Leisure in the Civilising Process,* Oxford: Blackwell.

—— (1998a), *On Civilization, Power and Knowledge,* eds Mennell, S. and Goudsblom, J., Chicago: The University of Chicago Press.

—— (1998b), *The Norbert Elias Reader*, eds Mennell, S. and Goudsblom, J., Oxford: Blackwell.

—— (1983), *The Court Society,* Oxford: Blackwell.

Ellington, Duke, quoted by Eyles, John (1999), "'Ragatal" and "Indo-Jazz Fusions 1 and 2'", *Avant,* Issue 10 (winter).

Foucault, Michel (1981), *The History of Sexuality, Vol 1. An Introduction,* London: Penguin.

—— (1977), *Discipline and Punish: The Birth of the Prison,* trans. Sheridan, A., New York: Vintage.

Fromm, E. (1991), *The Fear of Freedom,* London: Routledge.

Gabrielsson, A. (1987), *Action and Perception in Rhythm and Music,* Stockholm: The Royal Swedish Academy of Music.

Gefou-Madianou, D. (ed.) (1992), *Alcohol, Gender and Culture,* London and New York: Routledge.

Giddens, A. (1990), *The Consequences of Modernity,* Cambridge: Polity Press.

—— (1991), *Modernity and Self-Identity,* Cambridge: Polity Press.

Gleichmann, P., Goudsblom, J. and Korte, H. (eds) (1977), *Human Figurations: Essays for Norbert Elias,* Amsterdam: Amsterdam Sociologisch Tiijdschrift.

Goffman, E. (1961), *Encounters: Two Studies in the Sociology of Interaction,* Indianapolis: Bobbs-Merrill.

—— (1990), *The Presentation of Self in Everyday Life,* London: Penguin Books.

Grinspoon, L. and Bakalar, J. B (1976), *Cocaine: A Drug and its Social Evolution,* New York: Basic Books.

Grosz, E. (1995), *Space, Time and Perversion: Essays on the Politics of Bodies,* London and New York: Routledge.

Hebdige, D. (1979), *Subculture: The Meaning of Style,* London: Methuen.

Keil, C. and Feld, S. (1994), *Music Grooves: Essays and Dialogues,* Chicago: University of Chicago Press.

Lakoff, G. (1987), *Women, Fire, and Dangerous Things: What Categories Reveal about the Mind,* Chicago: The University of Chicago Press.

—— and Johnson, M. (1981), *Metaphors We Live By,* Chicago: The University of Chicago Press.

Leary, T. (1990), *The Politics of Ecstasy,* Berkeley: Ronin.

—— Metzner, R. and Alpert, R. (1970), *The Psychedelic Experience a Manual Based on the Tibetan Book of the Dead,* Secaucus: The Citadel Press.

LeDoux, J. (1999), *The Emotional Brain, The Mysterious Underpinnings of Emotional Life,* London: Phoenix.

Lee, M. A. and Shlain, B. (1992), *Acid Dreams the Complete Social History of LSD: The CIA, The Sixties, and Beyond,* New York: Grove Press.

Lyotard, J.-F. (1984), *The Postmodern Condition: A Report on Knowledge*, Minneapolis: University of Minnesota Press.

—— (1988), *Le Postmoderne Expliqué aux Enfants: Correspondance 1982–1985*, Paris: Galilée.

Malbon, B. (1999), *Clubbing: Dancing, Ecstasy and Vitality*, London and New York: Routledge.

Mauss, M. (1979), *Sociology and Psychology: Essays*, trans. Brewster, B., London: Routledge & Kegan Paul.

Mcdonald, M. (ed.) (1994), *Gender, Drink and Drugs*, Oxford: Berg.

Merleau-Ponty, M. (1994), *The Phenomenology of Perception*, trans. Smith, C., London and New York: Routledge.

Mirbeau, O. (1989), *The Torture Garden*, San Francisco: Re/Search.

Montagu, A. (1986), *Touching: The Human Significance of the Skin*, New York: Harpers & Row.

O'Rourke, P. J., (1992), *Give War a Chance*, London: Picador, pp. 115–16.

Plant, M. (2001), 'UK Teenagers hit Drugs and Alcohol Harder', *Guardian*, 20 February.

Redhead, S. (ed.) (1993), *Rave Off. Politics and Deviance in Contemporary Youth Culture*, Aldershot: Avebury.

—— Wynne, D. and O'Connor, J. (eds) (1997), *The Clubcultures Reader: Readings in Popular Cultural Studies*, Oxford: Blackwell.

Rojek, C. (1995), *Decentering Leisure: Rethinking Leisure Theory*, London: Sage Publications.

Sartre, J.-P. (1993), *Being and Nothingness: A Phenomenological Essay on Ontology*, trans. Barnes, Hazel E., New York: Washington Square Press.

Shilling, C. (1993), *The Body and Social Theory*, London: Sage Publications.

Shils, E. (1981), *Tradition*, London: Faber & Faber.

Shore, B. (1996), *Culture in Mind: Cognition, Culture and the Problem of Meaning*, Oxford and New York: Oxford University Press.

Szasz, T. (1973), *The Second Sin, Personal Conduct*, New York: Anchor Press.

Thornton, S. (1995), *Club Cultures: Music, Media and Subcultural Capital*, Cambridge: Polity.

Turner, B, S (1996), *The Body and Society*, London: Sage.

Vaneigem, R, (1983), *The Book of Pleasures*, London: Pending Press.

Willis, P, with Jones, S., Canaan, J. and Hurd, G. (1990), *Common Culture: Symbolic Work at Play in the Everyday Cultures of Youth*, Milton Keynes: Open University Press.

Music

Dirty Beatniks. (2000), *Feedback*, Wall of Sound Records.

K. C. and The Sunshine Band. (1975), *Get Down Tonight*, T. K. Records.

Index

abandonment, 61, 135–41
  emotional, 137–8
  physical, 136–7
  social, 138–9
adventure, 43, 102–3
advertising, 161
alcohol, 58–63, 76, 141, 143–4
  and gender, 60
  chemically assisted drinking, 59
all-back-to-mine, 87, 107–8, 144
altered states of consciousness, 124
Alternative Miss World, 164
Alvarez, A., 2
amphetamine, 69–71
amplification, 27
anger, 90
attitude, 95–6

bass, 28–30
Bakalar, J.B., 69–70
Bataille, G., 22
Baudrillard, J., 159
beats-per-minute (BPM), 30–1
Blake, W., 79
bodily techniques, 65, 89, 116–17, 126, 139
body, 1–2, 5, 20–2, 30–3, 158
  and city, 66, 89–91
  and culture, 155, 117
  Appolonian, 15, 21, 23
  communicative, 106,
  Dionysian, 15, 20, 23, 27 142, 143
Bourdieu, P., 4–5, 23, 115–19, 141, 149,
  163–4
brain processing, 124

cannabis, 73–4
capitalism, 158–64, 173
chemical intimacy, 144–51
chemical literacy, 84–5
civilising process, 121–3, 171, 173
Claperede, E., 125–6

clothes, 47–50
  and sensual transformation, 52–4
  as costumes, 51–2
cocaine, 62, 69–71
  fight or flight mode, 70–1
  overindulgence, 71
Collin, M., 78, 120
communication, 94, 100, 104, 137, 142
community, 173, 161
consciousness, 124–5
consumption, 92, 158–63
  experiential, 159–60
Cornelius, R., 90
courtesy, 94–5
crack, 56
crowds, 103–7

Damasio, A., 5, 64–5, 90, 92, 124, 127, 156
dance, 15–24, 27, 137, 172
  and gender, 15–17
  social structure of, 17–20, 22
dance floor 15–19, 21–3, 31
death, 160, 166, 169
Dennett, D., 156
door codes, 51
dressing-up, 47–54
drugs, 55–85, 88,
  and addiction, 80–1
  and balance, 83
  as mainstream, 56–8
  pattern of usage, 74–84
  discovery, 75–7
  excess, 79–82
  honeymoon, 77–9
  reassessment, 82–4
  social experience of, 55–6, 144–50
  war on, 57
  see also alcohol, amphetamine, cannabis,
    cocaine, crack, ecstasy, heroin, ketamine,
    LSD, psylocibin
dub, 29

Index

Eco, U., 88
ecstasy, 1, 3, 15, 16, 62–8, 92, 145, 171
  evangelism, 78
  fear, 64–5, 66
  social effects 63–6, 141–4
  touch, 68
ego, 70, 146
Ekman, P., 97
Elias, N., 121–3
embodied metaphors, 129–30, 163
emotion, 33, 121–2, 126, 129, 145,
  and consciousness, 124
  and ideology, 166
  and memory, 125–8
  background, 127
empathy, 62, 64, 90
escapism, 130, 136, 139, 163
everyday world, 22, 55, 75, 80, 84, 121, 123,
  151

Feld, S., 27
Foucault, M., 43, 108–11 152
freedom, 21, 23, 162–5, 172
Freud, S., 69
friends, 55, 87, 104, 138, 140, 144–5, 147–8
Fromm, E., 162

Gabrielsson, A., 31
gaze, 49, 103, 108–10, 171
Geffou-Madianou, D., 60
gender relations, 16–17, 141–4
God, 22, 169–70, 174
Goffman, E., 48, 49, 88
Grinspoon, L., 69–70
Grosz, E., 152
guilt, 116–17

habitus, 4–5, 55, 36, 87, 116–21, 124, 149,
  159, 163, 171
happiness, 137–8
Hebdige, D., 52
hedonism, 136, 140, 173
heroin, 56
hierarchy, 95, 100
hyper-reality, 88

idealised cognitive models (ICM), 130–1, 153,
  163
identity, 100–2, 155–8

ideology, 5, 155, 166, 169
individuality, 156–8
Institute of Alcohol and Health Research, 57

Johnson, M., 129

Keil, C., 27
Kesey, K., 97
ketamine, 72
key-connections, 105
kinaesthetic-sense, 18–19

Lakoff, G., 129, 130
language, 129–30
Leary, T., 45, 72
LeDoux, J., 5, 66–7, 124, 125, 126, 129, 166
Lee, M.A., 57
leisure, 67, 123, 157
licensing laws, 59, 67
LSD, 72–3, 124
Lyotard, J.-F., 156, 159

McDonald, M., 60
Malbon, B., 22, 102, 115, 141, 159
Mauss, M., 116, 149
meaning, 165–70
meaningfulness, 28, 166–7, 169
meeting people, 103–7
Merleau-Ponty, M., 137
Mirbeau, O., 122
monogamy, 165
Montagu, A., 68
morality, 3–4, 33, 151–3, 171
  Protestant-Christian, 3, 15, 36, 60, 151, 171
multiple-drafts, 156
mushrooms, 72
music, 25–34, 172
  and acceleration, 30–2
  and drugs, 32–4
  and embodiment, 26–8

names, 100–1
National Statistics, 147
Nietzsche, F., 4, 15, 25
night, 2

objectification, 48–9, 53
oceanic-experience, 22
Owen, T., 42, 44

participation, 18, 33, 43, 51, 91–3
  and drugs 92–3
Plant, M., 56
pleasure, 3–4, 128, 139, 140, 169, 172
practice, 4, 33, 55, 117–19, 122, 157
  logic of 118–19, 142
proto-self, 90, 92, 124, 125, 156
psilocybin 73
psychedelics, 72–3
pubs, 61–2

rationality, 164
Redhead, S., 115
resistance, 48, 102, 119
rhythm, 29–30
ritual, 22, 6,167
Rojek, C., 108

safety, 16–17
Sartre, J.-P., 156
scripts, 100
self-confidence, 110
sensual landscape 20–3, 28, 33, 85, 115, 128,
  167
sensuality, 1–2, 17, 35, 141
set and setting, 71, 72, 120,
sex, 21, 24, 35–46, 148–9
  anal, 116–17
  and drugs 44–6, 73
  morality 151–3
sex clubs 41–4, 165
  ethnography of 37–41
Sex Maniacs' Ball 42
Shilling, C., 155, 166, 169
Shlain, B., 57
shopping, 160
Shore, B., 100

single people, 147–8
sleep-deprivation, 67
smile, 96–8, 126, 127
social networks, 105–6, 147,
sociality, 1–2, 78–9, 131–2, 138, 141, 145
  aspirational, 87, 89, 102
  party, 82, 88–91, 103–6, 158
socio-sensual, 2, 48, 55, 76, 135, 167
strangers, 19, 75, 88–90, 94, 101, 109, 127,
  138, 140
subcultural capital, 24–5, 28, 96, 159
super-facial, 94
superficiality, 63, 65, 94
symbolism, 5, 48, 52–3, 155–8, 159, 161, 166,
  169

Thornton, S., 25, 96, 100, 101, 115, 157,
  159
tolerance, 98–9
touch, 146
trainspotters, 26
Transformer, 49
Turner, B., 15

Urbach-Wiethe, 64
urban environment, 66

Vaneigem, R., 161 171
violence, 60, 99, 110, 121, 123, 171

water-sports, 152
weddings, 140
Willis, P., 157, 168
work, 67, 102, 168
Wouters, C., 157

youth-studies, 2–3